THE BUILDING BLOCKS OF PRESCHOOL SUCCESS

The
Building
Blocks of
Preschool
Success

Katherine A. Beauchat
Katrin L. Blamey
Sharon Walpole

THE GUILFORD PRESS
New York   London

© 2010 The Guilford Press
A Division of Guilford Publications, Inc.
72 Spring Street, New York, NY 10012
www.guilford.com

Printed in the United States of America

This book is printed on acid-free paper.

Last digit is print number: 9   8   7   6   5   4   3   2   1

Library of Congress Cataloging-in-Publication Data

Beauchat, Katherine A.
    The building blocks of preschool success / by Katherine A. Beauchat,
Katrin L. Blamey, and Sharon Walpole.
        p. cm.
    Includes bibliographical references and index.
    ISBN 978-1-60623-693-2 (pbk.: alk. paper)
    ISBN 978-1-60623-694-9 (hard cover : alk. paper)
    1. Preschool teaching. 2. Language arts (Preschool)   I. Blamey, Katrin L.
II. Walpole, Sharon. III. Title.
    LB1140.3B43 2010
    372.1102--dc22

                                                                2010003724

We dedicate this book to our families
who continue to support us through all of our endeavors:
Tracey, Keegan, Chloe, Chad, Owen, Andrew, Kevin, and Pete,
and to the preschool teachers with whom we work
and who continue to inspire us.

About the Authors

Katherine A. Beauchat, EdD, is Assistant Professor at York College of Pennsylvania, where she teaches undergraduate and graduate classes in literacy education. Her research interests include professional development for preschool educators in the area of literacy and language instruction and effective techniques and strategies to bolster oral language and vocabulary development for at-risk preschool children. Her recent publications include the article "Building Preschool Children's Language and Literacy One Storybook at a Time" (2009), published in *The Reading Teacher,* and the Literacy Coaching Clearinghouse brief "Facilitating Teacher Study Groups" (2008).

Katrin L. Blamey, PhD, is an early childhood literacy coach at the Delaware Center for Teacher Education in Newark, Delaware, and also coaches preschool teachers at a Head Start center. Her research interests include finding effective, practical ways to implement professional development in the preschool setting and developing instructional techniques for building the language and literacy skills of preschool-age English language learners. Her recent publications include the articles "Building Preschool Children's Language and Literacy One Storybook at a Time" (2009) and "Elementary Literacy Coaches: The Reality of Dual Roles" (2008), both published in *The Reading Teacher.*

Sharon Walpole, PhD, is Associate Professor at the University of Delaware School of Education in Newark, Delaware, where she teaches in both the literacy and educational leadership programs. She provides professional development for schools engaged in extensive change efforts and studies the work of literacy coaches in preschools, elementary schools, and middle and high schools. In 2007, she received the National Reading Conference Early Career Achievement Award. Her publications include two coauthored books on literacy coaching, *The Literacy Coach's Handbook: A Guide to Research-Based Practice* and *The Literacy Coaching Challenge: Models and Methods for Grades K–8,* and two coauthored books on differentiated instruction, *Differentiated Reading Instruction: Strategies for the Primary Grades* and *How to Plan Differentiated Reading Instruction: Resources for Grades K–3.* She is coeditor of a recent book on preschool reform efforts, *Promoting Early Reading: Research, Resources, and Best Practices.*

How to Use This Book

As we wrote this book together over the past year, we were constantly challenged to focus on individual teaching goals and opportunities and on embedding them into a playful, thematically rich instructional environment. We begin with an introductory chapter, followed by chapters on oral language and vocabulary development (Chapter 2), on comprehension (Chapter 3), on phonological awareness (Chapter 4), on print and alphabet awareness (Chapter 5), on emergent writing (Chapter 6), on assessment (Chapter 7), and on planning (Chapter 8). This organization made the best sense for the book, but it shouldn't distract you from considering the integration of all these opportunities. Each of these instructional opportunities is connected to the others, and the particular ways that you choose to make those connections will create your unique preschool community. It might be better to think of this book as a prism, with each chapter reflecting just a piece of the light that the entire prism can capture.

If you are reading alone, we recommend that you take a quick read through the entire book. You will find that what you read in Chapter 3 actually enhances your understanding of Chapter 2; for example, we constantly reference the potential of shared storybook reading and of creative play, while highlighting a different potential focus. Then go back through Chapters 2–6. Read only the section on whole-group instruction across the chapters; then read only the section on small-group instruction; then read only the center time section. Finally, read the stories of our composite teachers, one at a time, beginning in Chapter 1. You might then have a better sense of which approach will work in a setting more like your own.

If you can read this book with a colleague, first consider the suggestions above. But then go back to the lists of recommended print and Web-based resources. One of you can go to the library and find some of the books we have suggested; the other can use the Web to sample the sites and find the ones that seem most useful. Taking the time to decide on which resources to use, both from the library and from the Web, is really worth your effort. It will make your planning more fruitful and less harried.

When you have exhausted the content of the book and thought about and discussed it critically, it is time for planning. Chapter 7 invites you to plan an assessment system to inform your instruction and to share with parents. And Chapter 8 invites you to really think about the ways that you use time, grouping configurations, and the talents of your instructional team. We hope that there is something here that you can make your own and that it will build your sense of efficacy. We respect and appreciate your work with young children; we hope you will make support of young children's language and literacy development a career.

KATHERINE A. BEAUCHAT
KATRIN L. BLAMEY
SHARON WALPOLE

Contents

CHAPTER 1

The Realities of Preschool

As we began work for this book, we first considered our audience. We wanted to write directly to preschool teachers, but that is easier said than done. In fact, we think that preschools are perhaps the most diverse educational settings of all. They include half-day and full-day programs; school-based, church-based, home-based, and center-based programs; programs that target creative play; and programs that target basic skills. We consider these differences as positive—we do not want all preschools to look the same. What we do want, though, is to maximize the possibilities for social, emotional, language, and literacy growth for children regardless of the type of preschool they attend.

If you work in preschool, you are part of a growing workforce. In 2006, U.S. government employment data identified 437,000 preschool teachers and projected a need for 552,000 by 2016. Unfortunately, though, that growth is not accompanied by financial incentives—the median salary for preschool teachers is $22,680; less than the bottom 10% of elementary school teachers (Bureau of Labor Statistics, 2009).

If you work in a preschool, you work in an area that has garnered attention in federal policy. In 2002, the U.S. Department of Education began funding for Early Reading First, a competitive grant program designed to improve preschool experiences for the nation's poorest children. The targets of the grants were professional development for preschool teachers as well as improvements in classroom environments and in teaching practices. That effort has produced new information about effective practices in preschool and also revealed some of the continuing challenges that preschool educators face (Russell et al., 2007). We embed findings from Early Reading First throughout this book. If you want to know more about the initiative, we recommend *Promoting Early Reading: Research, Resources, and Best Practices* (McKenna, Walpole, & Conradi, 2010) that shares findings from multiple sites.

If you work in preschool, you work in an area of burgeoning research. In 2002, the same year that Early Reading First was authorized by Congress, the federal government also commissioned the National Early Literacy Panel (NELP) to identify interventions, parenting activities, and instructional practices that promote the development of children's early literacy skills. We also embed findings from NELP in the chapters that follow.

These research and policy initiatives are complicated, to say the least, and they are targeted only to specific parts of the preschool day. To start, then, we introduce three fictional preschool teachers. We have constructed these profiles from visits to and discussions about preschools with very different missions so that we can apply our research findings in the chapters that follow in ways that honor those differences.

MEET PAM, A PUBLIC SCHOOL-BASED PreK TEACHER

Pam is a prekindergarten teacher in a public school-based setting situated in a small school district in York, Pennsylvania. She teaches both a morning and an afternoon section; the morning section is funded by Title I, a federal program designed to provide support for children whose families are poor. The afternoon session is funded through the state budget. The program, which runs 5 days per week through the course of the school year, serves 15 students with two adults per classroom (one teacher and one paraprofessional).

This preschool is free for families, and we would consider it an intervention for children who might struggle in kindergarten. The students are selected by age and by need. They must be ready to feed into the public school-based kindergarten the following year, so they are 4 years old. First preference is given to those students who have been identified through the district's prekindergarten screening measure called the Battelle Developmental Inventory (BDI). The BDI is an early childhood developmental assessment that measures children's personal–social, adaptive, motor, communication, and cognitive abilities (Newborg, 2006).

Pam is afforded the same contract, benefits, and professional development opportunities as the district's K–12 teaching population. She must meet highly qualified status for her particular position, which includes having a bachelor's degree in early childhood education. Pam has the opportunity to attend graduate school classes and work toward her master's degree through district-funded stipends, as well as attend the districtwide professional development sessions for the kindergarten teachers. Additionally, the paraprofessional who works with Pam must also meet requirements for highly qualified aide status, which include an associate's degree or passing a state-approved assessment. Her paraprofessional attends monthly training and some districtwide professional development sessions that are applicable to her role in the classroom.

Because it is funded through state and federal funds, this preschool curriculum is more structured than other preschools. The curriculum is framed by the Pennsylvania academic learning standards, which include specific PreK standards. Pam uses curriculum materials chosen by the district to implement these standards: the Scholastic

Early Childhood thematic program (see Figure 1.1 for a list of themes), Everyday Math, Kid Writing, and Guided Reading. Pam formally measures the progress of her students three times per year using the BDI and the Phonological Awareness Literacy Screening (PALS; University of Virginia, 2004). Pam's total assessment plan includes more than these formal measures. She uses informal measures such as Kid Watching, anecdotal accounts, and work sampling strategies we explain later.

The results of the formal and informal measures allow Pam to plan for whole- and small-group time (see Figure 1.2 for a complete classroom schedule). Notice that, in addition to a whole-group instructional time, Pam has two distinct times for learning centers. During the first learning center time, students are able to select the center activity in which they'd like to participate. Pam and her assistant monitor and interact with all the students in each center. They also use this block of time to work with specific students on a one-on-one basis and collect anecdotal observations for record-keeping and planning purposes. The second learning center time is much more structured. Pam uses informal and formal assessment results to place students into one of three needs-based groups of students for small-group differentiated instruction. Each group meets with Pam for 15 minutes of literacy instruction while the other students visit the preselected learning centers. Pam's assistant works with students at one of those preselected learning centers on a specific literacy activity (e.g., concepts of print, alphabet awareness, phonological awareness).

Pam consistently plans targeted activities for her learning centers (see Figure 1.3 for a description of the classroom learning centers). She views her learning centers as a "hands-on" and engaging extension of her whole- and small-group instructional goals. Learning centers are unique in that they provide multiple opportunities for students to practice and apply skills, problem solve and use critical thinking skills, develop as independent learners, and collaborate with classmates.

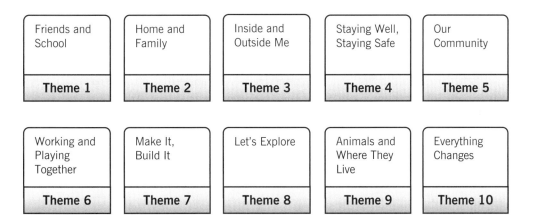

FIGURE 1.1. Themes in the curriculum.

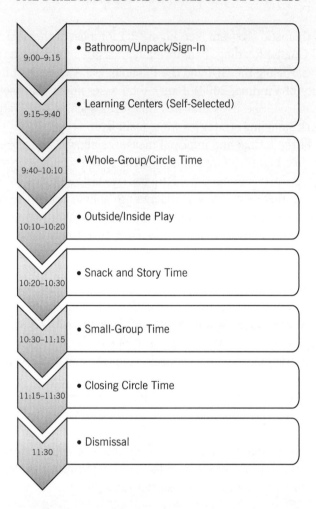

9:00–9:15 • Bathroom/Unpack/Sign-In

9:15–9:40 • Learning Centers (Self-Selected)

9:40–10:10 • Whole-Group/Circle Time

10:10–10:20 • Outside/Inside Play

10:20–10:30 • Snack and Story Time

10:30–11:15 • Small-Group Time

11:15–11:30 • Closing Circle Time

11:30 • Dismissal

FIGURE 1.2. Daily PreK schedule (A.M. sample).

Pam's classroom is inviting, bright, attractive, and stocked with a variety of print, books, children's work samples, and hands-on activities (see Figures 1.4 and 1.5 for products of whole-group instruction and student work, respectively). Notice that Pam includes intentional instructional routines in her whole-group instruction that target essential literacy components. For example, every day she includes a *Question of the Day*. She takes the opportunity to engage students daily in a shared writing and reading of these questions. She also writes down students' individual responses to the question through a language experience approach. These language charts are then displayed for subsequent use during whole-group time and for student use during center time. Within

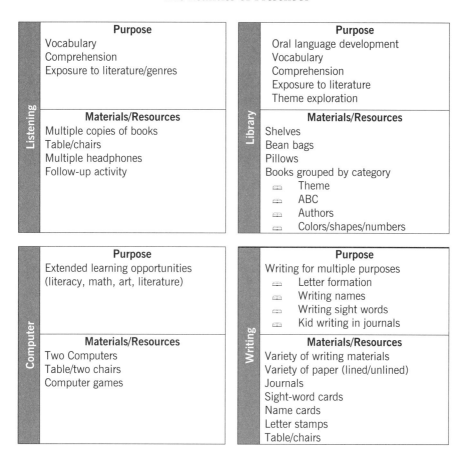

FIGURE 1.3. PreK learning centers.

this block of time Pam targets alphabet awareness, alphabetic principle, letter formation, concepts of print, and oral language development.

Pam is also aware that some of her students will require additional resources and assistance beyond that of her classroom instructional environment. Pam, as well as the parents, can refer students who demonstrate specific concerns (speech therapy, occupational therapy, etc.) to the local Intermediate Unit (IU) for further assessment and testing. If students are identified through this process, they can receive services at the IU outside of the regular PreK school day. The home–school connection is pivotal to the program and includes two home visits, several parent–teacher conferences, and monthly Title I parent workshops. When asked what the best aspect of being a prekindergarten teacher is, Pam answered, "I like it when they really get it. They come in with so little knowledge and they grow so much. It's an amazing transformation that takes place and brings tears to my eyes."

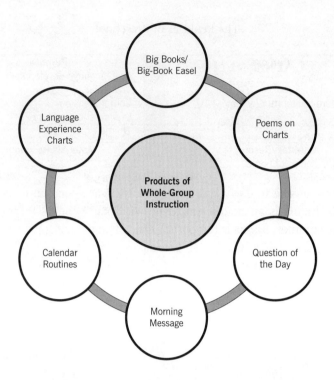

FIGURE 1.4. Products of whole-group instruction.

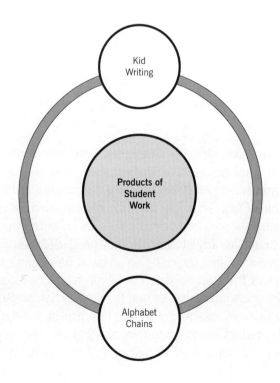

FIGURE 1.5. Products of student work.

MEET ELAINA, A HEAD START CENTER TEACHER

Elaina, a single mother in her early 40s, has been working for Head Start in Richmond, Virginia, for 7 years. Head Start is a federally funded agency charged with serving the needs of families with low incomes. Head Start provides early care and education for children ages 3 and 4 and supportive services for families. Elaina came to Head Start from a private preschool setting. She has an associate's degree and is currently working on her bachelor's degree in early childhood education at a local university. As a Head Start employee, Elaina is an hourly employee with paid benefits 9 months out of the year; during the summer, Elaina is temporarily laid off and must apply for unemployment benefits. To supplement her income, she manages a restaurant in the afternoons and evenings after her Head Start day.

There are three adults (head teacher, teacher's assistant, and classroom aide) and twenty 3- and 4-year-old children in Elaina's classroom. Students are accepted into Head Start if their families meet the low-income requirements and/or if they have an individualized education plan (IEP). The majority of Elaina's students are learning English as a second language; they speak Spanish at home with their families. The Head Start day begins at 9:15 A.M. and lasts until 1:15 P.M. (see Figure 1.6 for a classroom schedule). Head Start uses *The Creative Curriculum for Early Childhood* (Dodge & Colker, 2000). (see Figure 1.7 for a list of curriculum themes.)

Students are screened by professionals from the Child Find Educational Services for Children, a government organization tasked with early screening and diagnosing of students with disabilities, once a year in the fall, and students with IEPs receive special education services from the school district during the Head Start day. To keep open communication between home and school, Elaina conducts home visits twice a year, in the fall and spring, and invites parents into the classroom for a parent–teacher conference twice a year.

Head Start classrooms are required to attend directly to the health and hygiene needs of the children. Student schedules are punctuated with teeth brushing, hand washing, and healthy meals. Compared to Pam's schedule (see Figure 1.2), then, Elaina's instructional schedule (pictured in Figure 1.6) includes very similar items, but with fewer minutes overall.

However, you cannot see any evidence of time pressure when you look at the classroom. Elaina's classroom is a fun, colorful place to be. By the front door there is a counter space with a sink for hand washing and tables for meals. The tables also function as art and manipulative game centers during center times. The rest of the room is divided into separate centers (see Figure 1.8 for a list of classroom centers). At the back of the room there is a large open space with a colorful rug and a big-book stand for large-group shared reading activities. On the walls, Elaina has posted student work (see Figure 1.9), including watercolor paintings, letter *K*'s written in paint, drawings of favorite items, and writing samples. She also displays group literacy projects, such as a thank-you note to a

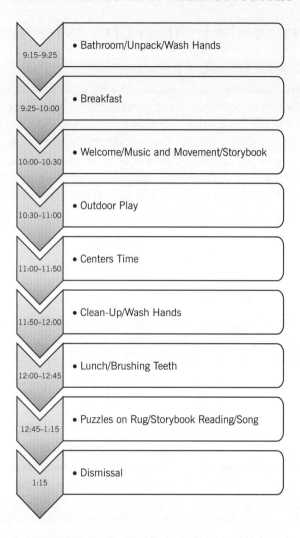

FIGURE 1.6. Daily Head Start schedule.

police officer who visited the classroom (see Figure 1.10 for a sampling of whole-group literacy activities).

To track students' progress throughout the year, Elaina uses several assessments. She makes informal observations of students' actions and knowledge in connection with 50 learning objectives identified by *The Creative Curriculum* (Dodge & Colker, 2000). She enters these data daily into a computer database in order to meet three checkpoint deadlines throughout the year. At each checkpoint, multiple observations per child are required.

When asked to describe her most important instructional goals, Elaina discussed the desire to "reach everyone's level" by planning instructional activities that all chil-

Back to School	Community Helpers	Transportation	Nutrition
• School • Making Friends	• People in your Neighborhood	• Cars • Buses • Airplanes • Boats	• Eating Healthy

Nursery Rhymes	Dinosaurs	Letters	Numbers
• Selection of Familiar Nursery Rhymes	• Animals that lived long ago	• Alphabet Letters	• Learning How to Count

FIGURE 1.7. Themes in Eliana's classroom.

Listening

Purpose
Alphabet knowledge
Vocabulary
Comprehension
Exposure to literature/genres

Materials/Resources
Multiple copies of children's books
Multiple copies of alphabet books
Table/chairs
Multiple headphones

Library

Purpose
Oral language development
Vocabulary
Comprehension
Exposure to literature
Theme exploration

Materials/Resources
Shelves
Couches
Tables
Stuffed animals
Books differentiated by theme and all others

Computer

Purpose
Extended learning opportunities (literacy, math, art)

Materials/Resources
Two computers
Table/two chairs
Computer Games

Writing

Purpose
Writing for multiple purposes
  Letter formation
  Writing names
  Writing sight words
  Writing in journals

Materials/Resources
Variety of writing materials
Variety of paper (lined/unlined)
Journals
Sight-word cards
Name cards
Letter stamps
Table/chairs
Alphabet books

FIGURE 1.8. Classroom learning centers. *(Continued on the following page.)*

Science

Purpose

Exploration of science and literacy concepts

Materials/Resources

Science journals
Writing instruments
Variety of materials
- Magnets
- Balance
- Magnifying glasses
- Class pet—fish
- Sorting rocks
Books related to science

Blocks

Purpose

Extended opportunities for literacy and spatial concepts

Materials/Resources

Rug
Vehicles
Road signs
Cardboard red brick blocks
Wooden blocks of different shapes and sizes
Gears
Connecting tubes
Legos
Books related to building/construction

Art

Purpose

Fine-motor skills
Literacy
Theme exploration
- Shapes
- Colors
Cognitive development

Materials/Resources

Table and four chairs
Multiple kinds of paper
Multiple kinds of instruments
Magazines for cutting
Books related to art

Sensory Table

Purpose

Extended opportunities for literacy and math concepts

Materials/Resources

Sand table with variety of materials
Objects to sort/find

Dramatic Play

Purpose

Extended opportunities for oral language and literacy

Materials/Resources

Multiple kinds of paper
Multiple writing instruments
Clipboards
Props related to theme
- Cash register
- Appointment book
- Costumes
- Tools
Books related to theme

FIGURE 1.8. *(cont.)*

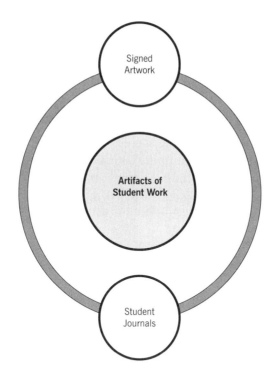

FIGURE 1.9. Evidence of student work.

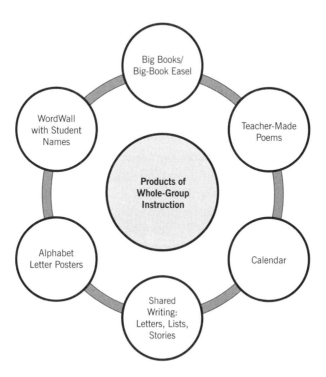

FIGURE 1.10. Evidence of whole-group instruction.

dren in her room, no matter their language ability, could participate in with ease. She also described one of her goals as designing learning opportunities in which the students could lead and direct with minimal teacher intrusion. She envisions the ultimate learning opportunity for preschoolers as being one in which the students have autonomy over their own learning. Elaina measures the success of her instruction by observing to see the progress each student has made in the course of the year. She explains that it is amazing to see students come in at the beginning of the year who are unable to recognize a single alphabet letter and are able to identify all of the letters by the end of the year—an accomplishment also important to Pam.

MEET SARAH, A PRIVATE PRESCHOOL TEACHER

Sarah works in a setting very different from Pam's or Elaina's. Her preschool, located in an affluent suburb of the city of Miami, Florida, is located in a remodeled warehouse owned by a local church. Sarah is married with two children of her own, and she returned to work 1 year ago when her youngest started first grade in another church-based school. She has a bachelor's degree in social work, but a social work job did not suit her.

Sarah teaches in the 4-year-old room, but her center includes daycare options for children as young as 18 months and two kindergarten classrooms. Most of the children live close to the center, and the parents have social connections with one another outside of school. Many of the mothers do not work outside their homes, but some have part-time jobs. Children pay tuition, and it is expensive. There are no admission requirements aside from the tuition; therefore, children who may eventually require services in the autism spectrum or for specific learning disabilities are a part of the school community, as are a growing number of Spanish-speaking children. The day lasts from 9:00 A.M. to 1:00 P.M., with an optional after-school daycare program that runs from 1:00 P.M.to 3:00 P.M.. This schedule allows Sarah to meet her own children at the school bus at 3:20 P.M. Children bring their own lunches and a morning snack and drink.

The daycare and preschool is the foundation of a new larger school that the church has begun as a reaction to its own parishioners' discontent with the local public schools. That school is just down the road, on the grounds of the church, in the classrooms formerly used only for Sunday school. This year, there are two sections each of first, second, and third grades, with plans to add fourth and fifth grades in the next 2 years. With the founding of the elementary school, the mission of the preschool/kindergarten has changed. There is growing pressure from parents to create a more seamless road from the 4-year-old program to the kindergarten to a successful first-grade experience. However, there is no formal plan for how to do this. There is a preschool director who manages the daycare, preschool, and kindergarten rooms, but she has no formal curriculum training. There is also a first-time principal of the elementary school (who taught third grade for 7 years in another private school) but both physical space and the complexities of their separate missions keep their work fairly separate. In fact, parents, church members, and teachers appear to have equal voice in plotting a course for both the elementary school and then for the preschool's and kindergarten's role in preparing students to be successful there. What is clear is that too many children who moved from the school's preschool and kindergarten to its first grade struggled in formal literacy instruction.

Sarah is in an awkward place this year. Her colleagues who take care of the younger children are not affected, but she has to rethink her mission and change her classroom from a daycare to a preschool. Last year's activities, focused squarely on projects linked to the seasons and the holidays, is not enough. She is determined to add literacy activities to her strong foundation in creative play and arts and crafts. To help her in this new mission, she has the support of the kindergarten assistant who will be with her for 1 hour each day, from 10:00 A.M. to 11:00 A.M. The kindergarten assistant is more experienced than Sarah, and she also has a sense of what previous kindergarten children have struggled with. The kindergarten team has asked that Sarah spend more time on fine-motor skills so that children will learn to form letters more easily in kindergarten.

Sarah has many strengths on which to draw. First, she is talented in dealing with young children who struggle in social situations, so parents of those children tend to seek out her classroom. She enjoys children's literature, having spent many hours reading to her own two children, and she knows the value of those one-on-one interactions. She is also very creative, easily able to turn a washing-machine box into a castle. To deal with the demands for more attention to fine-motor skills, she plans to build in more planned attention to children cutting, painting, and drawing on their own.

The center administrator has given them 2 days to plan. They have art supplies, blocks, puppets, and costumes, but no formal preschool curriculum materials aside from a relatively small collection of big books. Sarah typically goes to the local library every 2 weeks to take out additional big books and multiple trade books for her daily read-alouds. They begin by planning their themes for each month, again focusing on seasons and holidays. Their plan is presented in Figure 1.11.

Next, they plan a daily schedule to help them to figure out how they will work together. Since her new assistant will be available from 10:00 A.M. to 11:00 A.M., Sarah wants to have centers during that time. That way, both adults can work with small groups, and the rest of the children can work independently or in pairs. They come up with the schedule presented in Figure 1.12. Notice that Sarah has protected time for two read-alouds, because books are the easiest literacy materials for her to gather on her own and because she believes that read-alouds are the key to language development for 4-year-olds.

Space is tight, though, and Sarah knows that she can set up only four stations in her classroom. She sets them up so that they can be changed easily each month, as the theme changes, with the materials that she has available. With four centers and two adults, only two centers will be independent in each of the three 20-minute rounds. Sarah suspects that the adults will be more effective in direct language and literacy interactions in very

FIGURE 1.11. Planned monthly themes.

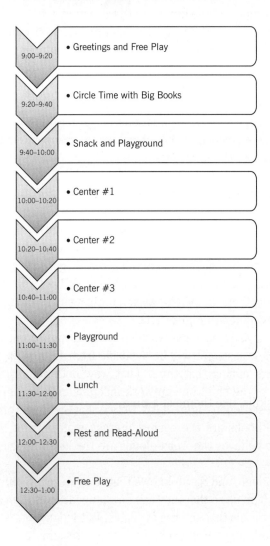

FIGURE 1.12. Sarah's new schedule.

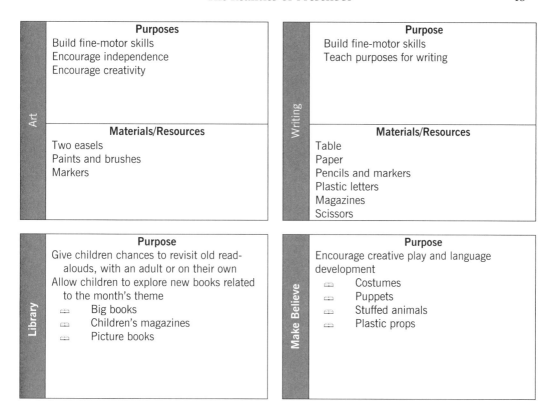

FIGURE 1.13. Sarah's learning centers.

small groups. She decides that she will spend time in a different center each day, inviting all the children to work with her at each one of the centers (see Figure 1.13). Her assistant will do the same.

   With a new schedule and a new partner, Sarah is poised for a year of learning for herself and her students. Her strong ties to the community outside of school mean that she has strong ties to the families of her students, and she can expect their support. She has purchased some professional books to use for ideas, and she is committed to developing her curriculum and skills, one theme at a time.

LOOKING AHEAD

In the next chapters of this book, look for a description of research particularly important for preschool and then suggestions for how teachers who work in settings like Pam's, Eliana's, and Sarah's might take those suggestions into their work with children. We consider applications during whole-group, small-group, centers, and other times.

CHAPTER 2

A Focus on Oral Language and Vocabulary Development

T he natural delight that parents and teachers of preschoolers take as their children's language unfolds is a marker of its importance and its rapid development during the preschool years. This natural development, though, can be bolstered by specific language experiences during the preschool day.

WHAT IS ORAL LANGUAGE AND VOCABULARY DEVELOPMENT?

Without a doubt, children's entrance into literacy begins at birth. This entrance typically begins with the oral language and vocabulary they are exposed to at home with their caregivers. Children's oral language development is natural, building over time and with exposure, and demands no formal instruction. Children are born ready to learn language and communicate with those around them. They have the innate ability to learn the rules of language as a communication tool and to absorb it from their everyday environment.

Children's oral language development typically develops in stages. While it may differ slightly from one child to the next, the stages provide a general developmental continuum against which to measure progress. Children typically say their first words between 12 and 18 months of age. Between 18 months and 2 years of age, they may say two-word sentences and understand simple questions and commands. Between 2 and 3 years of age, they begin to use pronouns, prepositions, and to name familiar people, places, and things. In addition, to their caregivers' dismay, they master the use of the word *no*. This stage marks a time of significant growth in both listening and speaking vocabulary.

Language and vocabulary also grow at a steady pace through the child's 4th and 5th years. Children tend to master the use of irregular nouns and verbs and to use complex sentences. A stranger can understand their speech, and they can carry on a conversation with a peer, even engaging in imaginative play that includes language. These formative years certainly represent a time of amazing language growth and accomplishment in a child's life (see Figure 2.1 for language development sequence). While the language learning process is one that is natural, children's specific language and vocabulary stores are highly dependent upon the language and communication to which they were exposed.

Children "store" words and meanings in their brains and are then able to access these words from their "store" and use them in both expressive and receptive language. They can learn only the language and vocabulary that they hear. As a result, children enter preschool and then kindergarten classrooms having had vastly different experiences, exposures, and stores of language and vocabulary. This surely should be on the minds of early childhood educators as they plan and implement learning experiences from the moment children enter the preschool classroom each day.

WHY IS ORAL LANGUAGE IMPORTANT?

Oral language and vocabulary exposures play a critical role in the language and literacy development of young children. Oral language and vocabulary exert a strong influence not only on children's listening and speaking, but also on their reading and writing ability. Listening, speaking, reading, and writing are interrelated rather than sequential (Whitehurst & Lonigan, 2001). In other words, early strength in listening and speaking skills tends to bolster reading and writing skills later. Conversely, weaknesses in listening and speaking skills may be associated with struggles in formal reading and writing instruction when it begins.

Preschool teachers must understand the roots of children's language and vocabulary development. What happens before a child enters the preschool classroom can have both a short- and a long-term effect on a child's literacy development. This idea, that what happens early really matters, was powerfully presented in the *Meaningful Differences* study by researchers Betty Hart and Todd Risley (1995). They recorded the conversations between parents and children in 42 families at different levels of socioeconomic status for 1 hour a month from the time the children spoke their first word to the time the children were approximately 3½ years of age. What these researchers found were truly meaningful differences.

The children in each group were similar in that they learned how to speak at roughly the same time and all developed the structures and rules of language needed to communicate effectively. But that is were the similarities ended. By the age of 3, the spoken vocabularies recorded for the *children* from the professional families were larger than those recorded for the *parents* in the poor families. The researchers also found that the children in professional families heard many more language encouragements as well as a higher quality of vocabulary. Looking at these numbers over the course of a year, a child

Stage	Language Development Discoveries
1–4 Months	• Coo, gurgle, and grunt to express feelings • Understand all the sounds in their native language • Blow bubbles and make raspberries • Repeat their favorite sound
6–9 Months	• Intact sight and hearing • Squeal, make bubbling sounds, repeat one syllable • Sometimes two syllables • Recognize different tones • Understand words that he or she cannot use • Recognize tone more than words • Begin to understand the meaning of "no"
10–11 Months	• Words and wordlike sounds are in use • May follow simple directions
12 Months	• Speak a few words including *mama* and *dada* • Respond to simple questions and commands
14 Months	• Vocabulary between 7 and 20 words • Practice inflection • Realize the importance of talk
16 Months	• Begin to produce many consonant sounds: *t, d, n, w, h*
18–20 Months	• Begin a rapid vocabulary growth spurt • Learn 10 or more words per day • Some add a new word every 90 minutes
20–24 Months	• Begin to use two-word sentences • Overextend words • Misuse pronouns • Understand 200 words • Begin to use three-word sentences
25–30 Months	• Experiment with volume • Start to understand pronouns • Use a speaking vocabulary will increase to 300 words • Understand 900 words • Form simple sentences • Speak in past tense although rules of grammar not understood
31–36 Months	• Carry on a sustained conversation • Adjust vocabulary, speech patterns, and tone to audience • Can be understood by a stranger
4 Years	• Talk continuously • Use a speaking vocabulary of 800 words • Begin to understand and use tenses • Begin to understand *won't* and *can't* • Ask why

FIGURE 2.1. Language development sequence. Data from National Institute on Deafness and Other Communication Disorders (2000).

SES Status	Words Heard by Children	
	By Hour	By Year
Professional	2,153	11 million
Working Class	1,251	6 million
Poor	616	3 million

FIGURE 2.2. Meaningful Differences: The numbers.

in a professional family would hear *11 million* words while a child from a poor family would hear just *3 million*. A child entering the kindergarten classroom could have heard *32 million fewer words* than his or her economically advantaged peers (Hart & Risley, 1995; see Figure 2.2 for additional findings from the *Meaningful Differences* study).

So what implications do these findings have for preschool educators? Again, the children who were spoken to far less often did learn to talk and eventually learned how to read and write. However, these early differences did indeed impact the children as they moved through formal literacy instruction. Their vocabulary stores were much smaller and they struggled through reading and writing well into their adolescence (Hart & Risley, 1995). These findings suggest that what happens early really matters because these oral language deficiencies remained consistent over time.

One of the characteristics of preschool, then, especially for children from poor families, is that it can be designed to provide the types and amounts of language that children from more advantaged families encounter. Preschoolers are primed for language learning; it is up to preschool teachers to provide the highest volume and quality of language experience possible.

Preschool educators can take away several critical insights as they plan and implement their everyday classroom instruction. Certainly an important aspect to growing children's language and vocabulary is the amount of talk occurring between children and caregivers—moment by moment. In order for language to grow, preschoolers need to engage in extended language interactions many times each day. Preschool educators can think about oral language and vocabulary as something that continues to grow, expand, and accumulate every day and know that their own choices about how and how often they engage children in language plays a major role in this process.

WHAT DOES LANGUAGE
AND LITERACY INSTRUCTION LOOK LIKE?

Teachers should view themselves as facilitators rather than directors of oral language and vocabulary development. This does not mean that the teacher should step back and watch the language process unfold and grow. Rather, the teacher has the demanding task of providing opportunity, encouragement, and an environment rich with language interactions throughout the preschool day. Children need consistent opportunities and encouragement to listen, discuss, and explore their own ideas, opinions, and reflections with both teachers and peers.

Given the realities of the preschool day, this may be more easily said than done. We think the key is seeing every moment of the day as a possibility for increasing students' language and vocabulary repertoires. In the following sections, we discuss what oral language should look and sound like. Specifically, we discuss how teachers can use whole-group instruction, small-group instruction, center time, and noninstructional times in the preschool day to grow and expand children's language and vocabulary—playfully and purposefully.

Whole-Group Instruction

Whole-group instruction represents an ideal time to grow and expand children's language and vocabulary. Whether this time is 10, 15, or 20 minutes, it indeed is a special time in the preschool day and every moment must be captured. It is a time when the preschool teacher has a captive audience. He or she has a large group of children, all grouped together at one time, and all focusing on the same topic or event. An especially rich opportunity for language development occurs within shared storybook reading. *Shared storybook reading* is a broad term, including all instances when an adult reads to a child or children, pausing to engage them in discussion about the text (Holdaway, 1979). That discussion includes ideas inside the text: the story, pictures, words, and letters—and outside the text: responses and connections to experience.

Storybooks and the interactions that surround storybooks lie at the heart of children's early literacy and language experiences, both at home and at school. One of our favorite maxims of Emile Buchwald is that "children are made readers on the laps of their parents." Reading storybooks to young children is highly valued and ritualized in the preschool setting (e.g., Justice & Kaderavek, 2004; Neuman, 1999) and therefore ties all preschool classrooms together. The International Reading Association and the National Association for the Education of Young Children (NAEYC; 1998) suggest that read-alouds are the single most important literacy activity during the preschool years.

So what role does storybook reading play in children's language and vocabulary development? During storybook reading, adults and children have opportunities to listen to new words and sentence structures and to engage in constant commentary on the story. An extensive body of research literature has documented the effects of storybook reading on language and vocabulary development. In general, these studies included storybook interventions that aimed to increase the frequency of the reading event, raise the level of adult–child participation and discussion, and target story vocabulary for elaborating word meanings. The findings suggest that storybook reading increases children's receptive, or listening vocabulary (e.g., Elley, 1989; Justice, Meier, & Walpole, 2005; Robbins & Ehri, 1994); expressive, or speaking vocabulary (e.g., Arnold, Lonigan, Whitehurst, & Epstein, 1994; Hargrave & Senechal, 2000); and both receptive and expressive vocabulary development (Beck & McKeown, 2007). Given these facts, we want preschool teachers to have strategies they can use to playfully, purposefully, and practically target and increase children's language and literacy experiences during whole-group storybook reading events.

An effective shared storybook reading involves lots of talk—the rich language of the book is enhanced with teacher talk and with discussion between the teacher and the children. The experience should be brimming with language. Talk may include discussion, questions, comments, opinions, reflections, ideas, and connections. Certainly, a teacher can initiate these wonderful exchanges, especially at first. Later, though, the children should also be initiators. In that sense, a storybook reading whose goal is to bolster language and vocabulary should be both teacher facilitated and child centered.

Genre	Description	Subgenre	Examples
Simple Fiction	• Experience in narrative, stories that are created from an author's imagination • Based on real happenings	Fantasy	*Abuela* (Dorros, 1997)
		Realistic Fiction	*The Hello, Goodbye Window* (Juster, 2005)
		Fairytales/Fables	*The Little Red Hen* (Galdone, 2006)
Simple Nonfiction	• Based on factual information about anything and everything like people, places, things, animals, and events	Informational Books	*Pumpkin Circle* (Levenson, 2004)
			Whose Toes Are Those? (Asim, 2006)

Type	Description	Examples
Rhyming	• Provides opportunities for children to listen for and identify rhyming words • Develops phonological awareness • Allows for children to sing or chant along during reading	*Down by the Bay* (Raffi, 1988)
		Llama Llama Red Pajama (Dewdney, 2005)
Cumulative Tales	• Presents action and/or dialogue that repeats and accumulates through the story • Allows children to become familiar and join and repeat the lines	*The Napping House* (Wood, 2000)
		There Was on Old Lady Who Swallowed a Fly (Adams, 2007)
Wordless Books	• Contains primarily art, although some may have very few words • Contains details in the illustration that tell a story • Allows students to develop language skills by engaging in storytelling and retelling	*Rain* (Spier, 2000)
		Look Book (Hoban, 1997)
		Good Night, Gorilla (Rathmann, 2000)

FIGURE 2.3. Storybook genres and types.

There are lots of options for choosing books for storybook reading. The first place to start is typically the theme that you are currently working on in your classroom. With your theme as the starting point, you'll have choices to make in terms of types and genres of literature (see Figure 2.3 for storybook genres and types). The preschool years are an ideal time to introduce and expose children to many types and genres; those that will be a part of their formal classroom instruction. Some of these choices include fiction, nonfiction, rhyming, alphabet, cumulative, and wordless books. Ideally, a teacher would have a healthy balance of each type and genre during the course of each theme exploration.

While storybooks are not the same, each offers opportunities for oral language and vocabulary development. Some storybooks contain many lines of text and have a more complex storyline and some may have only a few words per page. Wherever the storybook falls on that continuum, a teacher can look at it as a platform to consistently *model rich language*. The teacher can add to the story content by interspersing descriptive language while reading and explaining the story content. For example, after looking at the picture on the cover or after reading the first page, a teacher may say:

> "I notice that this story takes place in the city. I see gigantic buildings, lots of cars zooming down the street, and crowds of people walking down the sidewalks and across the streets. This story takes place in a city."

An ideal storybook reading is much more than just reading the words in the book.

The teacher can also use storybook reading to initiate discussion and teacher–child interactions. One way to accomplish this is to *ask open-ended questions.* In contrast to closed questions, which tend to limit children's talk to one-word responses, open-ended questions offer opportunity for personal thought and response and afford many students the chance to answer and expand on ideas. Open-ended questions often begin with *why* or *how*. For example, a teacher might ask:

> "How do you think he feels about that?"
>
> or
>
> "Why did the tabby cat decide to go home?"

The idea here is to consistently ask these types of questions during storybook reading events. We have found that it may work best to review the storybook before reading and place open-ended questions on sticky notes throughout the book. This will alert the teacher to ask a specific question in a specific or ideal spot in the selection.

There may be times during the storybook reading when the teacher has asked an open-ended question and a child replies with a limited, one- or two-word response. This is a natural, teachable moment. One thing the teacher can do is provide *language repeti-*

tion and expansion. The teacher repeats the child's response and then expands upon that response with rich language. For example, a child may respond after being asked how a character feels by saying, "He feels sad." The teacher can then repeat and expand by saying:

> "You're right that he is sad. I can tell he is sad because his head is down and he is starting to cry. He is sad because he left his teddy bear at the restaurant and now it is gone. He went back, searched for his bear, and couldn't find it anywhere. He now realizes that it is gone. That makes him feel sad."

Another way to encourage children to expand on a limited initial response is to provide *language follow-up prompts.* This entails a teacher prompting a child to increase the sophistication of his or her description of the story after an initial response. For example, after the child responded, "He feels sad," a teacher could encourage the child to stay with that idea and expand the response by saying:

> "Yes, you're right. He does look sad. Can you tell me why he might be sad? What happened in the story that made him feel so sad?"

The idea is to consistently use the storybook reading as a time for boosting language, while also offering realistic levels of challenge and constant encouragement. Continually setting that tone will allow students the opportunity to experiment with and feel supported in using rich decontextualized language. Decontextualized language is language that deals with concepts that are not visible or immediate. It may refer to the past or to the inner thoughts of characters. In information text, decontextualized language provides information about categories of nouns rather than about specific members of a category. For example, the sentence "Trucks are used to haul heavy loads across long distances" is different from the sentence "This truck is taking oranges to another city."

A final way that a teacher can bolster oral language development during storybook reading is to take on the *role of active listener.* In this respect, a teacher listens to students' comments and uses them to engage children in conversation surrounding the story. For example, when reading a selection about fixing a car, children may comment on their own experiences about car maintenance. A teacher might say:

> "Wow! You helped your uncle change a tire last summer, Cierra? That's great! Can you tell us how you helped? Why did the car need a new tire?"

This provides an ideal way to engage students and encourage rich and topic-focused adult–child interactions (see Figure 2.4 for five ways to boost oral language and vocabulary).

Whole-group instruction is a unique time in the preschool day. With all the hustle

1. Model Rich Language.	The teacher intersperses descriptive language while reading and explaining story content.
2. Ask Open-Ended Questions.	The teacher models and/or poses questions that include use of *why*, *how*, or other open-ended questions through the majority of the reading.
3. Repeat and Expand.	The teacher repeats a child's response and expands upon that response with rich language.
4. Provide Follow-Up Prompts.	After an initial question, the teacher prompts children to increase the sophistication of their description of the story.
5. Be an Active Listener.	The teacher listens to the students' comments and uses them to engage children in conversation surrounding the story.

FIGURE 2.4. Five ways to boost oral language and vocabulary in shared reading.

and bustle in the typical preschool schedule, it's a time when all the children can come together as a community of learners. Preschool teachers can use these times of focused attention to engage, encourage, and enlarge children's oral language and vocabulary one storybook at a time (see Figure 2.5 for storybooks by theme).

Another ideal time to develop children's language and vocabulary during whole-group instruction is circle time. Circle time is typically a 5- to 10-minute time block where the teacher and children complete daily classroom routines like the attendance, calendar, days of the week, and the weather. Another wonderful language-building activity to add to these more typical routines is called Question of the Day. This involves asking children a question and then having them respond by placing their name tag under the category of their choice. For example, a teacher may have a pocket chart with a question at the top that asks, "What color is your shirt?" Students can then place their name tag under the correct color category. This can be done as the children first come to school in the morning. The idea then is to take a few minutes during circle time to discuss the responses.

Another example of a Question of the Day might be "How are you feeling today?" Students can place their name tag under categories with picture representations like, "happy," "sad," "sleepy," "angry," or "excited." Then the teacher can take the time to expand children's language by having them explain why they chose this response. For example, a teacher may say:

"Sandra, you placed your name under the 'excited' category. Why are you feeling excited today?"

Make It, Build It
- *What Does a Construction Worker Do?* (Boekhoff, 2006)
- *This Truck* (Collicutt, 2004)
- *I Drive a Bulldozer* (Bridges, 2005)
- *Construction Countdown* (Olson, 2004)
- *Alphabet under Construction* (Fleming, 2006)
- *Hard Hat Area* (Roth, 2004)
- *·B Is for Bulldozer: A Construction ABC* (Sobel, 2006)
- *Dig Dig Digging* (Mayo, 2006)

Animals and Where They Live
- *Animals Animals* (Carle, 1999)
- *Over in the Meadow* (Keats, 1999)
- *Little Quack's Bedtime* (Thompson, 2005)
- *Big Red Barn* (Brown, 1991)
- *Old MacDonald Had a Farm* (Hawkins, 2003)
- *Is Your Mama a Llama?* (Guarino, 2006)
- *Four Fur Feet* (Brown, 1996)
- *Animal Babies* (Gregor, 1959)

Investigating Nature
- *We're Going on a Bear Hunt* (Rosen, 2003)
- *Who's Hiding Here?* (Yoshi, 1998)
- *The Very Hungry Caterpillar* (Carle, 1986)
- *The Very Busy Spider* (Carle, 1989)
- *A Tree Can Be....* (Nayer, 1994)
- *Wonderful Worms* (Glaser, 1996)
- *Under One Rock, Bugs, Slugs, and other Ughs* (Fredericks, 2001)
- *I Wish I Were a Butterfly* (Howe, 1994)

FIGURE 2.5. Storybooks by theme.

The teacher may also use this as a time to encourage peer-to-peer language interactions as well. For example, a teacher might add a question to this exchange like:

"Let's try to help Sandra have a great day. Tell Sandra what we can do to make her have a very special day today."

Of course, the storybook reading selection and the Question of the Day strategy could be used in tandem. For example, an ideal storybook to read with the emotion question or theme could be *A is for Angry* by Sandra Boyton (1987), *Alexander and the Horrible, No Good, Very Bad Day* by Judith Viorst (1972), or *Today I Feel Silly: And Other Moods That Make My Day* by Jamie Lee Curtis (1998; see Figure 2.6 for example Questions of the Day and accompanying storybooks). Children can then expand on their responses on

How do you feel today?
- *Peter's Chair* (Keats, 1998) ·*A Is for Angry* (Boyton, 1987)
- *Alexander and the Horrible, No Good, Very Bad Day* (Viorst, 2009)
- *If You're Happy and You Know It* (Raffi, 2005)
- *The Very Lonely Firefly* (Carle, 1995)
- *What are You So Grumpy About?* (Lichtenheld, 2007)

How did you get to school today?
- *School Bus* [Crews, 1993)
- *The Car Trip* (Oxenbury, 1994)
- *The Train* (McPhail, 1992)
- *Truck* [Crews, 1991)
- *Flying* [Crews, 1989)
- *Boats* (Barton, 1994)

What color is your shirt?
- *.A Rainbow of My Own* (Freeman, 1978)
- *Brown Bear, Brown Bear, What Do You See?* (Martin & Carle, 2007)
- *Colors* (Ehlert, 1989)
- *Is It Red? Is It Yellow? Is It Blue?* (Hoban, 1987)
- *Little Blue and Little Yellow* (Lionni, 1995)
- *Planting a Rainbow* (Ehlert, 1992)

What letter does our first name begin with?
- *Alphabet under Construction* (Fleming, 2006)
- *Alphabet City* (Johnson, 1999)
- *Alphabetics* (MacDonald, 1989)
- *Alphabet Adventure* (Wood, 2001)
- *Chicka Chicka Boom Boom* (Martin & Archambault, 1989)
- *Eating the Alphabet: Fruits and Vegetables from A to Z* (Ehlert, 1994)

What do you want to be when you grow up?
- *Hands: Growing Up to Be an Artist* (Ehlert, 2004)
- *Jobs People Do* (Maynard, 1997)
- *Community Helps from A to Z* (Kalman, 1997)
- *My Dentist* (Rockwell, 1987)
- *I Want to Be a Doctor* (Liebman, 2000)
- *Fire Fighters A to Z* (Demarest, 2003)
- *A Visit to the Post Office* (Ziegler, 1989)
- *I Can Be a Police Officer* (Matthias, 1985)
- *Pet Doctor* (Sobol, 1988)

How many people are in your family?
- *The Family Book* (Parr, 2003)
- *All Families Are Special* (Simon, 2003)
- *Snow Family* (Kirk, 2002)
- *Hello Baby* (Rockwell, 2000)
- *The New Baby* (Mayer, 2001)
- *Annie Rose Is My Little Sister* (Hughes, 2003)
- *Let's Eat* (Zamorano, 1999)

FIGURE 2.6. Example Questions of the Day and accompanying storybooks.

the chart and compare their emotions with those of the character. Again, the idea is to use these times to their fullest extent. These are not just a quick "yes" or "no" answer, but a springboard for rich discussion and exchange. Just think of all the language and vocabulary opportunities for children if teachers used these procedures systematically every day!

Small-Group Instruction

While whole-group instruction represents a unique time to work with your community of learners, small-group instruction is a time to work more directly with smaller groups of students. In many cases, children are placed in small groups based upon need. These areas of need are often identified through formal or informal literacy measures. For example, students may be grouped because they have similar levels of knowledge of letters, letter sounds, or phonological awareness skills like rhyming or initial sounds. In the case of oral language and vocabulary, though, students may be best placed in mixed-ability groups so that students with smaller vocabulary stores may talk with those with larger stores.

A small-group oral language session, usually 10–15 minutes, is typically centered on a central concept, storybook, or target vocabulary words. Certainly, a teacher can follow the same shared storybook reading routines discussed in the previous section on whole-group instruction, but with a greater chance for each child to participate. This is a highly effective way to extend whole-group instruction and really focus attention on those students who may not have participated during whole group but are in critical need of language and vocabulary development.

Teachers can read the same book read in that particular day's shared reading session or they can choose to reread a familiar selection from weeks and themes past. The great thing is that children love to have their favorite book read time and time again. This practice is often viewed as building a feeling of comfort and familiarity. This love of repetition also has its advantages in the context of shared reading: it fosters oral language and vocabulary development. Children who have been exposed to repeated readings of one book gradually increase the sophistication and the amount of talk related to the selection after each subsequent reading (McGee & Schickedanz, 2007). They can be observed providing responses that are more interpretive and elaborative, and making more judgments about the characters, events, and resolutions (e.g., Bus, 2001; Morrow, 2009). Children may also begin to narrate the story on their own as the teacher conducts the small-group shared reading (Ivey, 2002) and can often be observed engaging in pretend readings of that selection during self-selected literacy center time (Sulzby, 1985).

Another playful and purposeful way to engage students in small groups is to have a focused discussion centered on target vocabulary words. *Target words* are individual words chosen from the current theme that allow for rich and varied discussion. For a

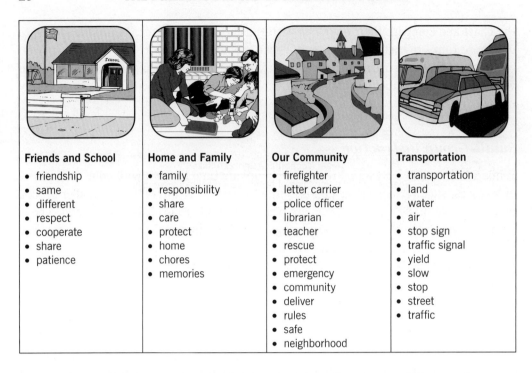

Friends and School	Home and Family	Our Community	Transportation
• friendship	• family	• firefighter	• transportation
• same	• responsibility	• letter carrier	• land
• different	• share	• police officer	• water
• respect	• care	• librarian	• air
• cooperate	• protect	• teacher	• stop sign
• share	• home	• rescue	• traffic signal
• patience	• chores	• protect	• yield
	• memories	• emergency	• slow
		• community	• stop
		• deliver	• street
		• rules	• traffic
		• safe	
		• neighborhood	

FIGURE 2.7. Example preschool themes and thematic target vocabulary words.

book about firefighters, they can be nouns (air mask), verbs (rescue), adjectives (courageous), or adverbs (bravely). Target words are words that add to a rich understanding of the current content and theme as well as words that add to students' vocabulary stores.

For example, the students could be exploring a theme centered on community helpers and the current shared storybook could be about the neighborhood fire station and the role of a firefighter. Some examples of target vocabulary might include the words *rescue, danger, safety, air mask,* and *courageous* (see Figure 2.7 for more examples of themes and thematic target words). Beck and McKeown (2001, 2007) suggest a set of procedures for teachers to use to introduce and engage students in a rich discussion surrounding a target word (see Figure 2.8 for a list of procedures).

A small-group lesson centered on the word *rescue* might look and sound like this. A teacher might say to the group:

> "This is a picture of a firefighter rescuing a person from a house that is on fire. The word that we will be talking about today is *rescue*. What word?"

The children will then all repeat the word *rescue*. Research suggests that this is an impor-

Target Vocabulary Repeated
Teacher asks children to repeat the target words after she has said them to establish a phonological *representation*.

⇩

Target Vocabulary in Child-Friendly Terms
Teacher explains all target word meanings in child-friendly terms.

⇩

Target Vocabulary Contextualized
Teacher explains meaning of target words as they were used in or related to the story.

⇩

Target Vocabulary in Other Contexts
Teacher provides examples of each of the target words outside of the story context.

⇩

Target Vocabulary Extended
Teacher encourages students to construct their own examples or make judgments about the target words.

⇩

Target Vocabulary Repeated
Teacher asks the children to repeat the target words after she has said them to establish a phonological *representation*.

FIGURE 2.8. Small-group target word procedures. Based on Beck, McKeown, and Kucan (2002).

tant first step in helping children remember and recall a specific word. The teacher will then provide a child-friendly definition of the target word, or one to which children can easily attach meaning. The teacher might say:

> "Rescue means to help someone by taking him or her away or freeing that person from something that might hurt him or her."

The next step includes providing the meaning of the target word as it was used in the storybook previously read to the students. A teacher might say:

> "In the story we read today, the firefighter rescued a cat from high up in the tree and then he rescued the boy from the apartment that was on fire. The firefighter

rescued the cat from falling from the tree and rescued the boy from getting hurt in the fire."

The fourth step includes providing multiple examples of the target word outside the context of the story. This procedure helps children to have a flexible and multifaceted understanding of the word. The teacher might then provide two or three additional examples of the target word *rescue*. The teacher might say:

"I remember watching a television show about some people who were rescued when their boat wouldn't work in the ocean. The coast guard, men and women with the special job of helping and rescuing people in the ocean, drove out on their boat and found the people who were stuck. They helped them off of their boat, put them on the coast guard boat, and pulled the boat to shore. They rescued them. I also remember the time I needed to rescue my brother because his car broke down on his way to work. I drove my car, picked him up, and drove him to work. I rescued him."

The teacher could then offer one or two more examples of the target word.

The fifth step includes encouraging the children to discuss their own examples, judgments, or connections to the target word. It might be helpful to also have the children hold some objects or pictures that represent the target word. The teacher might then say:

"What does it mean to rescue someone or something?"

"Have you ever seen or heard of anyone getting rescued?"

"Why might you need to be rescued?"

After this specific set of procedures and multiple exposures and examples of the target word, children are often ready and prepared to discuss their connections and understandings of the word. This surely is the purpose of this small-group instructional time. The sixth and final step includes having the student repeat the target word again to root that word in their memory. It is important that students are able to use (expressive vocabulary) and understand (receptive vocabulary) the target word in multiple situations. Teachers can also consider having a teacher assistant working with another group of students using the same procedures. Teachers can think of vocabulary as something that must live outside of the preschool classroom so that it makes its way into the daily lives and experiences of preschool children.

Center Time

Oral language and vocabulary development opportunities continue during children's center-time exploration. Center time is a time for children to explore, discover, create, practice and apply skills, problem solve, and use critical thinking skills, as well as to collaborate and interact with classmates. This is a unique aspect of center time—the peer-to-peer interactions that are facilitated through carefully planned center-time activities. One center in particular, dramatic play, lends itself well to language and vocabulary exchanges with fellow classmates.

The dramatic play center is one that can take on a total transformation based on the current theme. It can be a doctor's office while covering a theme on health and then a post office while working on a community helpers' unit. So, what do these thematic transformations have in common with oral language and vocabulary development? They help to facilitate rich and focused language interactions through role play. They provide an avenue for using and extending the specific language and concepts that are developed within the theme. When preschool children engage in role-playing activities their creativity, imagination, and language are strengthened. With a little imagination and creativity themselves, teachers can help make this possible.

Let's take for example a thematic unit surrounding cooking and nutrition. The dramatic play area could be transformed into a diner. It might look like this: a sign over the area that reads "Our Class Diner," table and chairs with plastic tablecloths, plastic vases with artificial or real flowers, and menus on the table. These can be brought into class from real restaurants or they can be teacher-made (See Figure 2.9 for a teacher-made

FIGURE 2.9. Teacher-made diner menu for dramatic play.

menu example). You can also have plastic food, plates, and cutlery that would match the food from the menu or the healthy food suggestions from discussions during your whole- or small-group time. Props such as a clipboard with paper and pencil for the waiter/wait- ress or a bell for the cook/chef also can be added. So, the scene has now been set. That's the easy part! What you want to ensure is that children will use the setting and props to increase their language and vocabulary repertoires. This is where the idea of modeling and role playing comes in as a critical component.

Whole-group instruction is an ideal time to model productive and purposeful role play. Continuing on the theme of healthy eating in *Our Class Diner,* the teacher can introduce the various roles in the diner experience and have a few students role play with him or her for the whole group. The diner roles include the *waiter* or *waitress, chef/ cook, host* or *hostess, cashier,* and of course, the *customers.* What may work is to make a necklace or a badge for each role with the matching picture (see Figure 2.10 for diner role-playing badges). The teacher can then show the children each role on the necklace, explain the role, and then model what it might sound and look like while they were in the "Class Diner." The necklace or badge then serves as a reminder of a specific role in the diner experience. The teacher can then assign roles for the diner during whole- group time by having each child put on the badge or necklace. For example, a teacher might say:

"This is a customer badge. This is a picture of a customer eating a meal and this is the word *customer.* A customer is someone who comes into the diner to eat a meal.

FIGURE 2.10. Our Class Diner role-playing badges.

When you come into the diner as a customer, a host or hostess asks you how many people are coming to eat today, and then takes you to a table and gives each of you a menu. The customer then reads the menu and then tells the waiter or waitress what he or she would like to eat. That is called giving a waiter or waitress your order. The waiter or waitress will then write down your order on paper and then give the paper to the cook or the chef. After your food has been prepared in the kitchen by the cook, the waiter or waitress brings your order to the table. Be sure to thank him or her for your food. You then eat your food while talking with your friends at the table. Have any of you ever had an experience like this at a restaurant or diner? The waiter or waitress then gives you the bill. You need to read the bill and then pay the cashier. Remember that we have pretend money in dramatic play. So, if you are a customer in the diner, don't forget your money! Okay, who can remind me what a customer is and what a customer should do when visiting Our Class Diner?"

The teacher can then role-play this scenario for the whole group. Further explanation and model role play will be necessary for the other roles as well.

It may be helpful to begin with only two or three roles and then gradually introduce new roles during whole-group time as the theme progresses and you are sure that children are engaging in productive and language-rich role play up to that point. It may also be helpful for the teacher as well as the teacher assistant to take on one of the roles each day to directly model and engage students in rich language exchanges. It really is fun and children love seeing their own teachers engaging in creative role-play scenarios. Teacher modeling is key for language and vocabulary enhancement in these dramatic play areas. Of course we want children to insert their own creative flair while playing in Our Class Diner but they also need the practical guidance and explanation from the teacher for purposeful, appropriate, and targeted language exchanges.

Additional Opportunities

As we have previously discussed, the preschool day is packed with instructional opportunities to focus attention on children's language and vocabulary development. It is important not to let any moment pass by—each one is a language exchange just waiting to happen! With that in mind, we also discuss how some otherwise unstructured times of the day, like mealtime and outdoor play, can also be a perfect opportunity to fit in those conversations.

Mealtime

Surely, mealtime is a time of the day to ensure that children are getting proper nutrition for healthy bodies and minds. Something that always goes well with a good meal is *good*

1. What did you do this weekend?
2. What is the weather like today?
3. What was your favorite center you visited today? Why?
4. What was the story about that we read today?
5. What is your favorite kind of animal? Why?
6. What book are you going to read next in the library center?
7. What foods on our table are crunchy? Chewy? Sweet?
8. What made you smile so far today? Laugh? Giggle? Cry? Why?
9. How do you help your mom, dad, grandma at home?
10. If you could be any animal in the world for a day, which would it be? Why?
11. What is your favorite color? Why?

FIGURE 2.11. Mealtime conversation starters.

conversation. Spills and mealtime challenges aside, this is also a healthy philosophy for the preschool mealtime schedule. Teachers, who include all adults in the classroom—teacher, teacher assistant, as well as parent volunteers—can enact this philosophy by sitting among the children during every mealtime and initiating language-rich conversations. There may be times when there is a natural dialogue that emerges on a particular day. Other times, you may need some help to get that conversation off the ground.

For example, a teacher assistant sitting at one of the tables might say, "Jamal, what did you do this weekend?" After Jamal comments, a teacher might extend Jamal's comments by asking him further questions, asking other children to comment on the topic of this response, or asking other students at the table what they did this past weekend. It may be helpful for the teacher to also comment on his or her weekend and model rich language. The key is to increase the amount of talk. Ideally, there would be one adult per table among the children modeling, initiating, and sustaining language-rich interactions. In Figure 2.11 we have provided a variety of conversation starters to help your mealtime include lots of tasty talk.

Outside Play

The preschool day offers opportunities for children to get outside, get some fresh air, and engage in some form of exercise. Traditionally, the focus of outside play in the preschool setting is activities associated with gross-motor skill development. While this is a critical component of any preschool curriculum, outdoor play also offers an abundance of language and vocabulary opportunities. A starting point for thinking about an outside activity is your theme. Consider an activity that combines gross-motor skills but also ties in a language-building component.

Let's explore the theme that investigates nature. One idea may be to take your children on a *nature walk*. A nature walk that builds language might include the classroom teachers modeling rich language during the walk, students asking questions, students providing observations, and the teacher facilitating peer-to-peer conversations. The central idea is that you have focused your children's attention to using language centered on what they see in nature. They have a purpose for this walk. A language-rich nature walk might look and sound like the following. *Before the walk*, a teacher might say:

> "We have been working on the nature unit. We have been talking about nature and reading many books about things and objects that we might find in the nature around us. So, today we will go on a nature walk. We will walk around outside the school and the park next to our school. Your job is to observe the nature around us, talk to your friends about the things that you notice or observe, and collect some objects that are a part of nature. Everyone will get a nature collection bag to collect some of these objects. When we come back to the classroom we will all have a chance to share our observations and talk about the interesting objects that you were able to collect. What are some things that we might find? Think about what we have been reading and discussing this week."

During the nature walk, the teachers and parent helpers can model rich language about some aspects of nature that they are noticing. For example, a teacher might say:

> "I notice the trees around us. The leaves on these are just beginning to bloom. The leaves are different shades of green. I even hear some birds chirping. Nature is coming alive after the winter!"

The teachers can also encourage the children to ask questions, make observations, and talk to peers about the things that they see and hear in nature. Children should also use this time to choose objects to collect for their nature bag.

After the nature walk, children can come together to discuss all the happenings and artifacts from the experience. This is an excellent time for purposeful and engaging language interactions. A teacher might begin by asking students to discuss their observations from the nature walk and encourage children to comment on one another's observations. It is important that teachers take on the role of facilitator; children should be doing the most talking. Teachers might consider recording the responses on chart paper to revisit after the discussion or the next day. The experience could end with a *Nature Show and Tell*. Children can pull out one of their objects from the nature bag and describe and discuss the object and explain why they chose it. The teacher can then add a comment to the child's response and encourage other students to ask a question or comment on the child's object. (Some of the objects might include leaves, grass, rocks, flowers, acorns, pebbles, twigs, etc.). Again, the idea is to use this thematic outdoor experience as a platform for engaging language and vocabulary interactions. Some websites that provide additional outdoor activities that promote language development are the following:

- *science.preschoolrock.com*
- *www.education.com/activity/preschool/outdoor*
- *www.brighthub.com/education/early-childhood/articles/38384.aspx*
- *www.preschoolrainbow.org/preschoolers.htm#Preschool%20Activities*

IMPLEMENTATION IN THREE CLASSROOMS

A Public School-Based Preschool: Pam

Pam places a special importance on her children's language and vocabulary development and it is evident in every aspect of her classroom instruction. She works with a population of children who may struggle in kindergarten and she feels this responsibility to prepare them for what lies ahead. Because of her rich pedagogical knowledge regarding children's language and vocabulary development gained from her degree in early childhood education and intensive professional development experiences, she realizes that the parental role in this component is critical. So, she gets her parents "on board" with this piece even before the school year begins.

Pam conducts home visits with her children's parents throughout the month leading up to the first day of school. As a part of this visit, Pam begins to lay the foundation with parents in regard to how both parents and teacher can assist each other to grow children's language and vocabulary stores. Pam talks to the parents about the importance of talk. She discusses some of the activities that she has planned to include lots of talk in her classroom and then moves to how parents can support their child's growth.

Pam informally talks to the parents about increasing the amount of talk and vocabulary in typical family activities like going to the grocery store, taking trips in the car, getting dressed for school, mealtimes, and even taking a bath. She also shows them an example of a language-building activity that she will send home with their child every Friday called *Weekend Book Buddies*. Pam will send home a baggie with a book and some accompanying activities designed to increase language interactions between parent and child before, during, and after reading the storybook. There is also a parent log where the parents can write comments, reflections, and descriptions of the activity. To then connect the home to school, children conduct a *Show and Tell* during whole-group time about the experience following the weekend.

Pam also talks to the parents about the parent workshops that will be offered throughout the school year. She provides a rationale for these workshops and shows them some examples of make-it and take-it activities that have been made in past workshops. She also talks about opportunities for parents to volunteer in the classroom. From the very beginning, the parents feel supported and very much involved in their child's education, and more specifically, in their language and vocabulary development success.

A Head Start Center: Elaina

Of all the literacy goals discussed in this book, oral language and vocabulary is the most important and perhaps the most challenging to develop in the children who are learning English as a second language with whom Elaina works. Elaina knows that because her children are learning English as a second language, a language that is different from the language they hear in their homes and in their communities, she has only 4 short hours each day to build her children's English vocabularies and their capacity to use oral language appropriately. How does she approach this daunting task? It may seem silly but the first thing Elaina reminds herself and her entire classroom staff each day is to talk. She knows that if she and the other two adults in the classroom serve as language models it will go a long way toward helping her children build both vocabulary and oral language skills. Therefore, Elaina and her team talk with children nonstop throughout the 4 hours that the children are in the classroom.

In addition to talking more, Elaina also focuses on the quality of words she is using while talking. In order to build vocabulary, Elaina first identifies words that coincide with her classroom themes and activities. She strives to choose words that are useful to children, that they will come into contact with during play activities and storybook readings connected to the theme, and that can be defined in ways that children will understand. To teach these words after reading, she says the word and asks children to repeat it, tells them a child-friendly definition, reminds them how the word was used in the story, gives them an example of how to use the word outside the story, asks them for an example of how to use the word, and then asks the children to say the word again (Beck, McKeown, & Kucan, 2002). Elaina has found that the key to children learning and using these words on their own is for the adults in the classroom to use these same words throughout the day, during mealtime, while playing with children in the centers, or whenever appropriate during conversations.

Elaina wants her children to hear the sound of the English language as often as possible. She reads aloud repeatedly from a variety of books, including children's trade books that others might consider too complex for her preschool community. Those books contain language that is much more complex than the big books that she uses in her curriculum. However, she knows that her children must have exposure to as much rich language as possible. After each page that she reads from one of these more complex trade books, she shows the children the illustration and provides a simpler summary of some aspect of the content of that page. Elaina knows that her children can understand more English than they can actually use, so she is careful to spend a few moments each day expanding their exposure.

Small-group time is an essential language time. During small group, Elaina can provide more individualized supports for her children as they begin to use the language that they are hearing and learning. In small-group time, whatever her focus, Elaina is building language. She allows children to point to pictures and objects as they learn to express themselves, but she also provides her own narration as they do it. When they begin to use words and phrases as responses, Elaina repeats and extends the children's language to show them that they are communicating effectively and that their ideas can be expressed in even more words over time.

A Private Preschool: Sarah

As Sarah is thinking through her new plan for centers, she knows that she has two adults to use during that time. She decides that one will focus on language and one on literacy. She speaks with her assistant, who admits that she is more comfortable with literacy. Together they decide that their writing and library areas are best for literacy work, and the art and make-believe centers are best for language. Each woman will alternate between those two centers each day.

Sarah starts to plan for building oral language in the creative play center. She considers two options: staying outside the play and prompting the children to comment on it, or inserting herself into the play itself, facilitating language from within the fantasy. She decides that both might be useful, but decides to jump right in. Although her props are fairly limited, she thinks that playing directly with the children will provide them models for how to construct make-believe scenarios filled with language. Given the upcoming theme (fall), she prepares a short list of potential scenes to suggest for times when the children do not have an idea of their own. Her list is in Figure 2.12.

Creative Play for Fall
Let's play school bus.
Let's clean up leaves.
Let's pick the last vegetables.
Let's go to the grocery store.
Let's cut wood.
Let's get our school things ready.

FIGURE 2.12. Creative play ideas for fall theme.

Sarah is fairly sure that her art center will be a place where she can engage each child in an extended one-on-one language interaction about his or her work. She has set up the center such that two or three children can work there at a time, and she plans to let them first get started with the materials. Then she will ask the children (one at a time) to tell her about what they are planning in their day's project, and eventually to provide a description. That will give Sarah a chance to reflect and extend the children's language and to prompt them to use words that they are learning to develop for the month's theme. She will also collect language samples during this time, transcribing children's talk into a journal that she has marked for this purpose. That way she can reflect on children's language production over time.

WHERE CAN I FIND MORE INFORMATION?

Oral language and vocabulary development is such a critical component to the preschool experience. It's an interesting area of development because it has the potential to grow every day of a child's life—well beyond the preschool years. The following are sources for you to continue to grow your own knowledge and expertise in the exciting area of oral language and vocabulary development.

Web-Based

- A to Z Teacher Stuff—teacher resources, lesson plans, themes, tips, printables, and more
  atozteacherstuff.com/Lesson_Plans
- Preschool large-group and circle activities
  www.preschoolrainbow.org/activities-large.htm
- Lesson plans page—language arts lesson plans
  www.lessonplanspage.com/LAK1.htm
- Florida Center for Reading Research
  www.fcrr.org
- Read Write Think
  www.readwritethink.org
- Reading Rockets—reading comprehension and language arts teaching strategies for kids
  www.readingrockets.org
- Free teacher resources, lesson plans, interactive activities
  www.thinkfinity.org/EducatorHome.aspx

Text-Based

- Bennett-Armistead, V. S. (2009). *Literacy-building play in preschool*. New York: Scholastic.
- Morrow, L. M. (2007). *Developing literacy in preschool*. New York: Guilford Press.
- Roskos, K. A., Tabors, P. O., & Lenhart, L. A. (2009). *Oral language and early literacy in preschool*. Newark, DE: International Reading Association.

CHAPTER 3

Comprehension

C hildren are born wanting to understand the world around them. Infants and toddlers intently observe and scrutinize objects, people, and events. Young children constantly experiment, trying to discover why, how, and if things work. In fact, they use all five senses of touch, taste, smell, sound, and sight in order to understand what is happening to and around them. The desire to understand and comprehend is an inherent one. A similar desire resides in learning to read (although the mechanics of it are not natural). Children who see people reading want to read themselves in order to understand what the mysterious symbols and marks on a page or in a book mean. Children bring this hunger for understanding with them into their first experiences with comprehension, and we can marshal it into a powerful force.

WHAT IS COMPREHENSION?

Comprehension is the goal of all literacy instruction. We sing rhyming songs and blend and segment sounds to develop children's phonological awareness in order to help them eventually learn to read and spell words. We teach children the letters of the alphabet to facilitate their ability to read and spell words. We talk with children and build their vocabularies in order to help them understand the words that they will later read. We teach children how to hold a book and where to begin reading and how to turn the page. And we develop all of these prerequisite skills so that children will be able to pick up a piece of text and not only decode the words but also understand what they have read. Comprehension is the ability to read or listen and understand text (Snow, 2002).

How do good readers comprehend what they are reading? Pressley (2006) offers a nice summary of what we know from research about how good readers comprehend text. First, good readers are able to automatically recognize familiar words and decode unfamiliar words while reading. As they read, skilled readers separate the main ideas from the details in order to get a big picture of what they are reading. To do this, readers use background knowledge to make inferences about the information they are reading.

Good readers also use comprehension strategies, albeit sometimes unconsciously, before, during, and after reading. Before reading, good readers make predictions about what they will be reading and examine the structure and format of the text to get an overview. During reading, they clarify predictions, make new predictions based on clues, ask questions, use clues to make inferences, and visualize or create mental pictures. After reading, good readers recall and synthesize information in order to summarize what they have read. Many factors contribute to whether a reader understands what he or she has read, including vocabulary, decoding skills, fluency, background knowledge, motivation, and knowledge and use of strategies (see Figure 3.1). All but two of them (decoding skills and fluency) should be real targets of our preschool work. All but these two can be modeled and applied during read-alouds. Because comprehension is so important, we argue that it can and should be a focus right from the start of preschool.

WHY IS COMPREHENSION INSTRUCTION IMPORTANT?

Historically, preschool teachers have focused their instruction on oral language and vocabulary, phonological awareness, concepts of print, alphabet knowledge, and to a

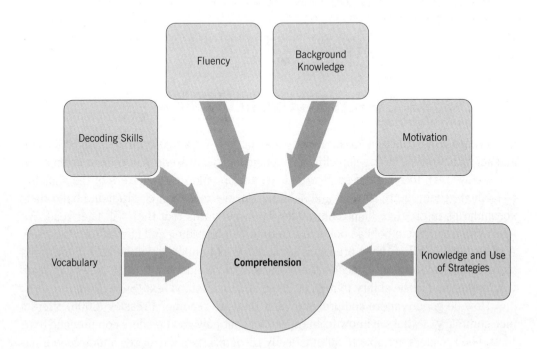

FIGURE 3.1. Factors that influence reading comprehension.

lesser extent, writing. For a long time reading researchers and educators did not empha-
size comprehension instruction in the preschool classroom. Comprehension was considered too complex a task for young children. Conventional wisdom dictated that because
children could not yet read on their own, there was no need to worry about their comprehension.

We now know that this way of thinking was shortsighted. Research in recent years
has indicated the important role preschool teachers play in developing the beginning
skills children can use in later reading comprehension (International Reading Association & National Association for the Education of Young Children, 1998; Snow, 1991).
By reading stories aloud to preschool children, teachers can begin to develop children's
comprehension. Reading to and engaging children in rich conversations about stories
can foster children's comprehension, vocabulary knowledge, and understanding of story
structure (Karweit & Wasik, 1996; McGee & Schickedanz, 2007; Morrow, Freitag, &
Gambrell, 2009; Paris & Paris, 2003; Pressley & Hilden, 2002).

If we wait to develop children's comprehension skills until they can read, we may do
them a disservice by not laying the foundational skills necessary to comprehend the text
that they are reading. If we can develop prerequisite skills necessary for later reading
comprehension, then we certainly should do so in playful, developmentally appropriate
ways.

WHAT DOES COMPREHENSION INSTRUCTION
LOOK LIKE?

It is challenging to envision comprehension instruction for children who cannot yet read.
So much of comprehension is intertwined with specific storybook readings. However, in
preschool classrooms teachers can build skills that will serve as the building blocks for
their future reading comprehension. Even young children can participate in activities
that develop the ability to make predictions, use clues to make inferences, and recall
events in a specific order—all strategies that good readers use while reading in order to
understand text. The activities shared below all support the development of prereading
comprehension skills and can be implemented during whole group, small group, centers,
and additional times in the classroom.

Whole-Group Instruction

Without a doubt, shared storybook reading is the ideal time for building preschool children's comprehension. Reading aloud to children has been called the "single most important activity for building these understandings and skills essential for reading success"
(International Reading Association & National Association for the Education of Young
Children, 1998). The potential of shared storybook reading lies in the rich interchange

that can occur between adults and children while reading a text. Therefore, it is essential that preschool teachers plan shared storybook readings that actively engage children (Whitehurst et al., 1994a). How can preschool teachers engage children while reading? Research indicates that conversation surrounding the book reading is the key for active child participation (Dickinson & Smith, 1994; Snow, Tabors, Nicholson, & Kurland, 1995; Whitehurst et al., 1988). "It is the talk that surrounds the storybook reading that gives it power" (International Reading Association & National Association for the Education of Young Children, 1998). So, what kind of talk should preschool teachers use while reading with children? We have chosen to highlight two kinds of talk that build children's comprehension—talk focused on asking open-ended questions and talk focused on modeling specific comprehension strategies that are developmentally appropriate for young children. Taken together, that talk about the story simulates or makes external the internal self-talk that will be the heart of reading comprehension later. A steady diet of such talk makes clear to children that comprehension is thinking with and about text ideas.

As you saw in the last chapter, the best storybook readings are not simply straight-through readings of the book from cover to cover. Instead, the most engaging storybook readings are those in which the teacher sprinkles well-planned, open-ended questions throughout the reading to engage children in discussion, making them active participants in the reading process. Open-ended questions are those questions that do not have right or wrong answers. Rather they are open to a range of answers. For example, "What do you think will happen next in the story?" is an open-ended question, for it has no right or wrong answer. Open-ended questions can be contrasted with closed questions. Closed questions have one right answer and all other answers are wrong. For example, "What color is the ball?" is a closed question, for it has one right answer based on the text. Figure 3.2 provides a comparison of open-ended and closed questions.

The power of open-ended questions is their ability to engage children in discussion. Since there is no right or wrong answer, children feel free to participate by providing their opinion. Open-ended questions are safe. Think about your own tendency to talk in large-group settings. Even as adults we are far less inclined to engage in discussion if we

Open-Ended Questions	Closed Questions
How do you think the character in our book is feeling? Why do you think that?	Who picked up the shovel?
	What tool is this?
Why do you think the bear did that?	What color is the plate?
What do you see happening in this picture?	What time is it?
Has anything like this ever happened to you? What did you do?	Where are they?
What do you think will happen next? Why do you think that?	How many raisins are there?
What would you do if you were in the same situation? Why?	

FIGURE 3.2. Example open-ended and closed questions.

are unsure of what we are supposed to say. In contrast, if we are asked about our opinion or a question that has no right or wrong answer, we are much more apt to participate. As children respond to open-ended questions they build confidence in sharing their opinions and understandings about the text. This confidence will help children when they are asked to respond to more advanced, higher-level questions as they develop their comprehension of text.

We are not suggesting that teachers should never ask closed questions during reading. In fact, closed questions have an important role in shared storybook reading. Closed questions help teachers determine quickly whether children have an understanding of basic vocabulary words found in the text or concepts in the illustrations. By asking his or her children what a certain tool is on the workbench in a book, a preschool teacher can determine whether the children know the word *hammer*. If children do not know the word *hammer* and it is integral to a deeper understanding of what the character in the book is doing, then the teacher can incorporate the word *hammer* into his or her vocabulary instruction. However, asking too many closed questions during a shared storybook reading has a stifling effect on children's ability to participate in discussion about the book. If a child answers the teacher's closed question correctly, then there is nothing further to discuss. Therefore, it is important to strike a balance between just enough closed and open-ended questions while reading. Our advice when in doubt is that erring on the side of open-ended questions is a good idea.

To help teachers incorporate a range of questions in their shared storybook reading, Whitehurst et al. (1994b) suggest using the acronym CROWD while planning questions for storybook reading. The *C* in CROWD stands for completion questions; these types of questions ask children to fill in a blank from a sentence taken directly from the text. Completion questions work well when children have been exposed to the text multiple times or when the text uses repetitive language that children can use as an aid for completing the sentence. "The bear used a _____ to cut wood" is an example of a completion question. Children would need to know the vocabulary word *saw* to complete the completion question. The *R* in CROWD stands for recall questions. Recall questions ask children to recall specific information from the book, sometimes in a specific sequence. For example, "What did the boy do first? second? last?" is an example of a recall question. Children would have to remember specific events from the story in a correct order to respond to the recall question. The *O* in CROWD stands for open-ended questions. Open-ended questions, as discussed above, are those questions that encourage children to participate in conversation about the book. Therefore, open-ended questions do not have one correct answer but instead have multiple right answers. "What do you think will happen next in the story?" is an example of an open-ended question because it asks children to use their knowledge of the story so far to make an informed prediction, but because children can have different opinions about what could happen next there is no right or wrong answer to the question. The *W* in CROWD stands for *Wh-* questions. *Wh-* questions ask children to provide specific information about the text. *Wh-* questions usually begin with *who, what, when, where, why,* or *how.* Many times *Wh-* questions are closed questions. There is a right or wrong answer and the answer usually involves specific vocabulary words. For example, "What tool is the bear holding?" is a *Wh-* question that requires children to provide a specific answer. Last, the *D* in CROWD stands for distancing. Distancing questions ask children to make connections between the text and their own lives. Sometimes distancing questions are also referred to as text-to-self questions. An example of a distancing question is "Has anything like this ever happened to you? How did you respond?" Figure 3.3 provides a summary of CROWD questions.

At this point, you may be wondering how many questions to include in your shared storybook reading and how to manage the questions during reading. The answer to the first question is highly dependent on the children and the text. As a teacher you must use what you know about your children's previous experiences with, background knowledge of, interest in, engagement with, and knowledge about the book you are reading to help determine the number and types of questions to ask. For example, if you are reading a book that the children have never seen that contains ideas with which children are very unfamiliar, then you may want to ask some very general open-ended questions to get children talking about the pictures and ideas in the book. Then on a second or third reading of the book, you can begin to ask more questions that focus on specific events or characters in the text itself. Also, with more and more practice reading to a specific group of children, you will begin to get a feeling for the number of questions needed to get children engaged in the story without breaking the flow of the reading too much. Our best advice for how many questions to ask is: know your audience.

Type of Question	Purpose	Example
Completion	Asks children to supply a word or short phrase into a sentence taken directly from the text.	The train went down the _____.
Recall	Asks children to recall what happened in the story.	What did the girl eat first? second? third?
Open-Ended	Asks children to engage in discussion about a text. These questions have no right or wrong answer.	Why do you think the mom asked the daughter to be quiet?
Wh-Prompts	Asks children to provide specific information about a text, using vocabulary words. These questions begin with *who, what, when, where, why,* and *how.*	Who is hiding behind the tree?
Distancing	Asks children to make connections between what is happening in the text and what has happened in their own lives.	Have you ever eaten at a restaurant? What was it like?

FIGURE 3.3. CROWD questions for storybook reading based on Whitehurst (1992).

Teachers at all grade levels have come up with a clever way to manage the questions they ask during shared storybook reading. Our teachers write down the questions they want to ask while reading on yellow Post-it Notes, which they place in the book they will read on the page that goes along with the question. While reading the text, the teachers have a written cue of the question they will ask on the correct page. This way the teachers do not have to memorize multiple questions and where to ask them. It also ensures that the questions are planned ahead of time and are not made up while reading. We have found that we and the teachers we work with are far more likely to include a range of question types if we preplan the questions rather than try to create questions as we read with children. The one caveat we will mention with the sticky-note system is that Post-it placement is very important. Remember to place the note in an unobtrusive spot around the border of the page, away from critical illustrations or the text itself. Blocking the illustrations will frustrate children who rely heavily on the pictures for comprehension, and blocking the text will frustrate you as you are trying to read.

Let's use all the information we have discussed about asking questions while reading together to consider a good example of a storybook reading in a preschool classroom. Notice the type of questions the teacher asks, when she asks them, how many she asks, and how she responds to the children's answers. Imagine that the teacher is reading *Planting a Rainbow* by Lois Ehlert (1988) for the third time to her children.

TEACHER: (*Reads pages 2 and 3 and then pauses to ask a question. Points to the picture.*) These are bulbs underground: what do you think is going to happen to them?

CHILD: I think they are going to grow up.

TEACHER: Carlos thinks these bulbs that are planted underground are going to grow up. Why do you think that, Carlos?

CHILD: Because we see plants.

TEACHER: Oh, good, Carlos, so you know that we see plants above the ground in our flower beds at school, so you think that these bulbs are going to grow up out of the dirt so that we can see them. Does anyone else have an idea about what will happen to these bulbs?

CHILD: I think they will grow down.

TEACHER: Why do you think these bulbs are going to grow down, Maria?

CHILD: I see roots.

TEACHER: Maria says she can see roots. That is a good observation, Maria. What do we know about what roots do?

DIFFERENT CHILD: Roots grow in the dirt.

TEACHER: That is right. We have been talking about how plants have roots and that the roots stay in the dirt to give plants water and food. So part of these bulbs may grow down. Does anyone else want to share an idea about what might happen to these bulbs?

CHILD: I think the bulbs are going to make flowers.

TEACHER: Madison says she thinks the bulbs may grow and bloom into flowers. Madison, why do you think these bulbs may make flowers some day?

CHILD: I planted some tulip bulbs with my dad and then we had flowers.

TEACHER: Wonderful. I bet that was a lot of fun planting bulbs with your dad. We are also going to plant some bulbs here at school to see what happens to them. We may be able to see the bulbs grow sprouts up out of the ground, grow roots down into the dirt, and eventually bloom into some flowers. Let's keep reading now. (*Reads and then pauses on page 5.*) What are these? (*Points to a picture.*)

CHILD: Seeds.

TEACHER: That's right, Mario. These are called seeds. How did you know these were seeds?

CHILD: They are small.

TEACHER: Yes, seeds are very small. We plant seeds in the dirt and they grow into plants. (*Continues reading and pauses on page 10.*) I see here that they put little sticks with the plants' names on them next to each plant. (*Points to illustration.*) Why do you think they put names next to the plants in their garden?

CHILD: To name them.

TEACHER: Yes, the stick with the plant's name written on it names the plant. Why would they want to name the plants, Mario?

CHILD: So they won't forget.

DIFFERENT CHILD: So they will remember.

TEACHER: Ah, they wrote the plants' names on little sticks to put beside each plant so that they would not forget, so that they would remember what each plant is. Why would they want to remember what each plant is?

CHILD: Maybe so that they can know where the flowers will be.

TEACHER: That is a good idea, Daniel. Maybe they wrote the plants' names down and labeled the plants so that they could have an idea of where flowers will bloom later. (*Continues to read and pauses on page 12.*) What happened to the plants?

CHILD: They got bigger.

TEACHER: Yes, they definitely grew. They got much bigger. How do you know that?

CHILD: They are bigger than before.

TEACHER: Let's look back a few pages. Look at how big the plants are here. Now, let's turn a few pages. Look at the plants now. Now, let's turn back to the page we are on. Look at the plants now. The plants are taller now than they were on the first page. What three things do plants need to grow?

CHILD: Water.

TEACHER: Yes, we have talked about how plants need water to grow. What else do plants need to grow?

CHILD: Dirt.

TEACHER: Yes, plants also need dirt to grow. So, we know plants need water and dirt to grow. What else do plants need in order to grow?

DIFFERENT CHILD: Sun.

TEACHER: Yes, plants also need sunlight to grow. Plants need water, dirt, and sunlight to grow bigger and taller like the plants in our book. (*Finishes reading book.*) I know Madison said she planted bulbs with her dad. Has anyone else planted bulbs or plants or flowers like the family in our book? (*Allows multiple children to respond.*)

The teacher in our shared storybook reading example above wove several questions throughout her reading. She did not simply read the book straight through, but instead engaged children in a discussion about the ideas found in the book by asking them thought-provoking questions. She also included a range of different types of questions into her reading. She asked a recall question ("What three things do plants need to grow?"), several open-ended questions ("What do you think is going to happen to them?" and "Why do you think that?"), a closed, *Wh-* question ("What are these?"), and a distancing question ("Has anyone else planted bulbs or plants or flowers like the family in our book?"). Through this line of questioning, the teacher was able to get a sense for how much children understood about the book and what words she may need to include in her vocabulary instruction. The range of questions allowed for different children to answer different types of questions, depending on their understanding of the story and comfort level with the question. The questions were also highly engaging to children, who were actively participating in the reading experience.

The second type of talk important to storybook reading with preschool children is talk centered around specific comprehension strategies. The large-group storybook reading offers teachers the opportunity to model by thinking aloud how to use comprehension strategies. We recommend using three comprehension activities with young children—taking a picture walk to build background knowledge, making predictions about the text, and retelling what happened in the story. During a picture walk a teacher guides children to look only at the pictures for clues about what the story will be about. The teacher does not actually read the text during a picture walk, but instead asks open-ended questions about the illustrations on every page. By participating in a picture walk, children build an experience with the ideas in the text before they hear the actual words. A picture walk is a great activity for the first day children see a new book, which will then be read on subsequent days. One comprehension strategy that good readers use while reading is to make predictions about what the text will be about and what will come next while reading. Preschool children can learn to make predictions about a storybook using clues from illustrations or from hearing the text read aloud by the teacher. After reading, children can retell what they remember about the story. Good readers use what they remember from reading to reconstruct the text in their own words. Even children as young as 3 and 4 years can begin to orally retell what they remember from listening to a story read aloud to them.

When introducing each of these three comprehension strategies to children, the teacher must model what the strategies are and how to use them appropriately. It would be ridiculous to ask children to plant a garden without first telling and/or showing them how to do it. The same thing is true for reading comprehension strategies. You cannot just ask children to make a prediction without showing them how to do it. A teacher can model using a comprehension strategy by thinking aloud and describing exactly what he or she is doing while reading. Here's how a preschool teacher could model how to make a prediction while reading:

> "Look at the picture on the cover of this book with me. I see a picture of a beach. I think this book is going to be about a day at the beach, because I see a little girl with her family on the beach. I see sand and waves. I see the sunshine in the sky. I see a little girl with a shovel and a bucket building a sand castle near the water. I see many people in their bathing suits. I see a little boy flying a kite. I see many things that I have seen when I go to the beach in the summer with my family, so I think that this book is going to be about a day at the beach."

A good structure to use while planning comprehension think-alouds is to plan what to do before reading, during reading, and after reading (see Figure 3.4). When using a comprehension strategy with young children, before reading make sure to introduce the strategy that you will be using during reading. Tell children what you will be doing and why you will be doing it in child-friendly terms, such as "Today I am going to make predictions while I read. Good readers use clues to make predictions while they read." As you read, use the comprehension strategy. Verbalize every step so that the children can hear what you are thinking. For example, "On this page I see a picture of a wagon full of plants. I know the little girl is planting a garden with her grandmother, because I just read that they planted flowers. I think they are going to plant these plants in their garden too." Finally, after reading review the comprehension strategy you used during reading. For example, "Today while I read I made predictions about what was going to happen next in the book. I used clues from the pictures and the story to make predictions."

Time of Reading	Purpose	Example Teacher Talk
Before Reading	Provide a preview of what strategy you are going to use while reading.	"Today I am going to make predictions while reading. Good readers make predictions while reading."
During Reading	Think aloud and verbalize every step of the comprehension strategy you are using.	"I see a picture of an elephant in a cage and a monkey in a cage. I predict that this book is going to be about the zoo."
After Reading	Summarize the comprehension strategy you used while reading.	"Today I used clues in the book to help me make predictions about what was going to happen next."

FIGURE 3.4. Before-, during-, and after-reading comprehension plan.

In addition to the kinds of talk teachers use to engage children with storybooks, research indicates that repetition also helps to build children's comprehension (Bus, 2001; McGee & Schickedanz, 2007). Children love to hear the same book read over and over again. Those of us who are parents have experienced our child asking us to read a favorite book over and over and over to the point that we could recite the text from memory. As children hear the same words and examine the same illustrations multiple times, they comprehend new things. We know from observations of children after repeated readings of the same storybook that comprehension improves because children's answers to questions become more sophisticated over multiple rereadings, adding more details in their responses and making more judgments about things that happen in the story (Bus, 2001; McGee & Schickedanz, 2007). In addition, after multiple rereadings children begin to help the teacher narrate the text as he or she reads the book aloud (Ivey, 2002).

So, what can repeated readings of the same storybook look like in the preschool classroom? Some preschool teachers read a storybook for 5 days in a row (Vukelich, Han, Buell, & Moore, 2009). Day 1 begins with recording children's predictions about what they think the book might be about and then taking a picture walk, examining the pictures but not actually reading the text. On days 2 through 4 of the reading, the teacher reads the text, pausing to ask a range of questions in order to engage children in discussions designed to aid comprehension of the story. Last, on day 5 of the sequence, the teacher may ask children to help him or her read the text or to retell the story either orally or with pictures or puppets or by acting out the story with props. Figure 3.5 reviews the focus of reading for each day during the 5-day sequence. We have also seen teachers who read one storybook for 2 to 3 days in a row. In a shorter rereading sequence, a teacher must make decisions about which skills to focus on. For example, with a limited number of days to reread a storybook, it may be less important for a teacher to devote an entire reading to a picture walk and more important for the teacher to read the book to the children while modeling a comprehension skill like retelling and asking open-ended questions. A 3-day sequence may involve asking children to make predictions and then

Day	Focus of Reading	Example Activities
Monday	• Modeling comprehension strategies • Building background knowledge	• Making predictions • Taking a Picture Walk
Tuesday	• Developing comprehension	• Asking a range of questions
Wednesday	• Developing comprehension	• Asking a range of questions
Thursday	• Developing comprehension	• Asking a range of questions
Friday	• Applying and assessing comprehension • Modeling comprehension strategies	• Inviting children to read the text along with you • Involving children in a retelling—orally or with props

FIGURE 3.5. Focus of reading during a 5-day reading sequence.

reading and asking questions about the book on the first day, reading the book and asking questions on the second day, and modeling the retelling strategy on the third day of reading. Some teachers find that a group of children really enjoy one or two specific books in the classroom and request these books often. In these classrooms, the teachers may reread a few favorite books multiple times across the entire school year. Each time a favorite book is read the teacher can focus on a new comprehension strategy, a new line of questioning, a new concept of print or text feature, or engage children in a new alphabet or phonological awareness activity using the text.

A common question about multiple readings is Won't children get bored with the same book? The answer is that children naturally like rereading books with which they are already familiar. In addition, the manner in which the book is read influences the children's engagement. If a teacher reads aloud well, then children will be engaged, whether it is the first reading or the fifth reading. So, what does it mean to read well? Figure 3.6 summarizes our six tips for reading aloud with children. First, be dramatic. Read as if you are an actor or actress on the stage and the children are the audience. Related to this is reading with expression, giving characters distinct voices, changing the tone and volume of your voice when appropriate, pausing to add suspense to the story, and using the punctuation as clues for how to add intonation to your voice. Be excited about what you read. If you are excited about what you read, then your enthusiasm will spill over to the children. It is also important to read fluently—not too quickly but not too slowly. Read with enough speed that children hear complete thoughts or sentences before you pause to ask a question. If you read too slowly or haltingly, the children will quickly tire of listening. To make sure that your reading is fluent, take a few short moments to read the storybook before you read it with the children. Make sure you know how to pronounce all the words correctly so that you do not have any surprises when reading in the classroom.

1. Be Dramatic.	Think of the children as the audience at your play.
2. Read with Expression.	Give characters different voices, raise and lower your voice at appropriate moments in the story, add suspense by pausing when appropriate.
3. Be Excited about What You Are Reading.	Excitement is contagious: if you are excited about the book, then your children will be excited.
4. Read Fluently.	If you read too slowly or too disjointedly, you will lose your audience. It is always a good idea to practice reading the book before you read in front of children.
5. Read Close to Children.	If you are too far away it will be hard for children to connect to the pages of the book you are reading. Sit close and create an atmosphere of familiarity.
6. Ask Questions.	Sprinkle in questions while reading the text to engage children in discussion about the storybook, allow multiple children to respond to your questions, and then know when to return to reading (before you have lost children's attention).

FIGURE 3.6. Tips for reading aloud with young children.

During reading, sit close to children either on the floor with the children around you or in a chair right in front of the children. Sitting together as a group creates a friendly, safe environment and ensures that all children can see the illustrations as you read. Finally, ask questions periodically while you read. Asking questions will engage children in discussion about the text and keep them interested in the activity. Ask a question, call on a few children to respond, and then move back to the reading before too much time has elapsed so that the discussion does not get too far away from the content of the book and that the reading is not too disjointed.

Of course it would be remiss of us to end this section on storybook reading without discussing the importance of the book in engaging children in comprehension instruction. Three factors about the book itself are important to consider when selecting texts to use with young children: format, subject matter, and quality. Format refers to the size of the book. Children's books for the preschool classroom come in multiple sizes, but two of the most common are big books (see Figure 3.7 for an example) and traditional-size or trade books. Both formats have advantages and disadvantages for use in the classroom. The advantage of reading a big book is that its larger size makes it easy for all of the children in a classroom to see the pages. The large print of a big book is especially nice for drawing children's attention to concepts of print, letters of the alphabet, text features, and the illustrations. A disadvantage of the big book is that it is sometimes hard to maneuver while reading and may require a poster stand or easel to hold it (see Figure 3.7 for an example). Big books are more expensive and harder to find, and not every chil-

FIGURE 3.7. Example of a big book and easel: *Rainbow Fish* (1992).

dren's book is available in big-book format. Trade books have several advantages; they are widely available, less expensive, and easy to hold while reading and discussing with children. However, trade books are more difficult for multiple children to see and have much smaller print that is hard to see from any distance. Figure 3.8 summarizes the advantages and disadvantages of the two book formats.

In terms of subject matter, it is always a good idea to choose books that relate to your current classroom theme. Reading children's books on themes studied in the classroom is one of the best ways to build children's knowledge and experiences with the themes. Connecting what children are playing in dramatic play with a book that is read during group time contributes to children's overall knowledge and comprehension of the theme, builds common vocabulary word knowledge, and interests and motivates young children to learn and play. The good news is that there are so many children's books available that it would probably be impossible to think of a theme for the preschool classroom that you could not populate with an array of appropriate children's books. The bad news is that there are so many children's books related to common preschool themes that it can be

	Big Books	Trade Books
Advantages	• Easily seen by multiple children in a classroom • Large print especially conducive to instruction focused on concepts of print, alphabet knowledge, and text features	• Widely available • Inexpensive • Easy to hold and maneuver
Disadvantages	• Tricky to hold and maneuver • More expensive • Not always available	• Harder to see • Smaller print

FIGURE 3.8. Comparison of book formats.

overwhelming to know which ones to choose. Therefore, book quality is an important factor when choosing what storybooks to read. When examining children's books for quality consider several factors: content, writing style, illustrations, and likeliness of child engagement. Figure 3.9 provides a list of questions to consider while examining the quality of children's books. In addition to examining children's books yourself for quality, one resource that is very helpful in making decisions about books is the American Library Association's (ALA) webpage (*www.ala.org*). Each year the ALA selects children's books for numerous awards and prizes. A list of current and past winners of each of the children's book awards is available on the webpage. Figure 3.10 provides a list of the children's books awards given by the ALA.

Small-Group Instruction

Small-group time offers a chance for the teacher to review and extend work on comprehension begun in whole group with children. As discussed in the previous section on whole-group instruction, the ideal context around which to build children's comprehension is through a shared storybook reading. Working with smaller numbers of children during small group, the teacher or teacher's aide may choose to read the same book read during whole group or practice using the same comprehension strategies modeled in whole group with a new storybook in small group. As when reading to children in a whole-group setting, talk surrounding storybooks read in small group should include open-ended questioning and comprehension strategy modeling. The benefit of shared reading in small groups is that the teacher can focus attention on individual children to determine areas in which a child excels and areas in which a child struggles and can then help the child where needed.

Small group also provides an opportunity for reading more sophisticated storybooks than may be appropriate in whole-group settings. McGee and Schickedanz (2007) developed a technique for reading storybooks with young children in small groups in which teachers read nonfiction and picture books that require children to make inferences about character's feelings and motivations, to make connections between causes and

---

Content
- What is this book about?
- Is there a central storyline for children to follow?
- Is the central storyline confusing? or misleading?
- Is the topic appropriate for use with young children (Is there violence?)?
- Are stereotypes used throughout the text (Are gender-related, ethnic, or racial stereotypes used?)?
- Is content in the book accurate or realistic?
- How well does the content connect to your classroom theme?

Writing Style
- Is the text written for children? Will children be able to understand the vocabulary words and ideas expressed in the text?
- Is the writing free of grammatical errors?
- Is the text written in such a way that it is enjoyable to read aloud?
- Does the text include interesting text features (e.g., rhyme, rhythm, alliteration)?
- Does the text include a variety of interesting vocabulary words?

Illustrations
- Do the illustrations support the ideas in the text?
- Do the illustrations provide clues to aid comprehension of the text?
- Are the illustrations aesthetically appealing or interesting?
- Are the illustrations jarring and distracting?

Likeliness of Child Engagement
- How much background knowledge will children need in order to connect with the story?
- How familiar will your children be with the topics addressed in the book?
- How long is the book?
- How big are the print and illustrations?
- Does the text lend itself to asking a range of comprehension questions?
- Are the text and illustrations compatible with modeling comprehension strategies?

FIGURE 3.9. Questions to consider while examining the quality of books for children.

effects in the story, and to use rich vocabulary words and concepts. Figure 3.11 provides a list of sophisticated picture books that are on our shelves. The reading technique, called repeated interactive read-alouds, organizes a reading into three events—before, during, and after—and includes specific reading behaviors during each event. Using this technique, a teacher reads the same storybook three times.

On the first reading, before reading the teacher provides children with a brief introduction to the book, describing the main characters and problem in the story. During reading, the teacher calls attention to several vocabulary words and connects the words to illustrations or gestures to help children understand their meanings. During the first reading, the teacher also makes comments about what the main character is thinking or feeling and asks questions that require children to reflect on the comments the teacher

Children's Book Award	Description of the Award
Batchelder Award	Given to an outstanding children's book published in a foreign language and then translated into English.
Belpre Medal	Given to an outstanding children's book that celebrates Latin culture.
Caldecott Medal	Given to the artist of the most distinguished American picture book for children.
Coretta Scott King Award	Given to African American authors and illustrators for inspirational and educational contributions to children's literature.
Newbery Medal	Given to the author of the most distinguished children's book.
Schneider Award	Given to an author or illustrator of a children's book that embodies the disability experience.
Sibert Medal	Given to the author and illustrator of the most distinguished children's informational book.
Theodor Seuss Geisel Award	Given to the author and illustrator of the most distinguished American book for beginning readers.
Wilder Medal	Given to the author or illustrator whose life's works have made a lasting contribution to children's literature.

FIGURE 3.10. American Library Association's Children's Book Awards. Data from American Library Association.

Aardema, V. (1975). *Why mosquitoes buzz in people's ears*. New York: Puffin.
Bang, M. (1999). *When Sophie gets angry—really, really angry.* New York: Scholastic.
Cronin, D. (2000). *Click, clack, moo: Cows that type*. New York: Scholastic.
DePaola, T. (1975). *Strega Nona*. New York: Scholastic.
Henkes, K. (1991). *Chrysanthemum*. New York: Greenwillow Books.
Lionni, L. (1963). *Swimmy*. New York: Scholastic.
Lionni, L. (1967). *Frederick*. New York: Random House.
Lionni, L. (1969). *Alexander and the wind-up mouse*. New York: Scholastic.
McCloskey, R. (1976). *Blueberries for Sal*. New York: Scholastic.
Rathmann, P. (1995). *Officer buckle and Gloria*. New York: Scholastic.
Ringgold, F. (1991). *Tar beach*. New York: Scholastic.
Rylant, C. (1985). *The relatives came*. New York: Scholastic.
Scieszka, J. (1989). *The true story of the 3 little pigs*. New York: Puffin.
Sendak, M. (1963). *Where the wild things are*. New York: Harper Collins.
Shannon, D. (1998). *No, David!* New York: Scholastic.
Steig, W. (1990). *Dr. De Soto*. New York: Farrar, Straus & Giroux.
Steig, W. (2005). *Sylvester and the magic pebble*. New York: Simon & Schuster.
Teague, M. (2002). *Dear Mrs. LaRue: Letters from obedience school*. New York: Scholastic.
Yolen, J. (1987). *Owl moon*. New York: Scholastic.

FIGURE 3.11. Sophisticated picture books on our shelves.

made while thinking aloud. After reading, the teacher asks a question about why something happened in the text and then models how to use information from the storybook to answer the question.

The focus of the second reading is building children's vocabulary knowledge and comprehension of the text. On the second reading, the teacher again provides an introduction to the book before reading, this time including a question about the characters or events to see what the children remember. During reading, the teacher provides definitions of the same words discussed during the first reading, makes comments about what other characters are thinking or feeling, and asks questions that require children to reflect on the comments the teacher made while thinking aloud. After reading, the teacher asks why something happened and invites the children to respond.

For the third reading, the teacher's goal is to help children reconstruct the text. On the third reading, before reading the teacher asks the children to recall the title of the book and to describe the characters and the problem. During reading, the teacher asks children to tell what is happening based on the illustrations in the book and to recall what will happen next in the story before turning the page. After reading, the teacher asks a different why question and invites children to respond. The sequence of reading behaviors before, during, and after reading provides a nice timeline for previewing a storybook, modeling how to think about information in the story, and asking children to apply what they have learned from hearing the teacher model and read the story repeatedly.

A nice graphic tool to use while working with children on retelling in small group is the story cluster (Hansen, 2004). A story cluster is simply a way to capture what children remember about the characters or events in a story. The most basic story cluster is a circle with the title of the book written inside and lines coming out of the circle like spokes on a wheel or rays on a sun. As children remember things about the story, the

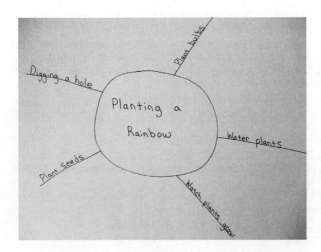

FIGURE 3.12. Example of story cluster.

teacher writes what children say on each of the lines coming off of the circle. Figure 3.12 is a story cluster completed by a 3-year-old after reading the book *Planting a Rainbow* by Lois Ehlert (1988). When using a story cluster with children it is a good idea to tell children before you begin reading that you will ask them to remember what happened in the story after reading. This information will help set the purpose for reading and will remind children that they will be asked to recall events. When using the story cluster with children for the first few times it is a good idea for the teacher to complete several spokes while thinking aloud and then to ask for children to volunteer information that they remember about the story. As children become more familiar with the story cluster format, you can ask for more and more input from children to complete it. Hansen (2004) suggests first asking children to recall anything they can about the story and as children develop their comprehension to begin to ask them to remember characters or events in order. The spokes of the story cluster can be numbered when working on specific recall in a sequence.

In addition to the story cluster, teachers may want to work on children's understanding of the underlying structures of text. A great way to introduce young children to story structure is to rewrite familiar storybooks in new ways using the same story structure. Some storybooks have structures that are dominant and predictable, making them perfect choices for developing young children's sense of story structure. For example, many of Bill Martin and Eric Carle's stories (e.g., *Brown Bear, Brown Bear, What Do You See?* [2007] and *Polar Bear, Polar Bear, What Do You See?*[1997]) follow a highly predictable sequence, repeating similar phrases or questions throughout. Using these texts as a model, children can write their own books using the same structure and incorporating their own ideas for new animals or actions. Figure 3.13 is an example of a class version of Martin and Carle's (2007) *Brown Bear, Brown Bear, What Do You See?* in which the children used the sentence structure from the original text but inserted their own colors and animals.

Teachers can also develop children's comprehension in small-group activities that are not directly linked to a specific storybook reading. Oral storytelling is a fun way to develop children's comprehension, either by listening to oral stories or by creating their own. When listening to oral stories, children practice their oral listening comprehension and are exposed to many of the same story elements that are involved in listening to a storybook reading. When creating their own oral stories, children practice applying their knowledge of the elements of a story, and give their oral stories characters, problems, and solutions. To incorporate oral storytelling in the classroom, we recommend modeling oral storytelling first by telling stories about things that have happened to you or stories that you make up to entertain children. We also recommend investigating whether your community has master oral storytellers—maybe parents or grandparents—who would be willing to visit the classroom to tell a story. Then as children become familiar with the process ask them to create oral stories to share with each other. At first, you may want to provide children with an object, a picture, or an idea to prompt their oral story.

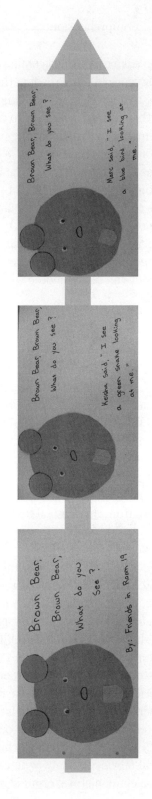

FIGURE 3.13. Class book based on *Brown Bear, Brown Bear, What Do You See?* (Martin & Carle, 2007).

Some of the best oral stories we have seen from teachers and children also incorporate music when appropriate to add to the entertainment experience. For example, a child told a story about what she did at home during a thunderstorm and the teacher asked other children in the small group to use musical instruments (cymbals and rhythm sticks) to make sounds for lightning and thunder. When first working on oral storytelling with children expect children's stories to be very short and hard to follow; this is completely normal for children still developing a sense of story structure. With practice over time you will notice an improvement in children's abilities to tell a coherent story with a beginning, middle, and end or at least with one character and one problem.

Center Time

Since preschool children cannot yet read on their own, creating activities that develop children's ability to comprehend during center time is challenging. If you think about extending comprehension, though, there are many possibilities. The best place to begin is with the storybook read during whole-group time. Consider whether there are activities that can be linked with the ideas found in the text. For example, does the text have an order of events or sequence that children can recreate with pictures? Is there a plot that children can retell using puppets or props? As you are planning for center activities, use the storybook as a guide for creating a center-time event that develops children's comprehension by asking them to review the storybook, retell events in a specific order, or act out events that occurred in the story.

As discussed in the previous section, young children love to read the same book over and over again. Rereading the same book helps build children's comprehension. In order to encourage children who would like to review a storybook read during whole group, place the storybook or a second copy of the storybook in the classroom library during center time. You may think that since children have just heard the book being read that they will not be interested in exploring the storybook again on their own. However, you will be amazed at how much interest is generated from placing a familiar storybook within children's reach. We have been in classrooms where children cannot wait to get their hands on the big book that the teacher has just read during whole group, and as a result we have witnessed several arguments over who gets to pretend to be the teacher first. Once children can take turns productively, allow them access to a spare reading pointer. Children will flock to the classroom library to pretend to be the teacher in order to use the reading pointer to "read" the big book to their friends. The child in Figure 3.14 is reviewing the big book read during whole group as an activity during center time. Even though she cannot read the words, she can look at the pictures and draw conclusions about the story by making connections between the pictures. Such practice develops comprehension by providing meaningful practice.

A second kind of center-time activity connected to a storybook is one that asks children to recall events that occurred in the story in a specific order or sequence. In

FIGURE 3.14. Child reading a big book during center time.

order to comprehend text, good readers must be able to recall events in order. Providing children with playful ways to put events in order is good practice for later when they are reading on their own. There are several creative ways for working on recall of events with children; however, the first step is making sure that the storybook you are working with has a sequence that can be put in order. Some books simply do not have a structure that can be broken down into a sequence of events, but instead provide general information on a topic or ideas that are more loosely connected (Figure 3.15 includes a list of children's books on our shelves that can be used for sequencing activities). Once you have determined whether the storybook you are reading has a sequential structure, then you can create an activity that develops children's ability to recall. One simple idea is to photocopy key images of events from the storybook and ask children to physically arrange the events in order. If you shrink the images into small squares, children can even order their images and staple them together with the help of an adult to create a little take-home version of the story. If your classroom has objects that represent events in a storybook, you can ask children to place these physical objects in a sequence as well. For example, in the book *The Very Hungry Caterpillar* by Eric Carle (1987), the caterpillar eats a different kind of food on each day of the week. Children can practice recalling the sequence of food the caterpillar eats in the book by placing plastic foods in order— one apple, two pears, then three plums, and so on. Many children enjoy playing with real objects as they practice recalling events in order (Hansen, 2004).

A general rule of thumb for sequencing is the younger the children, the fewer items to sequence. With very young children, two images may be more than enough to put in order. As children become better at recalling events from a story, they will be able to handle three and four and later five and six items to put in order. As children participate

Adams, P. (2007). *There was an old lady who swallowed a fly*. Auburn, ME: Child's Play International.
Brett, J. (1989). *The mitten*. New York: Putnam.
Brett, J. (2004). *The umbrella*. New York: Putnam.
Carle, E. (1987). *The very hungry caterpillar*. New York: Philomel.
Carle, E. (1989). *The very busy spider*. New York: Philomel.
Carle, E. (1996). *The grouchy ladybug*. New York: Harper Collins.
Carle, E. (1997). *From head to toe*. New York: Harper Festival.
Carle, E. (1997). *Today is Monday*. New York: Putnam.
Fleming, D. (1991). *In the tall, tall grass*. New York: Henry Holt.
Martin, B., & Carle, E. (1997). *Polar bear, polar bear, what do you see?* New York: Henry Holt.
Martin, B., & Carle, E. (2006). *Panda bear, panda bear, what do you see?* New York: Henry Holt.
Martin, B., & Carle, E. (2007). *Baby bear, baby bear, what do you see?* New York: Henry Holt.
Martin, B., & Carle, E. (2009). *Brown bear, brown bear, what do you see?* New York: Henry Holt.
Numeroff, L. J. (1985). *If you give a mouse a cookie*. New York: Scholastic.
Numeroff, L. J. (1991). *If you give a moose a muffin*. New York: Scholastic.
Numeroff, L. J. (2000). *If you take a mouse to the movies*. New York: Scholastic.
Numeroff, L. J. (2002). *If you take a mouse to school*. New York: Scholastic.
Numeroff, L. J. (2008). *If you give a cat a cupcake*. New York: Laura Geringer Books.
Taback, S. (1999). *There was an old lady who swallowed a fly*. New York: Scholastic.
Taback, S. (2004). *This is the house that Jack built*. New York: Puffin.
Wood, A. (2005). *The deep blue sea: A book of colors*. New York: Blue Sky Press.

FIGURE 3.15. Children's books with sequential structures "on our shelves."

in sequencing activities, they may need help. If a teacher or assistant is available, it is helpful to talk with children as they make decisions about the order of events. An adult can gently prompt children to think about the decisions they are making by asking questions such as "Why did you put that picture there?" or "Do you remember that part of the story; what was the character doing then?" It is also a perfect time to use vocabulary words such as *first*, *next*, *then*, and *last*: "Oh, I see you put the picture of the girl planting the seeds in the soil first. Then you put the picture of the girl watering the flower garden next." Sometimes an adult is not available, so placing a copy of the storybook in the center where children are sequencing is also a good help. Children can go back and look at the illustrations in the storybook itself to help them self-correct their own sequence.

A third activity for developing children's ability to retell events is to create a classroom center in which children can rehearse and perform their version of the storybook read during whole-group time. We have seen children retell stories using felt pieces and a felt board, premade puppets and a puppet theater, child-constructed puppets out of old socks and felt or construction paper and popsicle sticks, and by actually dressing up in costumes and acting out the story themselves. As in the sequencing activities described

For Girls	For Boys
• Dresses—Fancy and Casual	• Suit Jackets and Trousers
• Blouses and Skirts	• Ties and Bowties
• Coats, Hats, Mittens, and Scarves	• Coats, Hats, Mittens, and Scarves
• Pocketbooks, Purses, and Briefcases	• Top Hats
• High Heels	• Formal Shoes, Loafers
• Costume Jewelry and Eyeglasses	• Eyeglasses, Pocket Watches, Cuff Links
• Feather Boas, Formal Gloves, Silk Shawls	• Briefcases and Satchels
• Props/Tools Used in the Storybook	• Props/Tools Used in the Storybook

FIGURE 3.16. Costume trunk suggestions.

above, it is useful to have a teacher or teacher's aide in the center helping children retell the story by asking prompting questions or displaying a copy of the storybook the children are retelling in the center as a resource. Adults are useful not only as a resource to help children with their retelling but also to serve as the audience. Children will be much more likely to perform with an audience there to watch. In addition, the more well stocked the center and grand the stage, the more likely children are to play there. Encourage children to act out stories by providing them with costumes and a stage. By visiting a local thrift store you can find many affordable items to include in a costume trunk (see Figure 3.16 for costume suggestions). Stages can be as simple as a sectioned-off area on the rug to a more elaborate creation cut from a large refrigerator-sized cardboard box. One of the best stages we have seen was a grassy area between two trees outside in the play yard.

Additional Opportunities

Music activities designed to develop children's listening comprehension are important for later reading comprehension and easily implemented during transitional times in the classroom day. Simple activities that require very little time can be inserted in between whole group and center time, after a meal or snack, or before going outside to play. While simple, these activities are important for developing skills children will need for reading comprehension, skills such as listening, being able to follow directions, internalizing story structure, using clues to make inferences, and developing memory to recall events. For example, the song "Head, Shoulders, Knees, and Toes" asks children to touch the body parts used in the song in a particular order: head, shoulders, knees, and toes, knees and toes. Playing and performing this song with children not only helps develop their vocabulary knowledge of body parts but also works on their ability to follow directions and to perform actions in a sequence. The song "The Freeze" plays music and directs children to freeze when the music stops. At the beginning of the year many young children cannot freeze when asked to, but over time and as they begin to have more control over their bodies children will be able to follow the directions in the song.

Another listening activity that develops skills necessary for comprehension is asking children to listen to tapes or CDs of sounds and to use clues given in the sounds and what they know from their own experiences to make inferences about the sounds. For example, when working on a transportation theme with preschool children, a teacher could play a tape of different sounds related to transportation. Her tape might include a car horn beeping, a train passing over tracks, an engine revving, a motorcycle driving by, and windshield wipers moving. The teacher could create the tape herself with a tape recorder and a blank tape. When she plays the tape for the children the first time they will be delighted. The activity is a puzzle to figure out or a mystery to be solved. There will be many giggles and also many ideas proposed by different children trying to identify the sounds. Using clues to make inferences is an important reading comprehension strategy, so developing children's abilities to make inferences orally first is an important stepping stone for their future reading comprehension.

One of our very favorite transitional activities in the classroom is an oral rendition of *We're Going on a Bear Hunt* by Michael Rosen and Helen Oxenbury (1989). In this delightful storybook a family decides to go on a bear hunt, and along the way they encounter various obstacles. For example, the family comes to a grassy field and must walk through it, next they come to a cold river and must swim through it, and the story continues in this manner until the family makes it to the bear's cave. The family tiptoes through the bear's cave, meets the bear, and decides that meeting a bear is not a good idea after all. Therefore, they must run back through all of the obstacles they encountered on their way to the bear's cave until they are safe at home in their own bed. The language in the story is repetitive, "We can't go over it, we can't go under it, we've got to go through it," and descriptive. The grass swishes, the water splashes, and the mud squelches. The story's structure presents an initial sequence and then reviews the same sequence in reverse order as the family retraces its steps away from the bear.

Teachers use the bear hunt story as an oral activity with her classes year after year with tremendous success. The children love the story—it is expressive, uses interesting language, and makes them laugh. When using the story with children, the teacher begins by telling them the story herself and showing them hand motions to use to represent going through the different obstacles. For example, the children move their arms like they are doing the breast-stroke to represent swimming through the water and they pat their hands up and down on their thighs to represent walking through the woods. The teacher is careful to repeat the same obstacles and hand motions in reverse order when the family is retreating home. After only one or two models from the teacher, the children are able to recite the actions in the song in order with the teacher. Once children have become familiar enough with the story the teacher asks for new obstacles to insert into the story. The children are able to make suggestions for things the family can encounter and for what to do with their hands or bodies to act out the story. We love this activity because it practices children's ability to recall events in a specific sequence, it builds understanding of story structure—the story has a beginning, middle, and end—and it is incredible fun.

IMPLEMENTATION IN THREE CLASSROOMS

A Public School-Based Preschool: Pam

Pam has gained rich pedagogical knowledge from her degree in early childhood education and intensive professional development experiences and realizes that the seeds of children's comprehension development need to be planted well before children can actually learn how to read. Consequently, you can often observe Pam asking lots of questions during the day—questions that allow children to think, reflect, and evaluate.

Let's take a look at some of the ways that Pam incorporates comprehension development into her instructional routine. Pam takes the time to review all of the books that she will read that day and places sticky notes on the pages in which she will pause and ask open-ended questions. Pam typically has two read-aloud sessions a day. The first is centered around a big book and the second is around a smaller trade book; both are connected to a central theme. The sticky notes help her to remember the specific questions and spots in the book ideal for language exchanges and comprehension development. She spends at least 3 days in her 5-day cycle with the big book devoted to oral language and comprehension development. She finds that this intensive focus on comprehension has strengthened her children's engagement, understanding, and connections to the text over the course of the week, as well as over the course of the school year. She realizes, though, that comprehension development does not end after a whole-group read-aloud session. Pam extends these opportunities into her learning centers.

Pam has recently attended a districtwide professional development training course for early childhood teachers that focused on developing learning centers that support children's early reading development. For example, she learned how to use the listening center, a traditional center in a preschool classroom, to support comprehension development. Pam transformed her listening center into a veritable comprehension station. Children are asked to make predictions about the book before they listen, stop at certain points in the selection to turn and talk to their partner about what has happened so far or make a prediction about what might happen next, and retell the story to a partner and discuss their favorite parts of the book. Children are provided the opportunity to discuss these ideas with a partner as well as draw or write down their thoughts and opinions. Of course, much planning and modeling must happen to make this work. Pam records her voice on a tape or CD at points where she wants children to turn and talk and makes journals for students to draw and write down their ideas and thoughts. She also models each one of these concepts during her morning circle time. She wants to ensure that children are on task and are aware of the roles and procedures for each learning center.

Pam also has added elements of comprehension development into her library center by adding props for acting out the stories and into her writing center by asking children to explain their picture and having them dictate a story surrounding the picture to her into the child's writing journal. It must also be noted that Pam's center time would not run smoothly without the assistance of her assistant, Cheryl. She and Cheryl sit down and plan with each other every Thursday afternoon. They discuss and plan both small-group and center-time instruction and who will fulfill each role during those blocks of time so that each child's needs are being met consistently.

A Head Start Center: Elaina

Working with a large population of children learning English as a second language, Elaina finds it extremely important to integrate all of the activities in her classroom, all of the events, and all of the storybooks around one central theme. Typically, Elaina continues a theme in her classroom for about 4 weeks. Elaina has discovered that the repetition and the sustained experiences encountering similar ideas and related vocabulary words helps build children's comprehension around a central idea or concept. To help organize her classroom, she has created several distinct physical spaces or centers in her classroom and with each theme provides a series of theme-related activities and props in each of these centers. In addition, she provides theme-related books in each of these centers to serve as resources for children playing in the centers and to reinforce the theme visually throughout the room. Elaina's themes come from the curriculum her preschool has adopted; however, the same structure of centers and integration of activities across the theme can be used in any classroom with any theme.

Let's get a glimpse of what Elaina's classroom looks like during a theme on transportation. During whole-group time, Elaina reads one big book repeatedly for 5 days, covering a total of four books per theme. All of her big books are related to the transportation theme, either about a particular vehicle or about traveling in general. In addition, each afternoon Elaina reads a second, smaller storybook. Again, each of these storybooks is related to the transportation theme. Elaina also considers the theme when selecting music to play, movements for the children to make, classroom routines, and transitional activities. For example, children sing songs like "The Wheels on the Bus," move around the playground like they are small cars or airplanes, and line up like a train with an engine, cars, and a caboose when leaving the classroom.

Within the classroom centers Elaina also includes activities related to the theme. The classroom library has transportation-related books and a class-made scrapbook with photographs of each of the parents' cars and the school bus for children to view. In the writing center, Elaina has placed license-plate templates for children to write their own license plates, postcards for children to write home if they are pretending to travel, and simple maps and paper for children to examine and create their own. In the blocks area, Elaina has a rug with roads and intersections blocked out, small vehicles of all different makes and models, and road signs and traffic lights on popsicle sticks that children have created themselves. The dramatic play center has been turned into a travel agency with glossy brochures of different places to travel, class-made passports with the children's photograph on them, pretend money, tickets, maps, guidebooks, suitcases, and a separate area to make-believe being on an airplane, boat, or bus. At the sensory table, Elaina has water and toy boats and gravel and toy cars to explore how the different vehicles move over different surfaces. At the art table children can design their own vehicles with construction paper shapes or make tracks by dipping toy cars in paint and driving them over the paper. In the science center children drive toy cars up ramps and down ramps, experimenting with speed and gravity. Finally, at the manipulatives center Elaina places puzzles, sequencing materials, and other toys and games related to transportation. As children play in each of these centers, Elaina, her teacher's aide, and a classroom assistant rotate through the room using theme-related vocabulary words to engage children in conversation.

A Private Preschool: Sarah

Sarah simply does not have the space or the materials that Elaina has, but that does not discourage her from planning strategies for building children's comprehension. In fact, Sarah's experience tells her that comprehension is the area in which her children differ the most; some of them have had extensive experience with read-alouds in their homes, building sophisticated vocabularies and experiences with different types of text, and others are learning English for the first time. Sarah's interest in and experience with children's literature is a real help here.

Sarah's focus for comprehension building centers on wide readings of books related by theme. Sarah has two read-alouds built into her daily schedule. The first uses one of the big books that she has managed to gather to fill her themes. Because of the format, she uses that book for her more conspicuous modeling, both of print concepts and of comprehension strategies; for themes where she has enough big books, she uses them on a 3-day rotation. However, she has to supplement with trade books because she simply does not have enough big books to maintain her children's engagement and maximize their experiences with concepts related to her theme. Her local librarian, Maria, is very willing to serve as a partner, and she calls in advance to arrange a time to check out a new set of trade books for the classroom library every 2 weeks. She is particularly interested in having both narrative and information books, at least some of which have photographs. She is also interested in varying the amount of text; some of her books are shorter, often highlighting rhyme or repetition. Other books are more sophisticated, providing greater opportunity for exploring sequencing of events and more developed retellings.

The CROWD acronym makes it easier for Sarah to plan comprehension-focused interactive read-alouds. She finds that if she uses the question types to guide her thinking, it is quick and easy for her to plan her questions in advance. She uses sticky notes to plan all of the read-aloud questions, and keeps the books in a special basket. Sarah uses her second storybook reading time to read from this collection, and she builds in an element of child choice. During lunch, she brings three of these special books to her child of the day. That allows her to select among the more sophisticated books for children with more developed language and comprehension, and less sophisticated books for her more novice comprehenders. She describes each of the books, and then allows the child to choose. After lunch, when children are resting, she reads aloud from this new selection, careful to highlight the fact that it was specially chosen, and to direct at least some of her CROWD questions to the child of the day. Once the book has been read, she removes the Post-it notes and places it in the classroom library. She finds that this selection becomes a quick favorite and that it is automatically associated with the child who selected it. During library center time, when her assistant has a chance to reread books with the children individually, they can then choose the ones that are especially interesting to them, explore them in greater detail, and develop their comprehension in a more supported setting.

WHERE CAN I FIND MORE INFORMATION?

Web-Based

- Association for Library Service to Children
  www.ala.org/ala/mgrps/divs/alsc/awardsgrants/childrensnotable/index.cfm
- Center for the Improvement of Early Reading Achievement
  www.ciera.org
- Florida Center for Reading Research
  www.fcrr.org/forTeachers.htm
- Literacy Web at the University of Connecticut
  www.literacy.uconn.edu/pkhome.htm
- National Institute for Literacy
  www.nifl.gov/publications/publications.html#pfr
- Reading Rockets
  www.readingrockets.org/atoz/comprehension

Text-Based

- Beck, I. L., & McKeown, M. G. (2001). Text talk: Capturing the benefits of read-aloud experiences for young children. *Reading Teacher, 55,* 10–20.
- Cunningham, A., & Shagoury, R. (2006). *Starting with comprehension: Reading strategies for the youngest learners.* Portland, ME: Stenhouse.
- Giorgis, C., & Glazer, J. I. (2008). *Literature for young children: Supporting emergent literacy, Ages 0–8* (6th ed.). Upper Saddle River, NJ: Prentice-Hall.
- Hansen, J. (2004). *"Tell me a story": Developmentally appropriate retelling strategies.* Newark, DE: International Reading Association.
- McGee, L. M., & Schickedanz, J. A. (2007). Repeated interactive read alouds in preschool and kindergarten. *Reading Teacher, 60*(8), 742–751.
- Morrow, L. M., Freitag, E., & Gambrell, L. (2009). *Using children's literature in preschool to develop comprehension: Understanding and enjoying books* (2nd ed.). Newark, DE: International Reading Association.
- Parkes, B. (2000). *Read it again!: Revisiting shared reading.* Portland, ME: Stenhouse.
- Whitehurst, G. J., Arnold, D. S., Epstein, J. N., Angell, A. L., Smith, M., & Fischel, J. (1994). A picture book reading intervention in day care and home for children from low-income families. *Developmental Psychology, 30,* 679–689.

CHAPTER 4

Phonological Awareness

Preschoolers are language users. They know that words have meaning and power. They delight in adding new words to their own stash and have natural curiosity about the world that they express through words. What they might not know, though, is that words are composed of a combination of sounds. One of the foundational literacy skills that we can develop in preschool is phonological awareness, a bedrock concept about the construction of words.

WHAT IS PHONOLOGICAL AWARENESS?

Phonological awareness sounds scarier than it is. We like to think of phonological awareness as a skill that can be developed playfully with no paper, no pencil, and no materials of any kind. It involves thinking about the sounds of language instead of the meaning of language (Lonigan, 2008). Phonological awareness is not the same as reading words; phonological awareness is working with the sounds in words separate from the written letters. As a result, phonological awareness can be developed in the dark. A preschool teacher leading his or her children in a song with rhyming words is providing phonological awareness experience. By singing and noticing or providing rhyming words, the children are experimenting with the sounds of words in their language, specifically words that sound the same at the end. A preschool teacher leading his or her children on a walk and talking about things they see that start with the same sound, such as a goose and a garden, is building children's phonological awareness. And the preschool teacher who tells his or her children that *cowboy* is a compound word made up of the words *cow* and *boy* is introducing his or her children to phonological awareness. Phonological awareness instruction is not scary. Most preschool teachers do some phonological awareness work naturally as they interact with their children.

It is useful, though, to be more intentional. In this chapter we provide some of the technical vocabulary you need to understand how to plan for phonological awareness development. Children's overall phonological awareness consists of four levels of awareness: (1) word awareness, (2) syllable awareness, (3) onset–rime awareness, and (4) phoneme awareness (Lonigan, 2008). Figure 4.1 provides an overview of the four components of phonological awareness. These awarenesses are progressively more advanced. Interestingly, as the knowledge becomes more complex, the parts of sounds that children are working with become smaller and smaller. Figure 4.2 provides a visual representation of the developmental sequence of the four components of phonological awareness.

The story becomes a bit more complex, for within each of the four components there are also levels of task difficulty. For example, some syllable tasks are harder for children than others. In addition to type of task, the type of words used in an activity also makes a task easier or harder (Yopp & Yopp, 2000). For example, in a syllable counting activity, counting syllables in one- and two-syllable words is easier than counting syllables in three- and four-syllable words. Preschool teachers must make conscious decisions about the type of task they ask children to complete, finding a task that is not too hard, not too easy, but just challenging enough. Levels of task difficulty are addressed below within descriptions of each component.

Word awareness is the most basic awareness. Although words are the building blocks of communication, young children may not perceive them as individual units. Rather, they experience a stream of speech, without breaks between words. Or they might confuse a syllable with a word. The trick is to realize that an individual word, regardless of the number of letters or syllables it has, represents an individual meaning. Word awareness requires children to think about an individual word as a unit of speech. Experiences that target word awareness include working with compound words ("What do you get

Term	Definition	Example Teacher Talk
Word Awareness	Knowledge that a word is a unit of speech.	Which word is longer—*cat* or *forest*? What do you get when you put *lip* and *stick* together?
Syllable Awareness	Knowledge that words are made up of parts called syllables.	Let's see how many syllables are in the word *construction*.
Onset–Rime Awareness	Knowledge that one-syllable words can be divided into beginning sounds and then the vowel and what comes after.	What sound do you hear first in the word *cat*? What comes after the /c/?
Phoneme Awareness	Knowledge that words are composed of individual speech sounds that blend together.	What word do you get when you put the sounds /d/ /o/ /g/ together?

FIGURE 4.1. Subcomponents of phonological awareness.

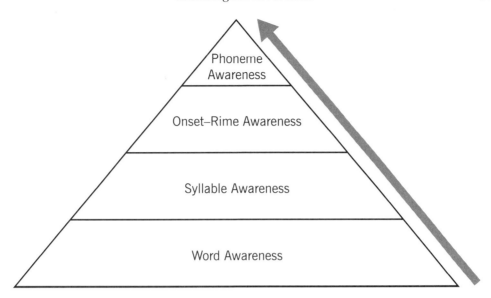

FIGURE 4.2. Developmental progression of phonological awareness skills.

when you put *tree* and *house* together?"), and counting how many words are in a sentence ("How many words are in the sentence—'The dog is chasing the ball'?"). See Figure 4.3 for a summary of word awareness tasks and a progression of difficulty. Note that these activities simply invite children to play with words.

Syllable awareness is the next developmental step. To develop syllable awareness, children understand that words are made up of parts called syllables. A syllable is a unit of sound anchored by a vowel, but preschoolers need not know those terms. Preschool teachers asking children to clap out the number of syllables in a word ("Let's clap out the number of syllables in Susan's name together: *su-san*."), comparing the number of syllables in different words ("Which has more syllables: the word *cat* or the word *hippopotamus*?"), or to delete a syllable from a word ("Can you say *pumpkin* without *pump*?") are building children's syllable awareness. See Figure 4.4 for a summary of syllable awareness tasks and a progression of difficulty.

Next, onset–rime awareness requires children to separate the beginning sounds (onset) from the ending sounds (rime) in a syllable. For example, the word *cat* has one syllable. In that syllable the /c/ is the onset and the /at/ is the rime. In the word *chime*, the /ch/ is the onset and the /ime/ is the rime. Preschool teachers usually use one-syllable words to target onset–rime awareness. They draw attention to beginning sounds in words by playing with alliteration in tongue twisters ("Can you say the sentence, 'Katie kangaroo kicked a kickball,' three times fast?") and ending sounds in words by playing with words that rhyme ("Which word does not sound the same at the end: *cat, lunch, bat*?"). See Figure 4.5 for a summary of onset–rime awareness tasks and a progression of difficulty.

Task	Description	Example
Counting	Ask children to count the number of words in sentences; the more words, the harder the task for children	"How many words are in the sentence 'The dog barked'?"
Identification	Give children a sentence and ask them to say one word in the sentence.	"Tell me one word in this sentence 'Today is Monday'."
Blending	Ask children to put two or more words together to create compound words.	"What word do you get when you put the words *rain* and *bow* together?"
Segmenting	Ask children to break a compound word apart into two words.	"What two words do you hear in the word *friendship*?"
Deletion	Ask children to say part of a compound word by taking away a word.	"Can you say *football* without the word *foot*?"
Substitution	Ask children what word they would have if they changed a word in a compound word.	"What word would you get if you changed the word *basket* in *basketball* to *volley*?"

FIGURE 4.3. Word awareness tasks.

Task	Description	Example
Counting	Ask children to count the number of syllables in words; the more syllables, the harder the task for children.	"How many syllables are in the name *Hunter*? Let's clap it out together."
Identification	Give children two words and ask them if they contain the same beginning or ending syllable.	"What parts of *rainbow* and *raindrop* are the same?"
Blending	Ask children to put two or more syllables together to create words.	"What word do you have when you put /sis/ and /ter/ together?"
Segmenting	Ask children to break a word apart into syllables.	"What parts do you hear in the word *candy*?"
Deletion	Ask children to say part of a word by taking away a syllable.	"Can you say *pumpkin* without the /kin/?"
Substitution	Ask children what word they would have if they changed a syllable in a word.	"What word would you get if you changed the /ber/ in *berry* to /cher/?"

FIGURE 4.4. Syllable awareness tasks.

Task	Description	Example
Identification	Give children three words and ask them to identify two that contain the same beginning sound.	"Listen to these words: *drip*, *drop*, *tin*. Which two words start with the same sound?"
Blending	Ask children to put an onset and a rime together to create a word.	"What word would you get if you put the sounds /b/ and /oat/ together?"
Segmenting	Ask children to break a word apart into onset and rime.	"What two chunks of sounds do you hear in the word *land*?"
Deletion	Ask children to say part of a word by taking away the onset or the rime.	"What sound do you get when you take /p/ away from *pig*?"
Substitution	Ask children what word they would have if they changed the beginning sound in a word.	"What would you get if you changed the /sh/ in *sheep* to /j/?"

FIGURE 4.5. Onset–rime awareness tasks.

Finally, phoneme awareness is the most complex skill, requiring children to identify individual sounds in words (phonemes). Instruction targeting phoneme awareness asks children to identify individual sounds in words ("What sounds do you hear in the word *cat*?") and blend individual sounds together to create words ("What do you get when you put /c/ /a/ and /t/ together?"). Phonemic awareness is so fine a level of phonological awareness that researchers debate whether it should even be taught to preschoolers (International Reading Association & National Association for the Education of Young Children, 1998). We have encountered some children who are ready to begin work with phonemes by the end of preschool; however, these children have already developed a strong foundation in alphabet knowledge and in word, syllable, and onset–rime awareness. See Figure 4.6 for a summary of phoneme awareness tasks and a progression of difficulty.

WHY IS PHONOLOGICAL AWARENESS IMPORTANT?

These fairly technical language tasks may seem to be a strange match for the language skills of preschoolers, but phonological awareness is important. Phonological awareness is an essential building block for successfully learning to read (Ball & Blachman, 1988). A child's phonological awareness predicts later reading skills, such as decoding, reading comprehension, and spelling (National Early Literacy Panel, 2008). Reading research shows that children who are good at segmenting syllables, rhyming, and blending phonemes become readers faster than their peers (Lonigan, 2008). Understanding why that

Task	Description	Example
Counting	Ask children to count the number of phonemes in words; the more phonemes, the harder the task for children.	"How many sounds do you hear in the word *pig*?"
Identification	Give children a word and ask them to identify the beginning or ending sound.	"What is the first sound in *foot*? What is the last sound?"
Blending	Ask children to put two or more phonemes together to create words.	"What word do you get when you put /c/ /a/ and /t/ together?"
Segmenting	Ask children to break a word apart into phonemes.	"What sounds do you hear in the word *hat*?"
Deletion	Ask children to say part of a word by taking away a phoneme.	"Can you say the word *pin* without the /p/?"
Substitution	Ask children what word they would have if they changed a phoneme in a word	"What word do you get when you change the /b/ in *bug* to /r/?"

FIGURE 4.6. Phoneme awareness tasks.

might be is a foundational idea for designing preschool phonological awareness experiences that make sense.

Decoding is a skill typically targeted in the middle of kindergarten. It makes sense that children who are able to play with sounds in words will have an easier time decoding words. When an individual encounters an unknown word, one way to "get it" is to make the individual sounds and then blend them together. This type of "sounding it out" involves two sets of skills: letter-sound knowledge and the phonemic awareness skill of oral blending. Conversely, children who have trouble with phonological skills struggle to make the connection between written words and the sounds in the words (Lonigan, 2008). The good news is that research indicates that preschool children can be taught phonological awareness effectively (Adams, 1990). The key to phonological awareness instruction at the preschool level is to make it playful and to use words that are meaningful to the children.

WHAT DOES PHONOLOGICAL AWARENESS INSTRUCTION LOOK LIKE?

Effective phonological awareness instruction in preschool does not have to be costly or time-consuming. The results of the National Reading Panel (2000) suggest that programs with less than 20 hours of phonological awareness instruction were sufficient for laying the foundation of phonological awareness skills children need. We now share ideas for phonological awareness instruction that require few materials and take 5 to 10 minutes of classroom time to implement. With a small amount of advanced planning, preschool teachers can incorporate phonological awareness instruction throughout the preschool day, during whole group, small group, centers, or even transitions and outdoor play.

Whole-Group Instruction

Whole-group time offers preschool teachers a perfect opportunity to teach phonological awareness. We have chosen to highlight two approaches to teaching phonological awareness during whole-group time—through song or poem and in connection with storybook reading.

Singing songs and reading poems that contain rhyming lyrics is a playful way of teaching preschool children to hear, recognize, and generate rhyme. Luckily, it is not hard to think of dozens of preschool songs that contain rhyme. To make a rhyming song meaningful to children in your classroom, we recommend trying to connect the song you choose to your current theme of study. For example, if you are studying animals at the zoo, you may want to teach your children the rhyming song "Willabee Wallabee Woo," which features an elephant. In that song, children first hear a silly situation: "Willabee Wallabee Woo, an elephant sat on you. Willabee Wallabee Wee, an elephant sat on me." Then the remaining verses are made to include children's names. For example, one verse could be "Willabee Wallabee Wowen, an elephant sat on Owen." Or, if you are working on an outdoor nature unit, you can sing "The Ants Go Marching" with your children. In that counting song, each verse includes a rhyme to go along with the number of ants marching. For example, the first verse begins, "The ants go marching one by one, hurrah, hurrah. The ants go marching one by one, hurrah, hurrah. The ants go marching one by one, the little one stops to suck his thumb. And they all go marching down to the ground to get out of the rain, boom boom boom boom." Children love to get up and march around the room as they sing this song and act out the rhyming actions.

While planning your instruction, it is important to locate song lyrics and, whenever possible, recordings of songs to play in the classroom. It is embarrassing to get halfway through a song and realize you have forgotten the lyrics. Figure 4.7 lists a collection of resources we have found useful when tracking down preschool song lyrics.

Once you have identified a song or poem to use, incorporate the song or poem into your daily routine. Do you sing or recite a poem in the morning before large group? Do you sing or recite a poem in the afternoon before going outside to play? Singing is a fun, developmentally appropriate way to engage children in playing with the sounds of the English language. And, the good news is that children love singing and reciting poetry. Introducing a new song or poem that fits with the current theme of study makes it meaningful to the children and can coincide with the content of your lessons. For example, we recently observed a preschool teacher using "The Caterpillar Poem" during a thematic unit on exploring nature. This poem is structured so that it reviews the life cycle of the

---

Text-Based

Church, E., & Hensley, D. (2000). *The great big book of classroom songs, rhymes, and cheers (Grades preK–1)*. New York: Scholastic.

Silberg, J., Schiller, P., & Berry, M. (2006). *The complete book and CD set of rhymes, songs, poems, fingerplays, and chants*. Lewisville, NC: Gryphon House.

Henry, L. K., & Moore, S. (2007). *Early learning with puppets, props, poems, and songs: Reproducibles and how-to's for dozens and dozens of easy activities that help children build background knowledge, vocabulary, and early concepts*. New York: Scholastic.

Web-Based

Creative Kids Crafts—
www.creativekidscrafts.com/preschoolsongs.html

Gayle's Preschool Rainbow—
www.preschoolrainbow.org/index.htm

KIDiddles Printable Songsheets—
www.kididdles.com/printables_home.html

Preschool Express—
www.preschoolexpress.com/music_station.shtml

FIGURE 4.7. Resources for discovering preschool song lyrics.

butterfly and includes rhyming words. First, she selected the poem because it coincided with her learning objective of teaching the life cycle of the butterfly. Second, she created a poster of the words to help her as she taught the children the poem and to serve as a visual representation of each stage in the cycle for children as they read. See Figure 4.8 for a photograph of the teacher's poem poster. Next, the teacher introduced the poem by explaining to her children that they were going to learn a new poem about the caterpillars and butterflies they had been learning about in class. The first day the teacher read the poem as she pointed to each word on the poster for the children. The second day the teacher read the poem first and then asked the children to say it along with her the second time. By the third day the children came into class saying parts of the poem they remembered, and as a class they could say the entire poem with the teacher. Through this poem, the teacher achieved two instructional goals. First, she helped reinforce the concept of the life cycle of the butterfly that she had been working on through large-group storybook reading and activities during center time. Second, she engaged children in playing with rhyming words.

One nice thing about teaching phonological awareness through a poem or song is that it is highly engaging to young children. While the teacher in our example was reading a poem with her children, the teacher's aide took time to set up activities for center time. Using classroom time and classroom personnel in this way maximizes time used for instruction. The teacher did not have to stop after reading the poem to set up centers, but could transition smoothly from reading to center time.

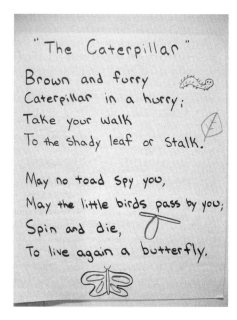

FIGURE 4.8. The Caterpillar Poem (Rossetti, 1988).

Phonological awareness instruction can also be incorporated effectively into large-group storybook reading. What better place to talk about rhyme, compound words, or syllables than when children encounter language in storybooks while listening? Phonological awareness instruction goes hand in hand with storybook reading because it is a natural, authentic context for encountering the sounds of language. The hardest part about incorporating purposeful phonological awareness instruction is choosing the best book. Figure 4.9 lists some of our favorite rhyming books, but there are millions more out there to discover and use. Our advice about choosing the right book is to find one that fits in with your current unit of study and one that will hold children's interest. Texts that are too long or involve complicated plots may require children to focus so much on comprehension that they are not able to attend to phonological awareness. Don't force phonological awareness activities with a book that is better suited to other activities; most books will provide you with some natural choices to develop attention to the sound of language, but doing so artificially will not be worthwhile.

The same teacher who read "The Caterpillar Poem" with her children continued the nature theme with her class the next week by reading Denise Fleming's *In the Tall, Tall Grass* (1991). Prior to reading to her class, the teacher read the book to practice reading dramatically and to look for rhyming pairs of words. She then decided to review the concept of rhyming words before reading, draw children's attention to the rhyming words during reading, and engage children in a rhyming activity after reading to informally gauge children's understanding. On the day of the storybook reading, the teacher calls

Andreae, G. (2001). *Giraffes can't dance.* New York: Orchard.
Barner, B. (1999). *Bugs! Bugs! Bugs!* New York: Scholastic.
Brown, M. W. (1947). *Goodnight moon.* New York: Harper Collins.
Brunelle, L. (1999). *The itsy-bitsy spider and a handful of finger rhymes.* San Francisco: Weldon Owen.
Christelow, E. (1989). *Five little monkeys jumping on the bed.* New York: Scholastic.
Donaldson, J., & Scheffler, A. (1999). *The gruffalo.* London: Macmillan.
Fleming, D. (1991). *In the tall, tall grass.* New York: Henry Holt.
Guarino, D. (1997). *Is your mama a llama?* New York: Scholastic.
Hoose, P., & Hoose, H. (1998). *Hey, little ant.* Berkeley, CA: Tricycle Press.
Martin, B., & Archambault, J. (1989). *Chicka chicka abc.* New York: Little, Simon.
Martin, B., & Carle, E. (2007). *Brown bear, brown bear, what do you see?* New York: Henry Holt.
Mitton, T., & Parker, A. (2003). *Tough trucks.* New York: Kingfisher.
Posada, M. (2000). *Dandelions, stars in the grass.* Minneapolis, MN: Carolrhoda Books.
Seuss, Dr. (1963). *Hop on Pop.* New York: Random House.
Shaw, N. (1986). *Sheep in a jeep.* Boston: Houghton Mifflin.
Slepian, J., & Seidler, A. (2001). *The hungry thing.* New York: Scholastic.
Westcott, N. B. (1992). *Peanut butter and jelly: A play rhyme.* London: Puffin.
Wood, A. (1999). *Silly Sally.* Boston: Red Wagon Books.
Yolen, J., & Teague, M. (2004). *How do dinosaurs count to ten?* New York: Scholastic.

FIGURE 4.9. Rhyming books on our shelves.

children to the rug and the teacher's aide sits on the rug with the children in order to help with child engagement. She sits on the rug in close proximity to a child she knows sometimes has a hard time paying attention during large-group activities. She is also available to children who need to ask a quiet question. With teaching staff and children in place, here is a glimpse of storybook reading.

"Good morning! Today we are going to read one of my favorite books called *In the Tall, Tall Grass,* but before we begin I want you to listen for a very special thing in our book. I want you to look for rhyming words. Remember rhyming words sound the same at the end like *cat* and *bat.* Will you listen for rhyming words in our book for me? Okay, when you hear a rhyming word, raise your hand."

Next, the teacher begins to read, weaving phonological awareness instruction in with her normal routine of pointing out print concepts and asking comprehension questions. On one page she reads, "crunch, munch, caterpillars lunch," and pauses, allowing children to hear the words. Two or three children raise their hands. The teacher calls one child's name.

CHILD: *Crunch* and *munch,* they rhyme!

TEACHER: That's right! *Crunch* and *munch* rhyme, they sound the same at the end. Is there another word we heard that rhymes with *crunch* and *munch*?

SECOND CHILD: *Caterpillars lunch.*

TEACHER: Which word rhymes with *crunch* and *munch—caterpillars* or *lunch*?

SECOND CHILD: *Lunch!*

TEACHER: That's right. *Crunch, lunch,* and *munch* all sound the same at the end. That means they rhyme.

The teacher and children continue this dialogue on every page with rhyming words. The teacher pauses after every two-page spread to allow time for children to hear and digest the words. The teacher notices while reading that some children know when words rhyme before she even begins reading, several children begin to catch on as they hear others find rhyming words, and a few children are not yet participating in finding rhyming words at all. As an informal assessment after reading, the teacher engages children in a rhyme odd-man-out activity. Let's listen in.

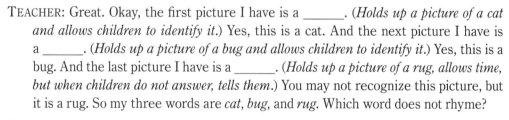

TEACHER: You all did a great job finding the rhyming words in our book. Now let's look at some more rhyming words. I have some pictures. Some of the words rhyme and some do not. On my way into school this morning my pictures got all mixed up. Do you think you could help me find which words rhyme and which do not rhyme?

CHILDREN: Yes!

TEACHER: Great. Okay, the first picture I have is a _____. (*Holds up a picture of a cat and allows children to identify it.*) Yes, this is a cat. And the next picture I have is a _____. (*Holds up a picture of a bug and allows children to identify it.*) Yes, this is a bug. And the last picture I have is a _____. (*Holds up a picture of a rug, allows time, but when children do not answer, tells them.*) You may not recognize this picture, but it is a rug. So my three words are *cat, bug,* and *rug.* Which word does not rhyme?

CHILD: Cat!

The teacher continued the activity with four more sets of words containing two rhyming words and one nonrhyming word for children to identify. Children's responses to the activity provided the teacher with informal data on child understanding. For example, the teacher noticed that some of her children energetically answered the questions correctly; she can reasonably conclude that these children are comfortable with rhyme and are ready for harder rhyme and other phonological awareness tasks. The teacher identified another group of her children who were eager to participate and answered some questions correctly and others incorrectly; these children need more practice. Four or five children in the class energetically answered, but their answers were consistently incorrect. The teacher plans to provide more explicit instruction and practice for these children. Finally, a few children were hanging in the back of the group not participating at all. The teacher suspects these children do not yet understand rhyme. She will build their understanding during small-group instruction.

The example of incorporating phonological awareness instruction into storybook reading we just shared focused on rhyme. You can focus instruction on any phonological awareness skill during storybook reading, not just rhyme. Let the storybook you are using help define which skill to target. Is there alliteration? Are there compound words? Is there a nice contrast between short sentences and long sentences that children can count and compare? Storybooks are ripe with possibilities for phonological awareness instruction. You just have to look at them in a new way.

Small-Group Instruction

Time set aside for small-group instruction provides teachers an opportunity for more individualized, needs-based instruction. When used to target phonological awareness, small-group instruction provides children a concentrated dose, targeting a skill with which they need more practice. This being said, phonological awareness instruction in small group should be fun, playful, and developmentally appropriate. And, like large-group instruction, it can be very brief, with as few as 5 or 10 minutes each day. The advantage for small group that preschool classrooms have over kindergarten classrooms is the benefit of multiple classroom staff. For example, in a preschool classroom with three adults, each adult can plan and run one small group. Conceivably you can have three small groups running at the same time, all targeting skills groups of children need to practice. Let's consider two examples of small-group activities, one focused on compound words and one on rhyme.

Early in the school year, compound word manipulation is a good phonological awareness skill to start with young children. They have fun recognizing smaller words they know in larger words and putting small words together to create large words. Of course you can play with putting compound words together and taking them apart with no materials; however, especially in the beginning when working with young children, it is often helpful to have some sort of physical manipulative or picture to represent the two parts of words. A manipulative or picture of each of the two words being put together helps to make the activity slightly less abstract for young children. Below is an example of a compound word small-group activity using manipulatives.

In October, a preschool teacher's aide used her 10-minute small-group time to work with six children on compound words. The children had been working on compound words for a few weeks in large group, and the teacher's aide wanted this group of children to have some additional opportunities for practice. Since the class was working on a thematic unit of seasons and weather, the teacher's aide chose compound words related

Common Preschool Theme	Related Compound Words
Outdoors/Nature/Insects	Baseball, birdbath, birdhouse, blackbird, bonfire, butterfly, campfire, doghouse, earthworm, firefly, flashlight, football, footprints, horsefly, housefly, ladybug, outdoor, outside, playground, underground, waterfall, wildlife
Transportation	Aircraft, airline, airplane, airport, breakdown, firefighters, firehouse, fireman, headlights, horseback, horsepower, houseboat, lifeboat, lifejacket, racehorse, railroad, roadblock, roadway, roadwork, rowboat, sailboat, suitcase, windshield
Food	Buttermilk, butterscotch, cookbook, cupcake, grapefruit, hamburger, milkshake, popcorn, watermelon
Doctor/Dentist/Health	Backache, backbone, eyeball, eyebrow, eyeglasses, eyelash, eyelid, eyesight, headache, healthcare, mouthwash, sickbed, toothache, toothbrush, toothpaste, toothpick
Seasons/Weather/Time	Afternoon, bedtime, daybreak, daylight, daytime, downpour, hailstorm, moonlight, naptime, nighttime, overcast, overnight, rainbow, raincoat, raindrop, rainfall, rainstorm, snowball, snowflake, snowman, snowplow, snowshoe, snowstorm, sunburn, sundown, sunlight, sunset, thunderbolt, weathervane
Building/Construction	Handyman, sandpaper, sawhorse, toolbox
Flowers	Buttercup, daylily, flowerpot, greenhouse, sunflower

FIGURE 4.10. List of common compound words by theme.

to this overarching class theme. See Figure 4.10 for a list of compound words organized by common preschool themes.

The teacher's aide began her small group by asking children if they remembered what a compound word was and reinforced their discussion by repeating and expanding the children's ideas. Then she provided each child in her group with a blue block and a red block. She explained:

"We are going to work together to build some compound words, or longer words that are made up of two smaller words. Your blue block is going to be the first word and your red block is going to be the second word, and when we put the two blocks together we are going to get a compound word. Watch me first. I have the word *snow*. (*Places the blue block so that it is on the children's left-hand side.*) My blue block is the word *snow*. Next, I have the word *flake*. (*Places the red block so that it is on the children's right-hand side.*) My red block is the word *flake*. When I put the two words together (*Moves the two blocks so that they are touching.*) I get *snow* ... *flake, snow* ...

flake, snowflake! My compound word is *snowflake*. Now I want you to try with your blocks. Put your blue block down to be the word *snow*. (*Children place blue blocks down in front of them on the left and say the word snow.*) Next, put your red block down to be the word *flake*. (*Children place red blocks down in front of them on the right and say the word flake.*) Now what word do you get when you put *snow* and *flake* together? (*Children push the blocks together and say the two words together.*)

During the short small-group period, the teacher's aide models several examples of weather-related compound words and then allows time for children to practice. At the end of the small-group session the teacher's aide may assess how children are progressing by asking children to complete one or two compound words without manipulatives to move or to explain what they are doing when they use the blocks to represent words.

Rhyme is also an important phonological skill to play with in a small-group setting. A *Rhyme Basket* is one of the most versatile small-group tools a preschool teacher can have, and it is easy to make your own. To make a Rhyme Basket, first find a basket, box, or bag to serve as the container. Next, collect concrete objects (pairs of things that rhyme) to place in the container. Use your creativity! For example, a sock that has lost its match and a rock from your garden or a small bell and a shell from the beach are objects that are easy to collect. You can also find small plastic toys that rhyme, such as a dog and a frog. Figure 4.11 provides some possible objects for the Rhyme Basket. Once you have your basket with between 8 and 12 rhyming pairs, there are many variations of activities you can do with your preschoolers.

Some rhyming tasks are harder than others. Figure 4.12 provides a summary of the progression of rhyming tasks from easier to most difficult. Typically, children can complete rhyme-identification tasks before rhyme odd-man-out tasks and odd-man-out tasks before rhyme-generation tasks. The great thing about a Rhyme Basket is that you can target all of the different levels of rhyme activities with one tool. Here are a few examples:

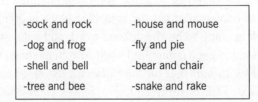

-sock and rock	-house and mouse
-dog and frog	-fly and pie
-shell and bell	-bear and chair
-tree and bee	-snake and rake

FIGURE 4.11. Materials for creating your own rhyme basket.

Type of task	Description	Example
Rhyme Identification	Children identify whether two words rhyme.	"Do the words *cat* and *bat* rhyme? Do the words *cat* and *dog* rhyme?"
Rhyme Odd-Man-Out	When presented with three words, children choose which word does not rhyme.	"Listen to these three words: *cat*, *dog*, and *bat*. Which word does not rhyme?"
Rhyme Generation	When given a word, children are asked to come up with a word that rhymes.	"Can you think of a word that rhymes with *bee*?"

FIGURE 4.12. Progressive levels of rhyming activities.

1. *Finding Rhyming Pairs—Teacher Directed.* For this activity, the teacher pulls out of the basket one of each pair of rhyming words and scatters the remaining objects on the table or floor. The teacher asks the children if they recognize what the items are on the floor and helps clarify all of the names to make sure children know each object. Then the teacher holds up one of her objects and says, "This is a _____. What object on the floor rhymes with _____?" Together the teacher and children locate all of the matching pairs of objects.

2. *Finding Rhyming Pairs—Child Directed.* For this activity, the teacher pulls out of the basket one of each pair of rhyming words and distributes the remaining objects to the children. The teacher asks the child to name the object he or she is holding and helps clarify the name. Then the teacher holds up one of the objects and says, "This is a _____. Does anyone have an object that rhymes with _____?" Together the teacher and children locate all of the matching pairs.

3. *Rhyme Odd-Man-Out.* For this activity, the teacher pulls out of the basket two objects that rhyme and one object that does not rhyme. The teacher asks the children to identify each object first and helps to clarify the names. Then the teacher repeats the three names and asks, "Which of these objects does not rhyme?" Together the teacher and children eliminate nonrhyming objects in groups of three.

4. *Rhyme Generation.* For this activity, the teacher scatters all of the objects in the middle of the table or floor. First, the teacher and children name all of the objects. Then, the teacher asks the children if they see any objects that rhyme. Children take turns finding two objects that rhyme. The teacher can then hold up the two objects that rhyme and ask children to think of other words that rhyme with those two words. This task, producing additional examples, is by far the most challenging.

Center Time

Phonological awareness activities that children can accomplish with or without a teacher's help are appropriate for center time and allow children to experiment with and practice the skills they have been learning during whole-group and small-group instruction. Believe it or not, there are child-directed activities that can help children develop their phonological awareness. The key to making center-time phonological awareness activities successful is to align the concepts being practiced with those to which children have previously been exposed. Since children's knowledge of phonological awareness will vary, it is also a good idea to have a range of center-time activities from which children can choose. And, of course, it is always a good idea if the activities connect whenever possible to the overarching thematic unit.

As an example, let's look at our classroom that is immersed in the nature theme to see what phonological awareness activities the teacher has included in center time. In the library, the teacher has added several rhyming books related to the nature theme, including *In the Tall, Tall Grass* (Fleming, 1991), *Hey, Little Ant* (Hoose & Hoose, 1998), *The Itsy-Bitsy Spider* (Brunelle, 1999), *Bugs! Bugs! Bugs!* (Barner, 1999), and *Dandelions, Stars in the Grass* (Posada, 2000). The children have heard these books read aloud, so they can engage in pretend readings of various types. The children are encouraged to browse, look at the pictures, and read the book with an adult when available. Also, in the library, the teacher has placed the homemade Rhyming Basket, described above, for children to explore. There is a laminated chart on the wall that is divided into two columns. Above one column the word *Word* is written and *Sentence* is written above the second column. There are individual laminated sentence strips with some words and

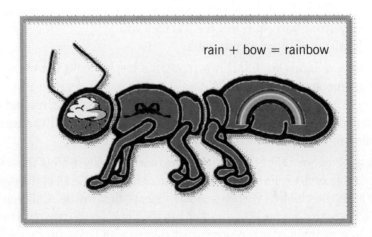

FIGURE 4.13. Ant sequencing: Compound words.

some sentences written on them. All of the words and sentences connect to the nature theme and review vocabulary words that the children have been learning. The children know the routine is to sort the single words into the "Word" column and the sentences into the "Sentence" column. Within the library center alone the teacher has included two phonological awareness activities, including rhyme and word awareness.

At the science center the teacher has included an ant sequencing activity. On one side of the simple, three-piece sequencing set the teacher has drawn an ant for children to piece together. On the other side of the cards are three pictures, one on each segment of the head, thorax, and abdomen. The first two pictures are of individual words that go together to create a compound word. The third picture is of the compound word itself. So, for example in Figure 4.13, the head piece has a picture of rain, the thorax has a picture of a bow, and the abdomen piece has a picture of a rainbow. Children work to put the sequencing cards in order to create concrete compound words with which they are familiar.

Finally, at the games center the teacher has placed two games designed to practice phonological awareness. The first is a game targeting syllable awareness. The teacher has hung a short string along the wall in the center and placed three clothespins on the line. One clothespin is marked with a number 1, the second is marked with a number 2, and the third is marked with a number 3. Scattered on the table are green leaves cut out of construction paper. Taped on each leaf is a picture that the teacher has printed from clip art on her computer of objects that are familiar to the children. Each object has one, two, or three syllables. So, for example, one leaf has a picture of a cat on it; one leaf has a picture of a pumpkin on it; and one leaf has a picture of a basketball on it. The children playing the game are asked to sort the pictures into groups by the number of syllables and attach them to the appropriate clothespin. Children would attach the leaf with the picture of the cat to the clothespin with the number 1 written on it, the leaf with the picture of the basketball to the clothespin with the number 3 written on it, and so on. The second game is a memory matching game with pictures that begin with the same initial sound. The cards are shaped like butterflies to connect with the nature theme; however, the pictures are of simple, concrete objects that children can recognize and determine the initial sound. For example, one butterfly has a picture of a sun and a second butterfly has a picture of a spoon. When a child finds both pictures beginning with the /s/ sound during his or her turn, it is a match, and the child gets to go again. The children play in this way until all the matches are made.

The teacher in the above example chose activities for center time that both practiced phonological awareness and included a range from easier to harder skills. Children working on words versus sentence and compound words were developing initial phonological awareness skills; children who were practicing rhyme and syllables were working on harder skills; and children who were matching by initial phoneme were developing the most complex skill along the phonological awareness continuum. It is important to provide enough choices for practice to engage all learners at their own level. The teacher in our example knows that some of her 3-year-olds are still learning and struggling with what a word is, while some of her children who are kindergarten-bound are beginning to experiment with initial sounds in words and can be challenged by some beginning phonemic awareness activities. Center time in the preschool classroom is a perfect time for providing children the differentiated instruction they need to develop further as emergent readers. As children rotate through centers, the teacher and teacher's aide also rotate through the centers engaging children in rich conversation to improve their oral language and vocabulary. They are also able to help children who are playing with phonological awareness tasks by playing along beside them, asking and answering questions about compound words and initial sounds, and informally assessing where individual children are in their phonological awareness development.

Additional Opportunities

Phonological awareness instruction need not be limited to the classroom. Outdoor activities are just as useful for practicing phonological awareness with young children. In fact, combining phonological awareness and movement helps many children learn the skills and become more motivated to do so. The good news is that many of the games with which children are already familiar can be modified to include phonological awareness. For example, consider the game Duck, Duck, Goose. You can change the game to focus on rhyme by having the child say rhyming words, even made-up rhyming words, and when they say a nonrhyming word they begin to run. Or, to practice phonemic awareness, the child can say all words that begin with the same sound and then say a word that begins with a different sound before running around the circle. Games with passing balls also work well with phonological awareness. Children can pass a ball to another child who then needs to say a rhyming pair or a word with a designated number of syllables or a word with a particular beginning sound before passing the ball on to another child. Another great physical activity is to use jumping, marching, skipping, and so on to count out the number of words in a sentence or the number of syllables in a word. Having children use their bodies helps them physically keep track of the items they are counting.

One of the best ways to weave phonological awareness instruction into outdoor time is to go for a class walk with a specific goal. The goal can be to find pairs of things that rhyme. For example, the teacher or teacher's aide leading the walk can say, "I spy something that rhymes with *ride*," and his or her children can say, *Slide.* Or the walk can be for the purpose of finding all of the things that they can that begin with a specific sound. If the sound is /s/, children can find *sun, sand, slide, sidewalk,* and so on. The same walk can be used for finding words that have a certain number of syllables or looking for compound words. Do not be afraid to be creative with your phonological awareness instruction, for it does not have to be formal to be effective.

IMPLEMENTATION IN THREE CLASSROOMS

A Public School-Based Preschool: Pam

Pam works with a population of children who may struggle with formal reading instruction when they enter kindergarten. Pam also knows that phonological awareness is a crucial foundation for children's early reading development. She has a strong knowledge base in early literacy development because of her degree in early childhood education and continues to learn how she can support children's growth in phonological awareness through professional development experiences offered in her district. As a result, Pam ensures that she draws explicit attention to areas of phonological awareness like rhyme, syllable, and alliteration during her instructional routine.

Luckily, Pam's district has adopted a research-based preschool curriculum that directs her to explicitly teach those essential elements in her whole-group shared reading and circle-time activities and provides some supplemental ideas for her learning centers. Pam knows that for some in her class though, it may not be enough. Pam uses the results of her district's screening tool, the PALS-PreK (Phonological Awareness Literacy Screening; University of Virginia, 2004), to identify those students who may need additional help in this area. PALS-PreK assesses some early elements of phonological awareness like rhyme and beginning sound awareness. Pam is able to use this valuable information to group students who need an extra dose of phonological awareness, and she works with them during small-group time.

Pam works with students on rhyming, syllables, and initial sounds. Pam knows that she has only a short time to work with these children so she takes advantage of each moment. She often uses the same instructional sequence. First, she will model the activity for the children. So, if they are working on a syllable activity, she will think aloud the process for deciding whether *elephant* has one, two, or three syllables. She will clap the syllables aloud and then match the picture to another picture on the sort that also has three syllables. Second, she will engage all of the children in the activity. Each child will clap, tap, or snap the syllables in his or her picture and then decide where it belongs in the group sort. Last, she will have each child sort his or her own picture and watch while the children move through the process. This serves as an excellent form of instruction as well as assessment. She also extends these instructional opportunities by sending the same lesson activity home with the children. Along with the materials, she provides directions for the parents so that they can actively engage their child in the phonological awareness activity.

Pam and her assistant Cheryl also use their monthly Title I Parent Workshops as a vehicle for bolstering children's phonological awareness. They know that parents are children's first teacher and they play a key role in children's reading success. During one of the first of these workshops, they introduce parents to an understanding of phonological awareness, discuss how they will address this area of literacy in the classroom, and provide some simple, but meaningful ways that parents can help build children's awareness of sounds while they are at home or "out and about" on a trip to the grocery store. Pam and Cheryl feel confident that because of their focus on phonological awareness throughout the preschool day, as well as support from parents, that they are setting up their children for future reading success.

A Head Start Center: Elaina

Given that Elaina works with a large population of children learning English as a second language, she must adapt her phonological awareness instruction differently from Pam and Cheryl. However, phonological awareness instruction for children who have no or limited English at the beginning of the school year is something Elaina has struggled with. How do you teach children to play with rhyme in a language they do not yet even know? The good news is that research indicates that developing phonological awareness in one language transfers to phonological awareness in other languages (Dickinson, McCabe, Clark-Chiarelli, & Wolf, 2004; Lopez & Greenfield, 2004; Manis, Lindsey, & Bailey, 2004). In Elaina's case, if her children develop a strong foundation in phonological awareness in their home language of Spanish, that knowledge will transfer into the language they are learning in the classroom—English.

While Elaina has a Spanish-speaking classroom aide in her room, the curriculum she uses is not bilingual. All instruction occurs in English with some Spanish used to help acclimate young children at the beginning of the year with classroom routines and personal expectations. Thus, in an English-only classroom the best way Elaina can support English language learners' (ELLs') phonological awareness development is by encouraging support of the same skills she is teaching in English in the classroom at home in Spanish (Yopp & Stapleton, 2008). She wants the parents of her children to know that by reading and talking about children's books in Spanish, by playing with tongue twisters, by singing rhyming songs, and by pointing out the sounds of letters and words that children come in contact with, parents can greatly support their children's language and literacy development (Yopp & Stapleton, 2008).

At the beginning of the school year Elaina knows the most important thing for her to do is to reach out to Spanish-speaking parents to give them the message of the importance of speaking with their children in Spanish. All too often Elaina has met parents who take English classes and try to speak with their children only in English to help them all to be successful. However, she knows that what her ELLs need most is a strong language role model in their native language in order to develop phonological awareness. Elaina has several opportunities for getting her message to parents.

First she makes an initial home visit to parents prior to the school year beginning in order to meet the children and families with whom she will be working. She brings an interpreter, usually a classroom aide or Family Service worker who speaks Spanish. At that initial meeting, Elaina works to create a relationship with the family and discusses with them the importance of fostering strong language-rich experiences in the home in order to support their children's language and literacy development. The Head Start center also hosts monthly parent meetings, and the classroom teachers are able to make suggestions for items on the agenda. Elaina uses these parent meetings throughout the year as an opportunity to introduce and reinforce ideas about language development that parents can use in the home with their children.

A Private Preschool: Sarah

Sarah knows that most of her children will need short, consistent phonological awareness experiences. She plans them four or five times each day. She takes responsibility herself for some of these opportunities, and she plans with Maria for others. Sarah works during and after her big-book read-aloud, after her afternoon trade-book read-aloud, and as a transition between the center rotations. Maria will address phonological awareness in the library center and the writing center.

Sarah's collection of big books provides ample chances to attend to syllables, rhymes, and alliteration. She knows to weave these into the reading, but she also wants to return to them afterward, pulling words or ideas out of the story environment to focus her children's attention on sound rather than meaning. She has a pocket chart and a collection of picture cards and she can almost always link her work to one of the central concepts in the book. For example, in a book about spring, she can then use the word *spring* to launch a 2-minute rhyming activity with *king*, *sing*, and *ring*. Her favorite activity with the children is to sing the Sesame Street song "One of These Things Is Not Like the Others" and present children with a set of three pictures and ask them to find the one that does not belong. First, she ensures that all children pronounce the picture names aloud, helping them to generate a strong phonological representation. Then, when they find the one that does not belong, she is careful to tell them why. This game works with all sorts of phonological tasks, including compounds and beginning sounds. Once the pictures have been introduced in this whole-group manner, she moves the pictures into the library center so that children can redo the tasks in pairs with the help of her assistant.

As a normal part of her afternoon trade-book read-aloud, Sarah selects a sentence from the book that represents an important idea or event. Then she writes that sentence on a sentence strip, and the children "read" it with her until it is memorized by all of them. Next, she cuts the words apart, careful to leave puzzle edges as clues. The individual puzzle pieces are then put into a ziplock bag with a photocopy of the book's cover and presented to the child of the day to further celebrate his or her book choice. After that day, the bag goes into the library center with the book so that other children can have a chance to reassemble and "read" the target sentence, developing their word awareness.

The use of rhyming songs is also an important part of Sarah's routine. As a way of transitioning between centers, Sarah uses songs, many of which include rhyme and alliteration. As the time for transition approaches, she sings the day's song in a very quiet voice. This is a signal for children to put away their materials. When they have done that, they join in the singing. This procedure makes the transitions regular and fun, and it gives the children a chance to use their voices in playful ways.

More targeted phonological awareness attention comes in the writing center. Sarah's assistant has picture cards and manipulatives to use. When she is working with word awareness, she asks the children to tell her what they want to write, and she draws lines for them. They "read back" the blank lines, developing their concept of words using language that they choose themselves. They also "write" by using pictures. She has sets of pictures that children can select to make rhyming books or books that highlight a special letter. When they do these activities, children use a set of pictures that includes some distracters. For example, on a day when they are making a book of favorite *P* words, they also have pictures of words that start with *S*. That way, children have to first decide whether the name of the picture starts with their target sound. They typically do this by saying the word over and over, and Maria can help them to accentuate and isolate the first sound.

WHERE CAN I FIND MORE INFORMATION?

Web-Based

- Center for the Improvement of Early Reading Achievement
  www.ciera.org/library/instresrc/index.html
- Florida Center for Reading Research
  www.fcrr.org
- Phonological Awareness Literacy Screening
  www.pals.virginia.edu
- Reading Rockets
  www.readingrockets.org/helping/target/phonologicalphonemic
- Washington Learning Systems
  www.walearning.com

Text-Based

- Adams, M. J., Foorman, B. R., Lundberg, I., & Beeler, T. (1997). *Phonemic awareness in young children: A classroom curriculum.* Baltimore: Brookes.
- Blevins, W. (1999). *Phonemic awareness activities for early reading success.* New York: Scholastic.

- Silberg, J. (2005). *Reading games for young children*. Lewisville, NC: Gryphon House.
- Strickland, D. S., & Schickedanz, J. A. (2009). *Learning about print in preschool: Working with letters, words, and beginning links with phonemic awareness* (2nd ed.). Newark, DE: International Reading Association.

CHAPTER 5

Print and Alphabet Awareness

A young boy who points to a sign that contains a letter in his name and yells, "Daddy, that says my name!" or scribbles on a piece a paper and proudly announces that it says, "I love my Nana" is beginning his journey to becoming a successful reader and writer. He is also demonstrating that he knows that print is an important part of daily life. Print and alphabet awareness are children's earliest understandings that written language carries meaning. These are also proficiencies that can be playfully and purposefully infused into the preschool day. In addition, these are proficiencies that should be nurtured in preschool for those children who have no other opportunities to learn them.

WHAT IS PRINT AND ALPHABET AWARENESS?

An essential component of children's early literacy development lies in the area of print and alphabet awareness (Ezell & Justice, 1998, 2000; National Early Literacy Panel, 2007). This area encompasses a number of critical skills such as knowledge of book conventions (e.g., ability to identify the title of the book), print conventions (e.g., left-to-right directionality of print), concept of letter and word (e.g., ability to match the written word with the spoken word), and alphabet knowledge (knowing the features and names of the letters of the alphabet). See Figure 5.1 for a definition of each component.

Generally speaking, print awareness refers to children's recognition of the rules and characteristics of written language. Print awareness includes children's ability to understand that words in print correspond to speech and that they must conform to conventions of directionality. Children with print awareness understand that print, not pictures, represents the words on a page and print has many practical uses in their lives. Alphabet awareness refers to children's ability to recognize and name the letters of the alphabet in

Book Conventions
A child can identify:

- Front of book
- Back of book
- Title of book
- Title page of book
- Role of the author
- Role of the illustrator/photographer

Print Conventions
A child can identify:

- Top line of the print on a page
- Bottom line of the print on a page
- Left-to-right progression of print

A child knows how to:

- Return sweep
- Track print on a page
- Count the words on a page
- Count the letters in a word

Alphabet Knowledge
A child can identify/name:

- Any letter on a page
- A specific letter/letters on a page
- A letter in his or her own name
- All letters in his or her first name
- The sound–symbol correspondence of a letter or letters

FIGURE 5.1. Print and alphabet awareness components.

isolation and within the context of words. This seems like a long list of isolated skills, but in fact they are developed concurrently as children learn how books are used.

It is important to note that children's development of print and alphabet awareness is not natural. Rather, it is an understanding that develops through direct and intentional intervention by adults, caregivers, and others who take the time to identify letters, parts of a book, and the many functions of print. The fact that these skills are not natural is not intuitive; children with extensive access to books and print and to adults who speak about books and print may appear to develop these initial understandings naturally, and this may cause some preschool teachers to wait for other children to develop the same understandings. In fact, children's understanding of print and alphabet awareness is constrained by their direct and active involvement with print as well as by the amount and type of access to print they have. Since children enter preschool and then kindergarten classrooms having had vastly different experiences and exposures to print, preschool teachers should be mindful of these differences as they plan and implement learning experiences that draw attention to the functions and purposes of print. The good news is that children who have not had these experiences prior to preschool *can* make up for that during preschool.

WHY IS PRINT
AND ALPHABET AWARENESS IMPORTANT?

Children with a firm grasp of print and alphabet awareness understand that written language has a reciprocal relationship with oral language. That is, what we say can be written down and then read back. This understanding brings with it the realization that, much like spoken language, the printed word carries a message and provides a source of enjoyment, information, and discovery. Children without this grasp of print functions may struggle with formal reading instruction. The National Early Literacy Panel (NELP) found that in addition to phonological awareness, print knowledge was one of the strongest predictors of a child's early success in reading (2007). Research has also found that children's knowledge of letter names and shapes is a reliable indicator of their future reading success (Adams, 1990; International Reading Association & National Association for the Education of Young Children, 1998). That makes sense. In order to read, children need to identify individual words, look at their letters, access the sounds of each letter, and blend the sounds together. However, growth in print and alphabet awareness is highly dependent upon exposure to and engagement with various print functions and forms (Neuman, 1996, 1999).

Many children have had a number of rich experiences and exposures to print long before they enter school. Parents or caregivers may have drawn their attention to signs, labels, and billboards during outings in the car or on the bus. They may have spent countless hours on their parents' or older siblings' laps reading books and learning (incidentally) about things like the title, the author, the front and back of the book, and how to turn a page. They know that you read the words on the page, not the pictures. They may have played with magnetic letters of the alphabet on the refrigerator and may quickly identify the first letter of their own name. They may have even observed their parents or grandparents reading and reacting to print both at home and in the world around them. Because of these experiences, these children have a firm understanding that print is important and meaningful. This awareness helps to lay the foundation for their future reading and writing success. See Figure 5.2 for websites that contain simple, yet purposeful home activities to build children's print and alphabet awareness.

Unfortunately, the truth of the matter is that not all children enter the preschool classroom with these valuable insights and experiences. Since research shows that children's performance on print and alphabet awareness tasks are predictive of children's future reading development, preschool instruction should be crafted to include an inten-

> - Kalkaska C.A.R.E.S (an Early Reading First Program)
>   *www.kalkaskacares.org/Print_Awareness/PrA_Home.html*
> - How to build print knowledge—family education
>   *school.familyeducation.com/reading/early-learning/46724.html*
> - Print awareness—storytime share
>   *earlylit.net/wordpress/category/adult-aside/print-awareness*
> - Reading Rockets: Print awareness
>   *www.readingrockets.org/teaching/reading101/printawareness*

FIGURE 5.2. Websites for home activities that support print awareness.

tional and daily focus to bolster that knowledge (Ezell & Justice, 2000). The encouraging news is that print and alphabet awareness is especially amenable to instruction. Targeted areas of print awareness, such as book and print conventions, concepts of letter and word, and alphabetic knowledge can be playfully and purposefully infused into preschool classroom instruction.

WHAT DOES PRINT AND ALPHABET AWARENESS INSTRUCTION LOOK LIKE?

Teachers play a key role in developing children's print and alphabet awareness. When teachers plan and implement experiences that draw children's attention to the print that surrounds them, they are providing a crucial stepping-stone for their children's reading and writing success. Of course, the key is to ensure that children are both actively involved in this process and see good models of this process in an intentional and meaningful way.

Given the realities of the preschool day, this may seem easier said than done. Again, we think the key is seeing and seizing as many opportunities as possible. In the following sections, we discuss what print and alphabet awareness instruction should look and sound like. Specifically, we discuss how teachers can use whole-group instruction, small-group instruction, center time, and noninstructional times in the preschool day to develop children's print awareness—playfully and purposefully.

Whole-Group Instruction

Whole-group instruction represents an ideal time to draw children's attention to the functions and forms of print. The wonderful aspect of developing children's print awareness is that it does not require a large block of time in your daily whole-group time. It simply needs deliberate attention for a few minutes each day. A little bit every day goes a long way.

Children initially grasp print awareness concepts through a few sources; their own names, active involvement in shared reading, and active involvement in the environmental print that surrounds them. Print concepts are learned through meaningful—not skill-and-drill type—activities and lessons. It is important to distinguish print concepts from conventional single-word reading. Preschool children need not learn to decode words; that can come much later. Rather, they need to learn what words are and how they are used to represent meaning. That early understanding about what words are can inspire children to do the sometimes difficult work required to learn to read them later.

A great introductory way to draw children's attention to print and the notion that print carries meaning is to *label the classroom* together. Instead of labeling the room before children come to school the first day, accomplish this meaningful experience together during whole-group time. Labeling the classroom means placing a printed word on an index card or sentence strip on a classroom object. For example, a teacher can show the children the word *door,* read the word to the children, and then label the classroom door with the word *door.* This provides children with an explicit connection between an object and a word—insights that are necessary to read. Teachers can choose a few words to label every day with the children during the first week or so of school until all objects have been labeled. Teachers can also extend this idea by creating a *word wall* and adding children's names to the word wall during the first week of school. As the school year progresses, children will not only recognize their own name but may learn the names of all the other children in the class.

Another optimal place to start children on their path to print awareness is within your daily shared storybook reading time (Beauchat, Blamey, & Walpole, 2009). You will remember from Chapter 2 that *shared storybook reading* is a broad term, including all instances when an adult reads to a child or children, pausing to engage children in discussion about the text (Holdaway, 1979). That discussion includes ideas inside the text—the story, pictures, words, and letters; and outside the text—responses and connections to experience.

So what role does shared storybook reading play in children's print awareness development? As children see their teacher model how print works within the storybooks and their attention is drawn to the forms and functions of print, they begin to understand how print works. The types of books that are ideal to develop these concepts are big books. These oversized storybooks with enlarged pictures and print are purposefully created to elicit interaction with children in a shared reading session (Holdaway, 1979). Big books that contain repetitive or patterned text that closely match the illustrations are especially helpful in developing and expanding children's print awareness. They allow children the opportunity to hear and participate in simple, predictable stories as well as see and interact with print on a page. Refrains such as "This is not my cat! Have you seen my cat?"

contained in the beloved big book *Have You Seen My Cat?* (Carle, 1997) are ideal for actively engaging children and drawing attention to print concepts on each page. To use these refrains to develop print concepts, teachers would draw attention to the refrain by reading it out loud, tracking the print with their finger or pointer, and asking the children to join along. Teachers could also pause and ask the children what they notice about the refrain. Children will begin to notice that they are saying the same refrain on each page and that the print in the refrain is also the same on each page. See Figure 5.3 for additional big-book titles that contain repetitive and patterned text.

Preschool teachers who are keenly aware of the print awareness potential of big books can be observed modeling concepts such as left-to-right and top-to-bottom progression, tracking print, differentiating between a letter and a word, and drawing attention to specific letters of the alphabet (International Reading Association & National Association for the Education of Young Children, 1998; Justice & Pullen, 2003). They also optimize the magical potential of big books and encourage children to become active, rather than passive, in the shared reading event. Children can come up to the big book to display their own print concept knowledge and attainments. These experiences not only develop children's sense of accomplishment and pride, but they help to pave the road toward becoming a successful reader. The trick is to make them brief but explicit, and to repeat them in many contexts.

Let's take a look at what a shared reading session that draws attention to print concepts like book conventions, print conventions, concept of letter and word, and alphabet knowledge might look and sound like. An ideal place to begin is the start of your shared reading session with a focus on *book conventions*. Children tend to grasp book conventions most quickly if they are introduced in daily shared reading sessions. The first component that should be introduced is the *front of the book*. At this time, the teacher can model or invite children to identify the front of the book. We can think about this process as a gradual release of responsibility whereby it may be necessary to model all of these concepts until they are familiar. But, as time and exposures increase, the teacher may

Brown, M. W. (1977). *Goodnight moon*. New York: HarperCollins.
Carle, E. (1987). *Do you want to be my friend?* New York: Harper Trophy.
Carle, E. (1992). *Brown bear, brown bear, what do you see?* New York: Henry Holt.
Dale, P. (1996). *Ten out of bed*. Somerville, MA: Candlewick.
Hennesy, B. G. (1992). *Jake baked the cake*. New York: Puffin.
Hoberman, M. A. (2007). *A house is a house for me*. New York: Puffin.
Hutchins, P. (2000). *Ten red apples*. New York: HarperCollins.
Martin, Bill Jr. (1988). *Barn dance*. New York: Henry Holt.
Metzger, S. (2008). *We're going on a leaf hunt*. New York: Cartwheel Books.
Williams, R. L. (1995). *Who took the cookies from the cookie jar?* Huntington Beach, CA: Creative Teaching Press.

FIGURE 5.3. Big books: Repetitive/predictable texts that develop print awareness.

elicit individual children over time to identify the specific print concepts. A teacher may say:

> "This is the front of the book (*pointing to the front cover*). When I start to read, I start at the front of the book."

The teacher may also ask an individual child:

> "Erica, can you show me the front of the book?"

The teacher can then elicit group participation by saying:

> "What part did Erica point to? That's right. She found the front of the book."

This same procedure can then be repeated with the *back of the book*. The key is to model these concepts initially, ask individual children to identify these concepts over time, and finally to invite all children to identify these concepts in shared reading sessions. Each of these segments of the shared reading event may take just a few seconds, integrated naturally into the routine.

The next book convention to introduce is the *title of the book*. The teacher models or invites students to point to and read the title of the book. The teacher can model by saying:

> "This is the title of our story (*pointing to the title*). It says, *Goodnight Moon*. What does it say?"

The teacher can also elicit individual children to participate by saying:

> "Kevin, can you show me the title of the book? Right. It says, *Goodnight Moon* (*pointing to both words*). What does it say?"

The teacher can then extend this concept by having the entire class read the title with the teacher or the individual student. There are a couple of things to note about this component. First, the teacher should also discuss the significance of a title and how we can use a title to think about what the story might be about. Second, a teacher can also consider infusing the concept of word practice by having the students point to each word as they read the title. This same process can be followed for identification of the *title page*.

The final book conventions to introduce are those of the *author and the illustrator*. For these concepts, the teacher models or invites students to discuss the *role* of the author and illustrator/photographer. The teacher can model by saying:

"The author of our story is Donald Crews. He is the person who wrote the words that we are going to read in our story today."

The teacher can then extend the concept by saying:

"What does the author do? What did our author, Donald Crews, do?"

This same procedure can be followed for the role of the illustrator and/or photographer. Note that the book convention concepts do not require an extended amount of instruction prior to the shared reading session. Students quickly grasp these basic concepts if attention is drawn to them repeatedly. See Figure 5.4 for a recap of the book conventions that are easily taught during shared reading.

Print conventions are more advanced than book conventions. In order to consider print conventions, a child must already have a handle on book conventions—print conventions refer to the rules for print within a book. The first print convention to introduce is the *top-to-bottom progression* of print. This concept can be introduced in the "during" phase of the shared reading session. The teacher can model or invite the children to demonstrate their understanding of top-to-bottom progression of print on a page. The teacher may say:

"There are five lines on this page (*pointing and counting each line aloud*). I read this

Front of the Book	*Teacher models and/or invites students to identify front of book and encourages entire group to name the part of the book.*
Back of the Book	*Teacher models and/or invites students to identify back of book and encourages entire group to name the part of the book.*
Title of the Book	*Teacher models and/or invites students to point to the title of the book.*
Title Page	*Teacher models and/or invites students to point to or name the title page.*
Role of the Author	*Teacher models and/or invites students to discuss the role of the author.*
Role of the Illustrator/ Photographer	*Teacher models and/or invites students to discuss the role of the illustrator/photographer.*

FIGURE 5.4. Book conventions to introduce before shared reading.

one first and this one last. When I read, I read from the top to the bottom. Watch me as I read each line."

The teacher can then extend this concept by eliciting individual students to identify the top versus the bottom of print by saying:

"Maria, there are five lines of text on this page (*pointing to each*). Which one do I read first? Which one do I read last?"

The teacher can then continue by introducing the concept of *left-to-right progression* of print on that very same page. The teacher can say:

"Right. I know that I need to start reading at the top of the page on this very first line (*pointing to the first line*). I also need to know where to begin reading on this first line."

The teacher can then model this concept by saying:

"When I read, I start here and then I move this way (*sliding finger from left to right*)."

The teacher can then extend this concept by asking individual children to show which way to read on a specific line of text. The teacher can say:

"Lily, can you show me which way I need to read? Show me with your finger on the line."

Finally, the last print convention, *return sweep*, can be introduced right after modeling and/or eliciting participation in the left-to-right progression concept. The teacher might say:

"Good. I know that when I read I need to go from left to right on the line. Now, I need to know where to go next at the end of this line. When I get to the end of the line, I sweep back to this side (*sweeping finger back to the left on the next line*)."

The teacher can then extend this opportunity to elicit individual student participation by saying:

"Tara, my finger is here at the end of the line. Can you show me where to go? Show us with your finger where we go next."

Top-to-Bottom Progression	*Teacher models and/or invites students to demonstrate top-to-bottom progression.*
Left-to-Right Progression	*Teacher models and/or invites students to demonstrate left-to-right progression.*
Return Sweep	*Teacher models and/or invites students to demonstrate return sweep.*

FIGURE 5.5. Print conventions to introduce during shared reading.

Note again that these print conventions do not require much additional time. However, these are concepts that require intentional modeling and active involvement from children to ensure they have a firm grasp of these essential print concepts. See Figure 5.5 for a recap of the print conventions that can be taught during shared reading.

The next, and most difficult level of print awareness concepts is *concept of letter and word*. These are the basic understandings that a word is a unit of meaning. A word can have one syllable or more than one. A word is composed of individual letters. You can see where a word starts and ends by looking for the white spaces around it. This component is typically one that children grasp over time through much active involvement and direct instruction. Teachers engage this involvement through *tracking print* during each shared reading session. Teachers track print while reading a shared storybook by pointing to each word as they read the text. This is a critical component to model as it allows children to begin to see the direct connection between oral language and written language (Morris, Bloodgood, & Perney, 2003). It allows the critical understanding that what I say can be written down and then read. It also draws direct attention to spacing between words and word boundaries (International Reading Association & National Association for the Education of Young Children, 1998). While tracking print may be an implicit action during shared reading, it can also be made explicit by simply thinking aloud. For example, a teacher might say:

> "Watch as I point to each word as I read this line. Each word that I say is written down on this line. 'Two cats play on the grass' (*pointing to each word as he or she reads the line*)."

The teacher can pause during the shared reading and invite individual children to track print on a page while the teacher reads the line aloud. The teacher might say:

> "Alaina, can you come up and point to each word as I read this line?"

It may be a good idea to start small. Begin with a two-word phrase and then gradually increase the number of words until children can track an entire line of print. It also makes it a little more inviting and motivating if children are given a special pointer stick to track print. Again, fingerpoint reading is an insight that children tend to grasp over time with many chances to participate.

The next print concept to target, *counting words,* goes hand in hand with tracking print. Counting words firms up the concept that words are separated by spaces. Teachers can model or invite children to count the words in the title or on a line of text. A teacher can model by saying:

> "I am going to count the words in our title. One, two, three (*pointing to each word as he or she counts the words*). There are three words in our title. How many? Let's count them together."

The teacher can then extend this opportunity by inviting individual children to count the words in the title or a line of text. The teacher might say:

> "Tracey, can you come up and count the words in the title? Good. Let's all count the words in the title as Tracey points to each word."

The final area to draw attention to is *counting letters in a word.* This is also a critical component to target as it allows children to see the difference between a letter and a word and that letters make up a word. The teacher can model this concept by saying:

> "This word is plant. I am going to count the letters in this word. One, two, three, four, five. There are five letters in the word plant."

The teacher can then extend this opportunity by inviting individual children to come up to count the letters in a specific word by saying:

> "This word is *flower.* Hunter, can you come up and count the letters in this word? Great. Let's all count the letters in this word together."

Collectively, the concept of letter and word are components that ultimately serve as a foundation for children's future reading and writing success. However, they are the most difficult of all print concepts for children and typically get the least direct attention in school (Justice, Bowles, & Skibbe, 2006). Preschool teachers play a key role in developing these insights by providing deliberate and direct instruction during shared reading as well as other print-focused times of the day. See Figure 5.6 for a recap of the concepts of letter and word to introduce during shared reading.

The final area of print concepts to target is *alphabet knowledge.* Children's alphabet

Teacher Tracks Print	*Teacher tracks print while reading a shared storybook (i.e., teacher points to each word as he or she reads).*
Students Track Print	*Teacher invites children to track print on a page while the teacher reads.*
Counting Words	*Teacher models and/or invites students to count words on a title or page.*
Counting Letters in a Word	*Teacher models and/or invites students to count the letters in a word.*

FIGURE 5.6. Concepts of letter/word to introduce during shared reading.

knowledge plays a crucial role in their future reading ability. Knowing letter names is directly related to children's ability to remember the forms of written words and their ability to treat words as a sequence of letters (Snow, Burns, & Griffin, 1999). A lack of letter recognition is also connected to children's ability to identify letter sounds, which is needed to read words. Preschool children need instruction that is crafted to help them gain knowledge of the alphabet. Children should begin to notice how letters come together to make words, phrases, sentences, and paragraphs, which come together to create stories. Preschool teachers can plan and implement meaningful activities that encourage children's alphabet learning.

Another critical goal of alphabet awareness instruction in preschool is for children to eventually grasp the alphabetic principle—that crucial understanding they will need for their formal reading instruction in kindergarten and first grade. When children have acquired the *alphabetic principle* they understand that there are predictable relationships between letters and sounds and that those relationships can be applied to both known and unknown words. It is truly a magical thing when children "unlock" their very first word by applying the alphabetic principle.

Preschool instruction can be crafted to ensure that children have this "lightbulb moment" fairly quickly when they begin formal reading instruction. Children tend to acquire alphabet knowledge in a sequence. It typically begins with knowledge of letter names, letter shapes, and finally letter sounds. See Figure 5.7 for the sequence of alphabet knowledge and ways that children typically acquire this knowledge. Shared reading during whole-group time is an ideal time to draw attention to letter names, shapes, and letter-sound correspondences.

Let's take a look at what alphabet awareness during shared reading might look and sound like. Teachers can take the meaningful experience of shared reading to draw attention to letters of the alphabet. Teachers have a choice as to when to draw attention to letters during the shared reading experience. For example, teachers might pause *before* the shared reading and discuss the letters on the cover of the book or the title page.

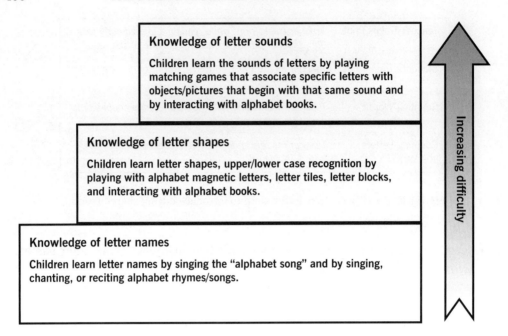

FIGURE 5.7. Sequence of alphabet knowledge and alphabet activities.

Opportunities can also be found *during* the shared reading to draw attention to letters while in the process of reading the story. Teachers can also go back into the story *after* the shared reading to draw explicit attention to letters. The key is to intentionally plan a time before, during, or after the shared reading to provide explicit attention to letters.

Teachers may begin this process, especially in the beginning of the school year, by asking children to *identify any letter of the alphabet.* Teachers can model or invite children to name any letter on a page. This is a great way to set up students for success and self-confidence. They have this opportunity to name any letter that they know on a page of text. Typically, children's very first letter is the first letter of their name. This is a great place to start, and then to nudge them a little to identify other letters in their name or other letters of the alphabet. The teacher can model by saying:

> "I am going to name some letters on this page. This is the letter *S.* I notice that it is squiggly like a snake. That will help you to remember the letter *S.* Here is another letter. This is the letter *M.* This letter looks like two triangles right next to each other. Let's name these two letters together."

The teacher can extend this time by asking individual students to showcase their letter knowledge by asking them to identify any letter by saying:

"Kiana, can you name any letters on this page? Come up and point to and name any letters that you know on this page. Good. What letters did Kiana name? Let's name them together."

Moving up the ladder of difficulty, the teacher can pause before, during, or after the shared reading and ask children to *identify a specific letter or letters of the alphabet*. The hard thing here is knowing where to start. We think that you should start with your curriculum resources. In many cases, preschool curricula will contain a scope and sequence of alphabet instruction and would have specific letters of the alphabet, usually two or three, to target every week. These letters are typically chosen to coincide with the theme exploration and to minimize confusion with their shape and sound. For example, letters *B* and *D* are not typically taught together. They are similar in both shape and sound and therefore can be quite confusing for the emergent reader. Current research points out that the *Letter of the Week* schedule, whereby letters are taught from the first letter to the last, is not necessarily best practice (International Reading Association & National Association for the Education of Young Children, 1998). See Figure 5.8 for a sample scope and sequence for alphabet instruction. The teacher can reinforce the scope and sequence during shared reading by saying:

"I am looking for the letter *K* on this page. We have been working on the letter *K* for the past 2 days. Here is the letter *K*. I see it in the word *King*."

Extending this opportunity, the teacher can ask individual children to identify a specific letter on a page. This is an excellent form of assessment. The teacher might say:

"Ben, can you point to the letter *B* on this page? Good. Ben, what is special about the letter *B*? That's right. It's the first letter in your name! What letter did Ben find?"

The last level of alphabet knowledge instruction that can be infused into whole-group shared reading is *identifying sound–symbol correspondences*. Remember, the ultimate goal of alphabet awareness instruction is eventually reaching that "lightbulb moment"—acquiring the alphabetic principle. That is not the same thing as sounding out

FIGURE 5.8. Sample scope and sequence for alphabet instruction. Based on Schumm (2006).

words. Rather, it is a necessary precursor to learning to sound out words: children need a basic understanding that the alphabet is used as a code before they can really benefit from conventional reading instruction. Teachers teach sound–symbol correspondences when they make a direct connection to a letter and the sound that it makes. They show or point to the letter, make its sound, have the students name the letter and make the sound, and provide words that begin with that sound. It requires explicit instruction. The teacher may say:

> "This is the letter *J*. This letter looks like a hook. What is the name of this letter? The letter *J* makes the /j/ sound. Make that sound with me. Right. I have some pictures here that begin with the letter *J* and make the /j/ sound. I have a picture of a jar. Say that word. I hear the /j/ sound when I say *jar*, /j/ /j/ /j/ *jar*. Let's say that together."

This process could continue with one or more target letters chosen for that shared reading session and corresponding pictures and/or objects that link to that letter. Teachers can then review all the letters, sounds, and then the pictures and objects that made that initial sound. In this respect, teachers have drawn explicit attention to the sound–symbol correspondence of a specific letter. Teachers can then extend this opportunity by having children think of other words that begin with that specific sound, but it is important to note that this is a fairly advanced skill. Another important thing to note is that not all of the print and alphabet awareness components would be a target in the same shared reading. Rather, teachers can use the shared reading event to meet the needs of the children. For example, in the beginning of the year, children may not have an awareness of book conventions like the front or back of the book. The teacher would be sure to draw attention to those very foundational and basic components of print. After children have mastered this understanding, the teacher may choose to focus on more sophisticated concepts like return sweep or letters versus words. The key is to meet

Identify Any Letter	*Teacher models and/or invites students to name any letter on a page/chart.*
Identify Specific Letter/Letters	*Teacher models and/or invites students to name a specific letter/letters on a page/chart.*
Identify Letter/Letters in Child's Name	*Teacher models and/or invites students to name a letter on a page/chart that contains a letter in their own name.*
Identify Sound–Symbol Correspondences	*Teacher makes a direct connection to a letter and the sound that it makes by showing the letter, having the students name the letter and sound, and by providing words that begin with that sound.*

FIGURE 5.9. Alphabet awareness introduced during shared reading.

children where they are in their development of these concepts over time. See Figure 5.9 for a recap of the concepts of alphabet awareness to introduce during shared reading.

The use of *alphabet books* during shared reading is also an effective and meaningful way to draw children's attention to the letters of the alphabet. Alphabet books were one of the earliest forms of illustrated picture books for children and they still represent a wonderful way to introduce the *ABC*s as well as capture minds and imaginations. Reading aloud alphabet books allows teachers the opportunity to build children's vocabulary and intentionally teach the letters and sounds of the alphabet. See Figure 5.10 for a list of alphabet books that are on our shelves.

There are some things to consider, though, when choosing alphabet books for the purposes of building sound–symbol associations. Not all alphabet books adhere to the rules of letter-sound correspondences. Be sure that the words used to represent each letter begin with the most common sound of each letter. For example, the letter *S* should be represented with a *sun* or a *salamander*, not a *ship* or a *sled*. When teaching letter sounds to emergent readers, it's best to avoid phonics patterns like digraphs (*sh, wh, ph, ch*) or blends (*bl, sn, tr*) to avoid unnecessary confusions. It's also a good idea to choose books with only one or two easily identifiable illustrations that directly link to the letter sound. Generally speaking, be sure that you have read and reviewed the alphabet book prior to the read-aloud and plan how you will explicitly draw children's attention to the shapes and sounds of the letters.

Ehlert, L. (1996). *Eating the alphabet.* New York: Harcourt Brace.
Elting, M., & Folsom, M. (2005). *Q is for duck.* New York: Clarion Books.
Ernst, L. C. (1996). *The letters are lost.* New York: Viking Press.
Feelings, M., & Feelings, T. (1974). *Jambo means hello: Swahili alphabet book.* New York: Dial Press.
Fleming, D. (2002). *Alphabet under construction.* New York: Henry Holt.
Hague, K. (1984). *Alphabears.* New York: Henry Holt.
Hoban, T. (1982). *A. B. See.* New York: Greenwillow Books.
Johnson, S. T. (1995). *Alphabet city.* New York: Viking Press.
Kirk, D. (1998). *Miss Spider's ABC.* New York: Scholastic Press.
Lionni, L. (1968). *The alphabet tree.* New York: Pantheon.
Martin, B. (1989). *Chicka chicka boom boom.* New York: Simon & Schuster.
Neumeier, M., & Glaser, B. (1985). *Action alphabet.* New York: Greenwillow Books.
Pallotta, J. (1986). *The icky bug alphabet book.* Boston: Quinlan Press.
Patience, J. (1993). *An amazing alphabet.* Hills, MN: Crescent.
Rankin, L. (1991). *The handmade alphabet.* New York: Dial Books.
Sendak, M. (1992). *Alligators all around: An alphabet.* New York: Scholastic.
Seuss, Dr. (1996). *Dr. Seuss's ABC.* New York: Random House.
Thomson, R. (1987). *All about ABC.* Milwaukee: G. Stevens.
Van Allsburg, C. (1987). *The Z was zapped.* Boston: Houghton Mifflin.

FIGURE 5.10. Alphabet books on our shelves.

Circle time is another block of time where teachers can draw children's attention to the *print that surrounds them in the classroom*. Research suggests that surrounding children with print and intentionally drawing their attention to the print in their environment provides a meaningful and critical backdrop for future reading and writing success (Adams, 1990). Consider the many types of print found in a preschool classroom, and more specifically, in the whole-group area of the classroom. You are likely to find an alphabet chart, a calendar labeled with the month of the year and the days of the week, a rocking chair labeled with the words *rocking chair*, a classroom-helper chart, an attendance chart with children's names who are present and absent that day, and a short poem or predictable text that coincides with the current theme exploration. The area is a veritable treasure chest of print awareness opportunities.

The key is to intentionally draw attention to the forms and functions of the classroom print. Simply surrounding children with the print is not enough. Be sure to *point out and discuss the print*. Talk about and point out print conventions like print directionality, word boundaries, capital letters, punctuation, and letters of the alphabet. Consider the example of using a short rhyming poem, "One Little Flower, One Little Bee," during a nature exploration unit. The poem reads like this

> One little flower, one little bee.
> One little blue bird, high in the tree.
> One little brown bear smiling at me.
> One is the number I like,
> you see.

Teachers can employ the same instructional routines with poems, charts, and songs that they would use with a big book. For example, teachers can begin by reading aloud the entire poem for the children and *track print* as they read. They can then extend by having children come up and track a line of print. Teachers can ask children where they should start reading, reinforcing the *left-to-right directionality of print*, and then ask children where to go at the end of a line, drawing attention to *return sweep*. Teachers can *count the number of words* on a line and ask children to *count the number of letters in a word*. Teachers can draw attention to the letter *O,* as it appears as the first letter on every line but one. They can even ask children to identify *specific letters or letters that are in children's names*. Children can also sing the "alphabet song" while the teacher points to each letter of the alphabet. The insights that children gain from an intentional focus on the print that surrounds them are numerous. The trick is to see every bit of print in their environment as an opportunity to develop children's print and alphabet awareness.

Small-Group Instruction

While whole-group instruction represents a unique time to work with your community of learners, small-group instruction is a time to work more directly with children. In some cases, children are placed in small groups based on a need identified through formal or informal measures of literacy development. In other cases, children may be placed in mixed-ability groups so that struggling children may work with other children with specific literacy strengths. In the case of print and alphabet awareness, children are most often placed in small groups based on informal measures of concepts of print and alphabet recognition. This allows teachers the opportunity to target individual children's needs in these areas that could not be met during whole-group instruction.

Let's first take a look at the area of print awareness and some examples of small-group instructional routines that could help bolster children's attainment of print concepts. So how would a teacher know whether children need help in the area of print awareness? Typically, preschool children take a print awareness assessment prior to or in the beginning of the school year; you will see an example in Chapter 7. This assessment involves giving a student a storybook and asking him or her to identify components such as the front of the book, a letter, a word, the first word of a sentence, and so on. See Figure 5.11 for a sample activity for assessing print awareness. The result of this quick assessment is a window on children's knowledge of print and the extent to which they have had print experiences and exposures. It also can direct the teacher's formation of needs-based, small-group instruction. See Figure 5.12 for a sample data chart of children's print awareness assessment results.

> Give a student a storybook and ask him or her to show you . . .
> - The front of the book
> - The title of the book
> - Where you should begin reading
> - A letter
> - A word
> - The first word of a sentence
> - The last word of a sentence
> - The first and last word on a page
> - Punctuation marks
> - A capital letter
> - A lower-case letter
> - The back of the book

FIGURE 5.11. A sample activity for assessing print awareness.

Concept	Pete	Chloe	Russel	Valerie
Front of Book	✓	✓	✓	✓
Title of Book	✓	✓	✓	✓
Where to Begin Reading				✓
A Letter	✓	✓		✓
A Word			✓	✓
First Word in Sentence		✓		
Last Word in Sentence				
First/Last Word on a Page				✓
Upper-case Letter	✓	✓		✓
Lower-case Letter		✓		✓
Back of Book	✓	✓	✓	✓

FIGURE 5.12. Children's print awareness data.

Small-group instruction focused on developing student print awareness, typically around 10–15 minutes, should strive to teach several components of print awareness. Again, teachers can use the same instructional routines with children used during whole-group shared reading but on a much more focused basis. Teachers have the flexibility to use the current shared storybook, books from past themes, or poems of repetitive or patterned text on chart paper or pocket charts. The important thing is to ensure that the children are interested.

Teachers often begin with such essential basics as book-handling skills like caring for books, positioning the book, and turning pages properly. This is an opportune time to get little books in children's hands so that they can practice what they are learning. Teachers can also treat this as a time to interactively read aloud to the children, while pausing to discuss the directionality of print, that we read the print and not the pictures, and that pages are numbered. Teachers can draw attention to word boundaries, and consistently discuss that the reason we read is for information, enjoyment, and discovery.

FIGURE 5.13. Letter and word frames.

Children can show teachers attainment of these concepts with their own little books or by coming up to a big book or a chart during this time, which serves as an excellent form of informal assessment.

When teachers are using big books or charts to reinforce print concepts during small group, it may be a good idea to use *letter or word frames.* Letter or word frames are circle-shaped frames made from tagboard, pipe cleaners, or wikki-stix (pipe cleaners covered in flexible wax) that children can use to highlight particular letters or words on charts or big books. In this respect, children are actively engaged and are able to practice what they are learning. This also is an excellent way to measure the individual print awareness progress of children over time. See Figure 5.13 for a picture representing the use of a letter or word frame.

Another engaging small-group activity beneficial for all children is the construction of a *classroom book.* Like shared reading, writing serves multiple purposes in the preschool classroom, so we include class books both here as a means for building book and print concepts and later in our writing chapter. Creating a classroom book is a great way for children to understand how books and print work as well as a feeling of accomplishment in publishing their own book. The central print concept that drives this activity is showing the children that their own words can be written down and then read. First, teachers will need to choose a topic or theme for the classroom book. A great idea would be to focus on the current theme exploration. See Figure 5.14 for additional ideas for publishing a classroom book.

Next, teachers will need to decide how they will execute this activity. We think it is important for teachers to explicitly talk and discuss with children the reason why they are doing any lesson or activity. So, during the first small-group time, teachers can talk to students about the purpose of the classroom book and then model the composition of the first page of the book. It might sound like this:

> "We have been learning about the ocean and sea life. We've read books about the ocean and all about the different creatures and things that we can find in the ocean. We even visited the aquarium yesterday and got to see and touch some of the many things we've discussed in the classroom. I know that you have so much new information to share about the ocean. A great way to share information is to write a book. Books are a way for you to share all the things that you have learned and discovered and a way for others to read about so many wonderful things. We do this every day when we read books in school and at home. So, we are going to make our own classroom book about the ocean. Everyone is going to get his or her own page in the book.
>
> "First, you'll draw a picture of something that you've learned about the ocean and sea life. Second, you will tell me or one of the teacher helpers what your picture is all about [this is an ideal project to enlist the help of classroom assistants or parent helpers] and we will write your words under your picture. Third, we will put all of

Class-made books can be created based on:

1. A recent class field trip.

2. A "get well" or "thank you" letter.

3. The letters of the alphabet based on a theme where each child would get his or her own letter.
   For example, *Our Spring Alphabet Book* may have a page that reads
   G is for green grass that grows in the spring.

4. A holiday.
   Thanksgiving Book: Children draw and dictate what they are thankful for.
   I am thankful for....

5. A book previously read in class.

6. Fill-in-the-blank *Ideas Book*
   When I grow up....
   In winter....
   If I had wings, I would....
   I knew it was fall because on Monday I saw one _____....

7. Patterned songs.
   For example, "The Farmer in the Dell" verses can be changed to a different theme, such as "The Zookeeper at the Zoo ... ; children would fill in the names of animals found at the zoo.

8. Patterned poems.
   For example, using the poem "Cloud Parade" children can write or dictate the word in the last line and then illustrate with white paint or cotton balls.
   When I look up into the sky, a cloud parade goes floating by!
   I love the pictures that I see.
   This one looks like a _____ to me.

9. End-of-year *Class Book*.
   Each child dictates one favorite thing or memory from the school year to create a memory book.

FIGURE 5.14. Class-made book ideas.

the pages of the book together and then make a class cover for the book. Last, we will read our book together during circle time. Everyone will have a chance to read their own page as well as each other's page. We will then put our classroom book in the library center so that we can read and visit the book as often as you'd like. This is going to be so exciting. I can't wait to see and read everyone's page in the book!"

The teacher can then model this process with his or her own page of the book. It might sound like this:

"I have drawn a picture of two seahorses next to a coral reef. Remember we learned that seahorses are often found around sea grass and coral reefs. We also learned that seahorses are usually brown so that they can camouflage, or blend in with their surroundings, but when they are with other seahorses, they sometimes change into bright colors. That's why I drew my seahorses in bright pink and purple colors. Now, I need to write a sentence about my sea life picture under the picture. I need to describe my pictures. I am going to write, 'Two seahorse friends are happily swimming around the coral reef.' "

The teacher can then say the sentence again slowly while writing each word, one at a time, on the page. The teacher can then read the sentence again while tracking print to reinforce the concept of word. This project could span a few days during small-group time and culminate in the publishing and reading of the book during circle time. Note that this activity not only promotes print awareness but also comprehension of content and rich oral language development.

Children can also make their own version of an alphabet book using the letters of their name. For example, children can create their own class-made version of *Chicka Chicka Boom Boom* (Martin, 1989). Children can draw pictures of the palm trees and then write the letters of their name in the trees. This idea can also be extended to target letters based on the theme or curriculum. Another fun idea for a class-made book is to create the book based upon a previously read book during whole-group time. For example, after reading the book *The Very Hungry Caterpillar* by Eric Carle (1987), children can dictate and illustrate an extension story about the places and foods that the caterpillar could also have visited and eaten along its journey. Teachers can also use a poem or patterned text based upon the story read and have the children fill in the blanks with their own word to complete the poem. Since each blank corresponds to one word, this activity is ideal for building the concept of word. Each child will have his or her own page with the poem and all pages will be put together to create a class-made big book. A poem that coincides with *The Very Hungry Caterpillar* is

Hungry Mr. Caterpillar
Was looking for a treat.
Said he to the _____,
"What's good to eat?"
_____ said to the Caterpillar,
"If you're hungry for a treat
Try a _____.
It's good to eat."

During small-group time, teachers can conduct a shared reading of the poem from a chart, reinforce the print awareness concepts, and then model filling in the blanks with their own words. Children can be asked to come up to the chart and identify specific print concepts and then be given their own pages to dictate their words and illustrate the poem.

Wordless picture books also allow for lots of opportunities to develop print awareness. For example, teachers could use a wordless book like *Pancakes for Breakfast* (DePaola, 1978) and go through each page and have the children first orally narrate the story. See Figure 5.15 for a list of wordless books on our shelves. Next, individual children could dictate their own sentence for each page of the book. Children can celebrate their authorship by a reading of the book during whole-group time. The best part is that children can revisit their book time and time again in the library center.

Small-group time is also an ideal time to focus attention on the letters and sounds of the alphabet. In some cases, preschool teachers have given children an alphabetic awareness assessment prior to or in the beginning of the school year. These assessments require children to point to and name the upper-case letters of the alphabet. Results of these assessments can guide the teacher's formation of small-group instruction.

Some children may need a focused introduction to the *concept of the letters of the alphabet*. Remember that children's initial understanding of the alphabet is the letter names only. They demonstrate this understanding by singing or saying the alphabet, a performance that adults encourage. We need to think about moving children from this earliest alphabetic understanding to the connection between the letter name and the let-

Carle, E. (1998). *1, 2, 3 to the zoo.* New York: Penguin Group.
DePaola, T. (1978). *Pancakes for breakfast.* New York: Houghton Mifflin Harcourt.
Hutchins, P. (1971). *Rosie's walk.* New York: Simon & Schuster.
Liu, J. S. (2002). *Yellow umbrella.* Brooklyn, NY: Kane/Miller Book Publishers.
Rathmann, P. (1977). *Good night gorilla.* New York: Penguin Group.
Speir, P. (1997). *Rain.* San Val, Inc.
Wiesner, D. (1997). *Tuesday.* New York: Clarion Books.
Wiesner, D. (2006). *Flotsam.* New York: Clarion Books.

FIGURE 5.15. Wordless picture books on our shelves.

ter shape. An ideal way to do this is by using an *alphabet chart*. Teachers can model singing the "alphabet song" and track each letter of the alphabet as they slowly sing the song. Be especially sure to slow down when you get to the *L, M, N, O,* and *P*! This draws an explicit connection from the known to the unknown; knowledge of the letter names in the song to knowledge of the letter shape. Children can then be presented with their own set of alphabet strips and can track each letter of the alphabet as they slowly sing the familiar "alphabet song." See Figure 5.16 for an example of an alphabet strip. This activity will require much practice, but children will truly see the connection between the song and the actual letters. This is a critical understanding needed for their reading success.

Small-group time is a wonderful time to allow children the opportunity to play with letters of the alphabet—in a meaningful way. A meaningful way for children to interact with letters is *playing with the letters in their name* and there are lots of fun ways to do this. One way is to read the alphabet classic *Chicka Chicka Boom Boom* (Martin, 1989). Provide each child with a bowl of alphabet tiles. As the teacher reads each page and names the letters, children pick out the letters and name them aloud. If one of those letters is in their own name, they keep the letter out on the table. After the story has been read, the children can then assemble the letters of their name in order and name each letter in their name aloud to a partner and to the teacher. Children can also stamp the letters of their names, use magnetic letters on a whiteboard, use letter-shaped sponges and stencils, toss bean bags onto specific letters and name the letters, and even try to write the letters of their names with shaving cream. These same activities could be applied to specific, or target, letters of the alphabet that teachers may be focusing on for a small-group session. Activities that draw children's attention to the letters of their names in their environment—in charts, books, posters, labels, and magazine pages—provide a crucial stepping-stone in their alphabetic knowledge success. See Figure 5.17 for a picture of a child playing with the letters during small-group time.

Small-group time also provides the opportunity to draw children's attention to the connection between letters and their corresponding sounds. This is the most difficult level of alphabetic awareness and the most critical understanding needed for formal reading instruction in kindergarten and first grade; it may be that you decide that letter

apple	boat	cat	dog	elephant	fish	gate	hammer
Aa	Bb	Cc	Dd	Ee	Ff	Gg	Hh

FIGURE 5.16. An example alphabet strip.

FIGURE 5.17. Child playing with letters during small-group time.

sounds are too sophisticated for your class. If your children already know their letter names, though, consider introducing at least a few letter sounds. Much like the concept of the alphabet names and letter shapes, learning the sounds of letters should also be meaningful and engaging. Activities that directly link the letter shape to the sound of the letter, typically through a picture or an object, are most effective in developing children's awareness that letters are symbols that represent sounds.

Children can create letter books that focus on a specific letter or letters that have the letter shape and pictures that they can draw or use from magazines that correspond to the letter sound. Teachers can also make posters with a large letter in the middle and children can paste pictures around the letter that matches the sound. As a final example (see Figure 5.18), teachers can make letter puzzles where the children match upper- and lower-case letters by matching the two sides of a picture that connects the letter to the sound the letter makes.

Children can also engage in sound-sorting activities on a regular basis. Children sort objects representing two or more letters into the correct container or pile; if the container is labeled with the letter and a picture, you are working both with phonological awareness and initial letter sounds. All of these instructional routines can be used

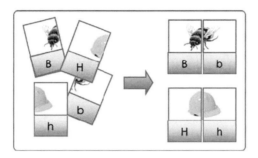

FIGURE 5.18. Letter-sound match puzzle.

repeatedly by simply changing the letter-sound focus. Many of these activities can also be transitioned into center-time activities once modeled during small-group time.

Center Time

Print awareness opportunities continue during children's center-time explorations. In many cases, the activities we discussed for small-group time can be transitioned to a center-time activity. The advantage is that children are familiar with the purpose and the procedures of the activity and can therefore demonstrate some independence with the skill in a center-time format. Overall, center time is an ideal time to encourage children to interact with and play with print. In order to encourage this play, teachers need to think about "stocking" *each center* with lots of print awareness supplies. Items like clipboards, paper, writing and drawing utensils, and books that match the theme that is being explored are wonderful ways to help children see that they can express their own ideas through print. We want to help children gain an insight that print is something that is important in their lives.

For example, in the *dramatic play center,* children can pretend to write a shopping list during a theme exploring healthy food choices. Teachers can supply "grocery lists" that say at the top, "My Shopping List," where the children can draw food items and pretend to write their own shopping list after gathering healthy foods in their food basket. Children can also write a letter to a friend or family member, put it in an envelope, place a "stamp" on the envelope, and "mail the letter" in the *writing center* during a theme exploring the post office and postal workers. Another fun idea is to ask parents, grandparents, aunts, or uncles to write letters to the children during this unit. Teachers or teacher assistants can take a few minutes during whole group or transition times to read the cards and letters from family members. Children truly delight in this special activity. Children can also be encouraged to work together to create traffic signs, like a stop sign or a railroad crossing sign, for the *block center* while exploring a unit on safety.

The *library center* is also a center that lends itself quite well to encouraging interactions with print. The library center is a center that should continually change with each thematic exploration. If the class is learning about the farm, the library center should be filled with lots of fiction and nonfiction books about life on a farm. In this sense, the library center is a spot that is engaging and exciting. It should be an area that children will be consistently excited about visiting during each new theme. Teachers can also think about making this area inviting and comfortable. Items like a carpet, pillows, and beanbags entice children to "curl up" with a good book. Teachers can even consider placing some stuffed animals in the center so that children can "read" their favorite book to a friend.

Often, children's favorite book to read is one that was just read during whole-group shared reading. In many cases, the book has been read several times and children are familiar with the characters, setting, and storyline. Teachers should consider placing a copy or copies of the selection in the library center for children to explore on their own. Children can often be seen engaging in pretend readings of a book after it has been read a few times during shared reading. It's a magical event to witness. See Figure 5.19 for additional center-time activities that encourage children's play with print. Again, we think that the key is for teachers to see each center in their class, no matter what it is, as an opportunity to develop children's print awareness.

Additional Opportunities

As we have previously discussed, the preschool day is packed with instructional opportunities to focus attention on children's print and alphabet awareness. It is important not to let any potential for print awareness instruction pass by. With that in mind, we also

Chicka Chicka Boom Boom **Tree and Magnetic Letters**	Make a "magnetic" version of the tree and place magnetic letters next to the tree in a bin. Children can put the letters of their name on the tree (or any target letters).
Letter-Snapping Cubes	Write letters with a Sharpie marker on unifix (snapping) cubes. Children can snap together the letters in their name, upper- and lower-case, or alphabetical order. This concept can be changed based on target skill.
Wikki-Stix Letters	Write target letters on construction paper and laminate it. Children can bend and twist wikki-stix or pipe cleaners into the letter shape.
Highlighting Letter Search	Provide children with highlighter markers and magazines. Have them search for and highlight any letters they know or specific target letters.
Book Baskets	Place baskets of books in the middle of your classroom tables. Book baskets can be filled with wordless books, ABC books, predictable books, magazines, etc. Children can take a basket and engage in pretend readings of their favorite book.
Read and Write the Room	Provide children with special pointer sticks and paper. Children can "read" and write the print that they are familiar with—calendar, days of the week, word wall, poems, children's names, etc. They can even search for as many letter *B*'s (or any letter) that they can find.

FIGURE 5.19. Additional center-time ideas that promote print awareness.

discuss how some otherwise unstructured times of the day, like transitional times, can be a perfect opportunity to engage children with surrounding print.

Transitions are an everyday component of the preschool day. Teachers and teacher's assistants alike routinely transition, or move, groups of children from an activity in the schedule into the next event of the day. This might include transitioning children from the carpet during circle and whole-group time to small-group or center-time explorations or from sitting at the tables during snack or lunch to getting into an orderly line to go outside or to use the bathroom. These are relatively short time segments of the day and as a result, often overlooked as noninstructional times just to get children from "Point *a* to point *b*" as quickly and quietly as possible.

Instead, teachers might consider these daily transitional routines as a perfect opportunity to engage children with print. For example, instead of just calling out children's names to go to specific centers, pull out children's names on cards from a basket and have them identify their names. They can then come up and get their name card and place it in the center pocket chart. You will be surprised how quickly children will learn not only their own name, but every other child's name in the class. Teachers can also use the alphabet strip to transition children. The teacher or teacher assistant can use a pointer stick and point to a letter on the alphabet strip and ask children to stand up quietly and go to their center if that is the first letter in their name.

Teachers can also incorporate print awareness in the game I Spy as a way to draw attention to the print that surrounds them and transition them smoothly to the next time of the day. For example, the teacher might say:

> "I spy the letter *M* on our Days of the Week chart. Who can show me the letter *M* on the chart? Good job, Georgia! What day of the week begins with an *M*? Right, it say *Monday*. Everyone that has a letter *M* in his or her name, stand up and get in line to go outside."

Teachers might also say:

> "I spy the word *sunny* on our weather chart. Who can show us where it says *sunny* on the chart? Excellent! Robert found the word *sunny*. What letter does *sunny* begin with? Right, it begins with the letter *S*. Everyone who has a letter *S* in his or her name can stand up quietly and get in line."

The teacher can even say, "I spy" on the cover of a book, or a title:

> "Who can find the title?"

This same idea can be continued with previously discussed book and print conventions like concept of letter, concept of word, and print versus pictures. Remember, print awareness need not take a large block of instructional time. In this sense, transitions lend themselves very well to this component of literacy instruction.

Teachers should consider drawing attention to as many forms of print in the classroom as a means to meaningfully engage children in print. This includes the calendar, poems on charts, word walls, environmental print, an alphabet strip, and the big book on the easel—every possible print source in the classroom. Teachers will most likely find that transitional times are much smoother because children are actively engaged and have a purpose. Teachers will also find that this focused attention will allow children's insights into how print works grow and expand.

IMPLEMENTATION IN THREE CLASSROOMS

A Public School-Based Preschool: Pam

Pam's focus on her children's print and alphabet awareness is evident throughout her instructional routines. She provides several meaningful opportunities for her children to engage in print activities throughout the day. Each morning and afternoon as children arrive, they "sign in" by writing their name on a card and placing it on the attendance chart. As a daily part of circle time, the children read the "Question of the Day" written on a sentence strip together and place their name cards under the answer of their choice, they read the days of the week, the months of the year, the weather chart, and the thematic poem on a chart. She also takes a few minutes each day to review the class word wall that contains the children's names and target vocabulary words chosen from past storybook read alouds. Children are then asked to find specific letters on the word wall and are invited to place highlighter tape on the letters. Pam tracks the print on these charts as she reads chorally with her children and also invites children to track print with a pointer stick as the class reads aloud together to reinforce concepts of print and word. They also sing the alphabet song while tracking the letters as they sing to help them connect letter awareness to letter identification. Children also use their name cards to choose a center from the learning centers chart every day. Children are also encouraged to visit the writing center several times a week to engage in invented writing activities with Pam and Cheryl. This practice reinforces the insight that oral language can be written down and then read. It also invites children to use what they know about letters and sounds. These are just a few snapshots of their daily print-related activities. From start to finish, print and alphabet awareness activities abound.

Pam uses her Weekend Book Buddies program, previously discussed in Chapter 2, to get parents on board and active in their children's print awareness. She realizes that, in many cases, parents and caregivers don't naturally draw attention to the forms and functions of print while reading to their child. So, she sends home a teacher-made index card (attractive with clip art pictures) with some tips and suggestions for parents and caregivers to do before, during, and after reading their Weekend Book Buddy book. See Figure 5.20 for sample Weekend Book Buddy print awareness cards. Pam feels confident

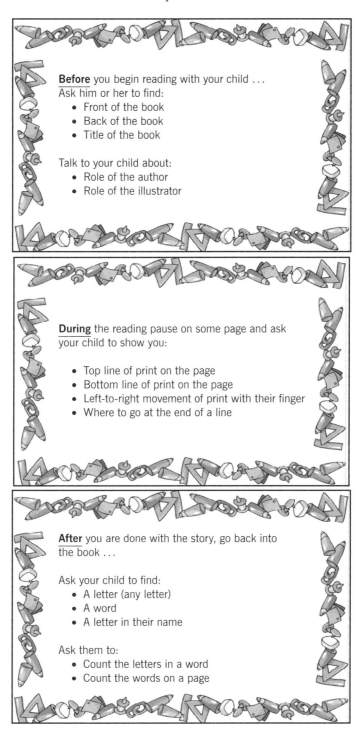

Before you begin reading with your child . . .
Ask him or her to find:
- Front of the book
- Back of the book
- Title of the book

Talk to your child about:
- Role of the author
- Role of the illustrator

During the reading pause on some page and ask your child to show you:

- Top line of print on the page
- Bottom line of print on the page
- Left-to-right movement of print with their finger
- Where to go at the end of a line

After you are done with the story, go back into the book . . .

Ask your child to find:
- A letter (any letter)
- A word
- A letter in their name

Ask them to:
- Count the letters in a word
- Count the words on a page

FIGURE 5.20. Sample "Weekend Book Buddy" print awareness cards.

Day	Alphabet Focus during Reading
Monday	• Introduces letter name and shape.
Tuesday	• Plays with magnetic letters or alphabet bean bags.
Wednesday	• Searches for letter in a big book.
Thursday	• Brainstorms and writes words that begin with the letter sound.
Friday	• Says alliteration tongue twister.

FIGURE 5.21. Elaina's alphabet instruction during storybook reading.

that her children's print awareness will grow and expand, not just because of her own instruction, but because of the support that children also receive at home.

A Head Start Center: Elaina

In order to support her children, many of whom who are learning English as a second language, develop understandings of print concepts and alphabet knowledge, Elaina includes a short, daily dose of each in her classroom instruction. She knows that sustained exposure over time is the best way to build children's understanding of these simple, but absolutely critical skills. To teach the letters of the alphabet, Elaina follows a set sequence for teaching letter names and shapes. She focuses on one new letter a week, but also includes a review of letters previously taught in order to build children's total alphabet knowledge. She weaves alphabet instruction into three parts of the day—large-group storybook reading, small group, and center time.

During large-group storybook reading, Elaina varies the types of alphabet activities she asks the children to do by day of the week (see Figure 5.21). On Mondays she introduces the letter by talking about its name, sound, and shape. She uses an alphabet strip to focus children on the letter's shape. On Tuesdays she forms the letter with magnetic pieces on her dry-erase board, talking through each line she uses to form the letter. On Wednesdays she asks children to help her find the letter in the print environment of her classroom. On Thursdays she asks children to think about the letter's sound by brainstorming and writing a list together of words that begin with the same sound. Because letter sounds are very difficult for young children, especially those learning English as a second language who have knowledge of different letter sounds in their home language, she again focuses on this skill on Fridays by asking children to play with a tongue twister using alliteration with the focus letter. Children love saying a funny tongue twister three times fast, and later in the year she even challenges her children to create their own tongue twisters to use in class.

Elaina uses small-group time for targeted alphabet instruction. Each month Elaina does a quick assessment to see what letters each child is learning and retaining and then uses this information to form her small groups. She places children together who are having difficulty with the same letters. The activities Elaina uses during small-group time are both playful and deliberate and focus on three to five letters at a time. The small-group time is devoted to work on letter identification, letter sounds, and letter formation and may be conducted by any member of the classroom team. First, she explicitly identifies the letters the children will be working with in their small group, by showing the letter and telling the children the letters' name and sound. Next, she asks the children to say each of the letter's names and sounds with her to practice. The next step is to a play a game that reviews letter names and/or letter sounds. She creates or uses premade games such as Fishing for Letters, Alphabet Bingo, searching for letters hidden around the room or in the sensory table, or sorting picture cards that begin with the different letter sounds. The last part of small group focuses on letter formation. During this time, she first models for the children how to form a letter by writing the letter and at the same time verbally describing each step she is making. Then she asks the children to practice forming the letters by writing on chalkboards, dry-erase boards, pieces of unlined paper, or even the sidewalk outside.

Last, Elaina always includes an activity that involves practice with the letters of the alphabet during center time. She has found creative ways to include letters in the blocks area, sensory table, writing table, library, science table, manipulatives table, and art center. Figure 5.22 provides a list of some of Elaina's favorite ways to incorporate the alphabet into her different centers. Ideally an adult is able to be with children in the cen-

Center	Alphabet Activity
Art	• Watercoloring letters of the alphabet • Tempura painting letters of the alphabet • Forming letters with construction paper shapes
Blocks	• Using blocks to build letters
Library	• Letter hunting in storybooks with highlighter tape • Playing with magnetic letters
Manipulatives	• Alphabet puzzles • Alphabet bingo • Sorting pictures beginning with different letter sounds
Science	• Making alphabet potato stamps
Sensory	• Finding alphabet letters in soil, sand, water, etc. • Fishing for letters • Selecting alphabet rubber ducks
Writing	• Forming letters on dry-erase boards • Forming letters on chalkboards • Writing letters on different types of paper with various writing utensils

FIGURE 5.22. Elaina's alphabet activities during center time.

ters as they are playing with the alphabet activities to help prompt the children to name the letters or to make the letter sounds. However, sometimes Elaina and her classroom assistants are busy in other centers, so the activities she plans builds on what children are learning during large- and small-group times.

Elaina primarily focuses on concepts of print during large-group instruction within the context of a storybook reading. Like alphabet knowledge, Elaina builds children's knowledge of print concepts by including daily instruction involving a range of print concept activities. She varies her activities by day of the week (see Figure 5.23). The activities occur before and while reading the storybook. Many of the concepts she teaches children repeat throughout the week since she finds that children are more likely to learn the print concepts through repetition across multiple storybooks.

In addition to classroom instruction, Elaina involves parents in building children's alphabet and concepts of print knowledge. Contacts with parents are both formal and informal, but they always include a reference to the specific concepts that the children are learning. If parents are able to come to the classroom, Elaina shows them the work that children are doing. She also sends work home. Elaina encourages parents to play letter hunts with their child as they are driving, walking, or shopping to find the letters of the month in the everyday environment. She also encourages parents to point out the

Day	Print Concept Focus during Reading
Monday	• Front and back of book • Title • Role of author • Role of illustrator/photographer
Tuesday	• Title • Title page • Role of author • Role of illustrator/photographer
Wednesday	• Title • Role of author • Role of illustrator/photographer • Top-to-bottom progression
Thursday	• Title • Title page • Left to right progression • Tracking print
Friday	• Title • Return sweep • Counting words • Counting letters in a word

FIGURE 5.23. Sequence of print concepts during storybook reading.

title, author, and illustrator before reading and to discuss where to begin and end reading while reading the book together with their child.

A Private Preschool: Sarah

Sarah and Maria are determined that all of their children master book and print conventions and learn the letters in their own names in the first 6 weeks of school so that they can have the rest of the year to use print as a vehicle for developing more extended alphabet awareness. They know that Sarah will be able to model book and print concepts during her daily shared readings, but they want to make it simple for Maria to follow up in the library center. They also choose an alphabet song that they have on a CD; they will use it as one of the center transitions, giving children a daily exposure to the letter names in a song that will give them a chance to sing and move. Maria will then focus on specific letter names in the writing center. They decide that the organization and materials in each center will be key to integrating these goals into the daily routine.

For the library center, Sarah is already rotating the collection by visiting the public library. She agrees that she will arrange the books by utility. She labels baskets to make it easier for Maria to direct children to books that are easy for reinforcing specific concepts. She has a *Point and Read* basket filled only with books that could be used to model and engage children in print concepts. None of these books has more than two lines of print on a page. She also has an *Alphabet Books* basket, a *Class Books* basket, a *Real Books* basket, and a *Storybooks* basket. During these first weeks, Maria will be sure to encourage children to select from the Point and Read basket so that she can reinforce print concepts in a one-on-one setting; once she knows that each child has print concepts, she will encourage them to choose from any basket.

In the writing center, Sarah and Maria agree on a two-pronged strategy. First, they make alphabet strips available in different formats. Small ones are attached to each clipboard. There are larger ones on the writing center desk. Next, they make a name puzzle for each child, writing the name on a sentence strip and cutting it apart. They put the pieces into a baggie with the child's picture. Maria will ask children to find their name bag, make their name, and then she will use the puzzle to teach each child the letters in his or her own name. That way, when Sarah is modeling alphabet awareness during her big-book readings, children will be able to demonstrate that they know the letters in their own names.

WHERE CAN I FIND MORE INFORMATION?

Print and alphabet awareness is indeed a critical component to the preschool experience. It's an interesting area of development because it's something that surrounds children every day—both in and out of the classroom. It's also an area that is especially "teachable" if given focused time and attention. The following are sources for you to continue to grow your own knowledge and expertise in the exciting area of print and alphabet awareness instruction.

Web-Based

- Birth to early childhood—for educators
  www.nifl.gov/earlychildhood/earlyeducator.html
- Reading Rockets: Print awareness
  www.readingrockets.org/teaching/reading101/printawareness
- Early language and literacy
  www.zerotothree.org/site/PageServer?pagename=key_language

Text-Based

- Justice, L. M., & Sofka, A. E. (2010). *Engaging children with print: Building early literacy skills through quality read-alouds.* New York: Guilford Press.
- Strickland, D., & Schickedanz, J. (2009). *Learning about print in preschool: Working with letters, words, and beginning links with phonemic awareness.* Newark, DE: International Reading Association.
- Venn, E., & Jahn, M. (2003). *Teaching and learning in preschool: Using individually appropriate practices in early childhood literacy instruction.* Newark, DE: International Reading Association.

CHAPTER 6

Emergent Writing

Preschoolers are interested in written messages. From an early age children begin to recognize the messages within environmental print—the isolated print that surrounds them in the form of signs and logos. Children know that the bright yellow *M* on the roadway sign is McDonald's. They quickly learn the graphic logo of their favorite cereal or candy. Children also know that it is special to receive a written message. Preschoolers delight in sending and receiving mail. Yet, because preschoolers' written messages do not necessarily look like conventional writing, teachers and parents are often at a loss for how to respond to them. This chapter explores methods for developing young writers.

WHAT IS EMERGENT WRITING?

Children begin to imitate adult writing long before they can write conventionally. This preconventional writing stage is referred to as emergent writing (Clay, 1975). Children follow a developmental progression within emergent writing. Sulzby (1990) described seven stages emergent writers progress through in their writing: drawing as writing, scribble writing, letter-like units, nonphonetic letter strings, copying from environmental print, invented spelling, and conventional writing (Vukelich & Christie, 2004). Figure 6.1 provides a summary and examples of the seven developmental stages of emergent writing. Recognizing these stages in individual children helps preschool teachers both celebrate and understand children's products and accelerate their progress.

In the first stage, drawing as writing, children do not understand that there are special forms for written communication. They focus on meaning, and they use their artwork to communicate ideas. To them, a picture is literally worth a thousand words. When asked to tell about their drawing, children can tell an entire story based on their artwork. As children begin to understand the differences between drawing and writing, they experiment with writing. During the scribble writing stage, their writing looks

Term	Definition
Drawing as Writing	Children tell stories by drawing pictures to represent their ideas
Scribble Writing	Children write by imitating what they see adults do when they write; the result looks like scribble lines
Letter-Like Units	As children begin to develop knowledge of the alphabet and concept of word, their writing begins to include some marks resembling letters that are separated into units with space in between
Nonphonetic Letter Strings	Children begin to write lists or strings of letters together in no certain order
Copying from Environmental Print	Children copy letters and more conventional forms from environmental print in the world around them
Invented Spelling	Children begin to use their understanding of letter-sound correspondence to write words using letters to represent the sounds they hear in the words
Conventional Writing	Children begin to use conventional spelling in their writing

FIGURE 6.1. Developmental sequence of emergent writing. Based on Sulzby (1990).

more like scribbles than writing, but it begins to have a left-to-right orientation. In addition, if asked what they are doing while scribbling, children in this stage will say they are writing rather than drawing. They see the activities as separate tasks. Children learning about letters in the alphabet begin to transfer this knowledge to their writing. In the letter-like units stage, children write units that are separated by spaces and that resemble, but are not quite yet, letters. That means that they begin to experiment with the straight lines, slanted lines, and curves that are used to form letters.

With further alphabet instruction children are able to form letters in the nonphonetic letter strings stage; at this stage, children string letters together in no certain order, experimenting with their new ability to form a conventional alphabet letter. The letters they choose are the letters they know—perhaps the letters in their name. There is no relationship between the sounds of the words they are "writing" and the letter they are using. Next they move to copying. Before children are able to use letter-sound knowledge to spell, they want to use their knowledge of the alphabet to write real words. In this stage, children rely heavily on written words in the environment in order to write. Essentially, children in this stage are copying letters they know in an order that they do not necessarily understand in order to write words.

A huge developmental leap occurs when children begin to make the connection between knowledge of the alphabet and knowledge that letters are used to represent sounds. When children have knowledge of letter–sound correspondence, they begin to use this understanding to write letters for the sounds they hear in words. The letters they choose are not always correct, and their phonemic awareness is rarely well-enough

Conventional Spelling	Child's Letter-Name Spelling
Car	Kr
Happy	Hpe
House	Hows
Peanut	Pnt
Pretty	Prite
Today	2da

FIGURE 6.2. Examples of children's letter-name spellings.

developed to hear all of the sounds, but they are still demonstrating a major accomplishment. Children in this stage are using invented spelling to write. In Figure 6.2 we show some possible examples of children's invented spellings. Notice that vowels are scarce; this is perfectly normal. With continued instruction, children's writing becomes more conventional with more accurate spelling.

WHY IS EMERGENT WRITING IMPORTANT?

Even though it may look like scribbles or a made-up language to us, children's emergent writing is an instructional gold mine. Children's writing is rich with clues about their understanding of the sounds in language and how sounds go together to create words. We know from research that children use their knowledge of the sounds in language to spell words (Read, 1971). When children use their knowledge of letters to represent the sounds they hear in words they want to write, they use invented or phonetic spelling (International Reading Association & National Association for the Education of Young Children, 1998). For example, a preschool child may write "hda" for *cheetah* or "prs" for *powers*. As children write using invented spelling, they experiment with the connection between the sounds of language and the letters that represent those sounds—the alphabetic principle. This experimentation in turn helps children develop skills that will aid them in beginning reading, such as segmenting and blending the sounds in words—phonological awareness. In fact, the efforts that preschoolers make to produce emergent spellings maximize and personalize their literacy learning (International Reading Association & National Association for the Education of Young Children, 1998).

In addition to developing phonological awareness, children's emergent writing also contributes to their understanding of the conventions and purposes of writing (International Reading Association & National Association for the Education of Young Children, 1998). As children begin to move from drawing pictures to writing letters and combining letters to create words, they develop an awareness of the print concepts we target in Chapter 5. Through their own writing, children also begin to internalize directionality—

writing from left to right on a single line. Perhaps most important, children learn through their beginning attempts that writing has a purpose. When a teacher or a parent asks a child to read what he or she has written or when the adult is able to read what the child has written, the child sees that writing has the power to communicate. Recognition of the purpose of writing creates a strong foundation and intrinsic motivation for children to be writers.

WHAT DOES EMERGENT WRITING INSTRUCTION LOOK LIKE?

Effective emergent writing instruction is *not* children completing handwriting worksheets. It is *not* writing the letter *A* 12 times in a row. Emergent writing instruction is *not* copying the word *pig* under a construction-paper pig made at the art table. It is also *not* asking children to sit at the writing center until they have composed an entire story. So what is developmentally appropriate emergent writing instruction? Instruction appropriate for developing emergent writers is nested within a social context (Burns, Griffin, & Snow, 1999). When children have an audience for their writing, they also have a purpose for writing. Children also need environmental and adult support as they learn to write (Love, Burns, & Buell, 2007). Equipping the classroom environment with children's and teachers' writing samples, writing examples from environmental print, writing aids such as cards with familiar pictures and words written out, writing tools such as different kinds of paper and writing utensils, and writing props to create a meaning for writing such as calendars, appointment notebooks, postcards, and envelopes all contribute to children's ability and desire to write. In addition, children need the guidance and support of their classroom teachers. When preschool teachers are sensitive to the needs of their children, they can provide just enough help and support to facilitate child writing while still allowing for independence (Love et al., 2007). Therefore, the activities shared below engage young writers in writing for a social purpose with environmental and teacher-provided support. The activities can easily be built into the preschool day, during whole group, small group, centers, transitions, or outdoor play.

Whole-Group Instruction

Whole-group instruction offers preschool teachers time to model what good writers do as they write. It is important for young children to see adults writing. Children need to see that adults write for multiple purposes and that there are conventions for writing—words are written from left to right and from the top of the page to the bottom, space is left between words, and sentences begin with capitals and end with a punctuation mark. It is also important for children to hear the message that the teacher is writing so that they can begin to see the connection between an oral and a written message (Vukelich

& Christie, 2004). We have chosen to highlight four ways in which preschool teachers can incorporate writing into their whole-group instruction: teacher dictation, predictable language charts, shared writing, and interactive writing.

Teacher dictation occurs when a teacher writes down on paper exactly what a child says. During whole-group time preschool teachers and children are usually gathered together to have a common discussion about a book that was just read or an event that happened or will happen in the classroom. This type of gathering provides a wonderful opportunity to also incorporate writing. Because children are talking, the teacher has a meaningful purpose for writing—to capture on paper what students are saying. Teacher dictation serves several instructional purposes. First, it illustrates to children that their spoken language can be translated into written words. Second, it relays the message that their words are important enough to write down. Third, it models conventions of print, such as capital letters, left-to-right directionality, and punctuation. Figure 6.3 provides an example of teacher dictation; the teacher asked children where they could go that day.

In order to make your teacher dictation successful, keep in mind this simple procedure. First, it is always a good idea to date your writing so that you, your children, and classroom visitors can look back across your writing to see how ideas have changed or evolved over time. Next, discuss what you are going to write down. Introduce the topic and write down a title; reread the title in order to focus children's thinking about the topic. Pause and give children time to think to themselves or to turn to a partner and discuss ideas. After a 1- to 2-minute interval, ask children the question again. Call on individual children to share ideas. Listen first. Ask any clarifying questions you may have in order to understand the child's idea. Then, repeat the idea back to the child to see whether you have it correct. Once the child has acknowledged that your interpretation

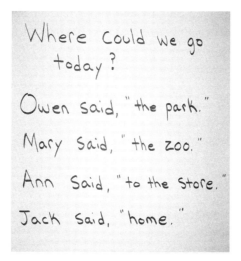

FIGURE 6.3. Example of teacher dictation.

is correct, begin to write. First, write down the child's name in order to give him or her credit for the idea. The child will probably be able to recognize his or her name in writing, even if he or she knows no other words. Then slowly write the child's idea; read aloud as you write. When you have written the entire idea, reading as you write, reread the entire sentence or statement again. Then you can move on to the next child's idea. More than likely you will not have enough time to write down each child's idea and retain high child involvement. Therefore, you may want to tell children ahead of time that you will only have time to write down four or five children's ideas this time but that you will call on different children next time so that everyone will eventually get a turn to share. We have found that children are very accepting of this explanation and it wards off any feeling of disappointment ahead of time. To conclude the teacher dictation, it is a good idea to summarize the topic and ideas that were shared. Last, it is important to hang the teacher dictation somewhere in the classroom so that children can see their ideas in writing and understand that their ideas are important.

Patterned language charts are an easy way to teach children about the structure of a sentence and the repetition in language. To create a patterned language chart, a teacher simply thinks of a sentence stem that could be repeated over and over again across multiple contexts. For example, "I feel ... " is a sentence stem that could be completed any number of ways by the children in a classroom. This sentence stem could be used on different days in connection with different events that occurred in the classroom, resulting in different answers. For example, on a day when children visit a local zoo answers to the sentence stem "I feel ... " would be very different from answers on a day when the classroom pet dies. Figure 6.4 provides a list of example sentence stems. We recommend writing the sentence stems on chart or poster paper and then laminating them. Once laminated, the patterned language charts can be used again and again for writing with dry-erase markers. Just as with the procedures for teacher dictation above, it is a good idea when using the patterned language charts with children to provide an introduction

| _____ said, "I feel _____." |
| _____ said, "I like _____." |
| _____ said, "I would like to _____." |
| _____ said, "I can _____." |
| _____ said, "I think _____." |
| _____ said, "I saw _____." |
| _____ said, "I wonder _____." |
| _____ said, "I wrote _____." |

FIGURE 6.4. Common sentence stems for predictable charts.

and purpose for writing, to listen to children's ideas, to talk aloud while writing, and to reread children's written ideas aloud. The completed charts can be posted and then reused when the sentence stem is again appropriate for the writing task.

We define shared writing as any opportunity for group writing in which the teacher acts as scribe, recording the message he or she and the children in his or her classroom decide on orally. This method for writing enables the children to be coauthors in the message without the burden of actually writing (Vukelich & Christie, 2004). In order to utilize shared writing effectively in your classroom, begin by planning an event or experience around which writing would be appropriate and meaningful. For example, Figure 6.5 is a shared writing sample in which the classroom teacher and children worked together to create a thank-you note for a police corporal who visited the classroom. The event of having a police officer visit the classroom and the resulting need to compose a thank-you note to send to the police officer created a very authentic purpose for a shared writing experience. Meaningful shared writing can occur in relation to a classroom visit, a field trip, a book reading, a sick friend, a new classroom procedure, an upcoming holiday, or almost anything you can imagine occurring in the classroom worth writing about.

On the day of the shared writing experience, gather children together on the rug. Introduce the purpose for writing the message. Children need to know why you are writing. Review the experience that you are writing about if it happened in the past or preview the experience if it will happen in the future. Next, discuss with children what they think the written message should include. For example, in the thank-you note written to the police officer above, the children wanted to thank the guest for coming to their school. The children also wanted to discuss what they liked the most from his visit—the car, the loud siren, and the police uniform. One key to making shared writing successful is to remember that it is shared; the content of the message should come mostly from the children with the teacher's input and not be teacher directed or teacher driven. Facilitate the children as they begin to brainstorm ideas for their message. You may need to ask

FIGURE 6.5. Example of shared writing.

guiding questions, such as *"What should we say next?"* and *"Is there anything else we need to say about this?"* You may also need to help children organize their thoughts by asking questions, such as *"Should we say this first or second?"* and *"When should we mention this idea?"* Once children have brainstormed and agreed upon a message orally, it is time to begin the work of writing.

In shared writing the teacher does all of the actual writing. Therefore, it is important to keep in mind the position of your children on the rug in relation to your writing. Every child needs to be able to clearly see what is being written. While it seems easy enough, it is actually very difficult to write in a way that enables all children to see. One suggestion is to prepare by choosing large poster or chart paper on which to write. Larger paper enables you to write in larger print, which is easier for young children to see. Similarly, select a writing utensil that is dark enough to see from a distance. A dark marker works better than a pen or pencil for shared writing. As you write try to position your body so that it is to the side and not in front of the paper. This may feel awkward at first, but with time and practice it becomes easier to manage. The teacher in Figure 6.6 does a nice job of keeping her body a little behind and to the side of the paper so that her body is not blocking the children from seeing the paper. She also keeps her arm below and not on top of the line of text she is writing.

Throughout the entire shared writing experience, you should be talking. As you write, think aloud what you are writing and the decisions you are making about print conventions, such as when to leave a space, when to make a letter capital, and when to include a period. Ask for children's advice on what the content of the message should be. Record children's ideas and think aloud your understanding of what writing looks like.

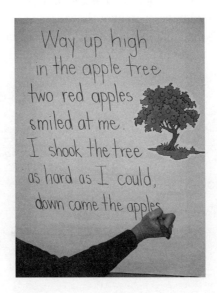

FIGURE 6.6. Preschool teacher modeling writing during whole group.

Write slowly. Children will need time to see that you are translating their oral message into written form. They will also need time to see what you are thinking aloud as it is being represented on the paper. You can involve children in the writing process by asking them to help determine what letter a word begins with or by stretching out the sounds in a word so that children may identify the letters in a word. After each sentence reread your work, pointing to each word from left to right as you read. Ask children if this is what they wanted to say. If children agree, then you can move on to the next part of the message. If children are unhappy with your written interpretation of their message, then shared writing offers a wonderful experience to show children that it is okay to edit and revise writing. Ask children how they want to change the sentence and then go back and revise accordingly. Keep the message short, limited to one piece of chart or poster paper in order to maintain a high level of engagement from all children. After writing, reread the entire message and then ask children to reread the message with you. Last, it is important to display the written message in the classroom so that children may return to reread the message at a later time.

Shared writing becomes interactive writing when the teacher invites the children to participate in some of the actual writing. The same procedures of shared writing are followed with the additional feature of the teacher periodically calling on individual children to help write letters, whole words, phrases, or punctuation marks. As a result, interactive writing engages children in the process of writing. It also helps to make the connection between sound and written language even more concrete, for teachers often sound out words to help children determine the appropriate letter for the sound in a word they are writing.

Figure 6.7 provides an example of an interactive writing first draft in which the teacher asked her children to help make a list of healthy fruits and vegetables that they like to eat. You can see that the first three items the teacher wrote herself; however, the fourth item was written by a child. The child used her knowledge of letter sounds (with extensive help by the teacher who was segmenting the sounds) to write the word *watermelon*. However, even with teacher help, the child left out both letter *E*'s in the

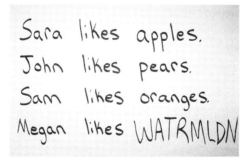

FIGURE 6.7. Example of interactive writing first draft.

word. If you try to segment that word, you will see why those letters are very difficult to hear. Without making the child feel poorly about her attempt at spelling, the teacher talked about how all writers make mistakes sometimes and that it is easy to fix words by going back to add or take things away. The teacher then simply inserted two arrows and wrote the letter *E* above the two places in the word *watermelon* where they belonged. In this way, the teacher was able to celebrate the child's contribution, teach about the importance of revising, and model the conventional spelling of the word.

In order to plan an interactive writing experience, the teacher has several decisions to make. McCarrier, Pinnell, and Fountas, authors of a resource book on interactive writing (2000), suggest that teachers decide "what to write, what to have the children write, and what to talk about" (p, 106). Especially with young children who are just beginning to understand the purposes of writing, asking children what they want to write is just not focused enough and will most likely leave the classroom in silence. Instead, the preschool teacher should decide on an overall topic for writing ahead of time. Good places to look for writing topics are in connection with storybook readings or classroom themes and events. Similarly, as children are contributing ideas with the support of the teacher thinking aloud during brainstorming and writing, the teacher must make decisions about when to ask a child to come up to participate in the actual writing. These decisions must be made during the writing based on the teacher's knowledge of the individual children. We recommend teachers strive for finding a skill that has the perfect balance between what a child can complete successfully while still offering some challenge. It is important that children can complete their task successfully in order to have a positive experience with writing. It is also important to find a task that will challenge the child so that he or she can learn from the experience. Lastly, the teacher could talk about every single aspect of writing, which could stretch out the interactive writing experience well beyond the young child's attention span. Thus, it is important to actively make decisions about what to talk about in a specific day's writing. Consider whether to talk about every word in-depth or to pinpoint certain elements of writing during the particular interactive writing experience. Let's listen in as a teacher uses interactive writing with her children to compose an invitation for parents to attend a classroom party. Note that these preschoolers have fairly well-developed alphabet knowledge.

TEACHER: Today I need your help to write an invitation to our parents asking them to come to our party on Friday.

CHILDREN: Okay.

TEACHER: What types of things should we say in our invitation?

CHILD: "Can you come?"

CHILD: "Please come."

TEACHER: Okay, so we should ask them if they can please come. Should we tell them the time?

CHILD: Yes, and where.

CHILD: The classroom.

TEACHER: So, we need to include in our invitation to come to the classroom at noon. Is there anything else we should write?

CHILD: Tell why to come. A party.

TEACHER: Good idea, we should tell them to come to a party for Earth Day. Okay, I think we have some good ideas to write about. I am going to start my invitation like a letter. I am going to write, "Dear ... " (*Talks while slowly writing.*) Who should I write the letter to?

CHILD: Mom and Dad.

TEACHER: "Dear ..., " then I am going to put a space before the next word, *Mom*, and space. Now I am going to write the word *Dad*. (*Talks while writing the words.*) D-ad, D-ad, D-ad. (*Slowly segments the beginning sound in the word.*) What sound do we hear at the beginning of the word Dad?

CHILD: /d/.

TEACHER: That is right. Carlos, would you like to come up and help me write the letter that makes the sound /d/? (*Child stands up and comes over to the chart paper to take the marker.*) What letter are you going to write for the sound /d/?

CHILD: *D*.

TEACHER: That's right. The letter *D* makes the /d/ sound. Go ahead and write the letter *D* here. (*Helps show child where to write the letter. Child writes the letter on the chart paper.*) Great job. This is the letter *D* that makes the /d/ sound at the beginning of the word *Dad*. Thank you, Carlos. I am going to write the rest of the word *Dad* for us. (*Rereads.*) "Dear Mom and Dad." Next I am going to write a comma and move to the next line. We said we wanted to ask our parents to please come to our classroom party for Earth Day. Let's begin this new line with a capital letter because it is the beginning of a new sentence. I am going to write a capital *P* to begin my word *please*. (*Talks while writing.*) Now I am writing the rest of the word *please*. After the word *please*, I leave a space, and write the next word, *come*. Then I leave a space and write the next word, to, space, *our*, space, *classroom*, space, *party*, space, *for*, space, *Earth*, space. (*Talks while writing.*) The next word I want to write is *Day*. (*Rereads.*) "Please come to our classroom party for Earth ... Day." Lily, could you come up and help me write the next word, *day*?

CHILD: Yes.

TEACHER: *Day* is one of the words on our word wall. We also see the word *Day* on our calendar each morning. If you need help, you can look over on our word wall to find the word *Day*. How do we write the word *Day*?

CHILD: (*Looks over at the word wall for support.*) *D-A-Y.*

TEACHER: Yes, the word *Day* is spelled *D-A-Y*. Go ahead and write the word *Day* right here after the word *Earth*. Make sure to leave a little bit of space between the two words. (*Watches as the child writes the word* Day.) Nice job, Lily. You wrote the word *Day* here. (*Points to the word as she says the word*.) Now I am going to go back and read what we have written so far....

As you can see from the example, interactive writing is a wonderful way to teach children about composing a message ("What types of things should we say in our invitation?"), word awareness ("I am going to put a space here before I write the next word." and "You wrote the word *Day*."), conventions of print (The teacher pointed to each word while rereading her sentence, showing left-to-right directionality and return sweep, and said, "I am going to begin the new line with a capital *P*."), sound–symbol correspondence ("What letter makes the /d/ sound?"), classroom resources for help with writing ("If you need help you can look at the word wall for the word *Day*."), and letter formation (Carlos and Lily both practiced forming and writing letters). In addition, the example illustrates how the teacher used her knowledge of Carlos and Lily to determine what types of writing tasks each would feel comfortable completing in front of the entire class. The teacher knew Carlos could write a single letter while Lily was able to write an entire word. Interactive writing requires preplanning and time in the classroom schedule, but in terms of the amount of literacy instruction accomplished it is well worth the effort. Figure 6.8 lists example topics and purposes for shared and interactive writing experiences with children.

Small-Group Instruction

Writing during small-group instruction enables the teacher or teacher's aide to provide one-on-one attention to a small group of children as they practice their own writing. While watching the teacher model the purposes and mechanics of writing in whole group, children can apply what they have learned in a safe, comfortable setting during small group. First, a few ground rules about working with individual children on their own writing. Writing is a very personal experience. Respect a child's writing by always asking whether the child would like to share with you rather than just assuming or demanding. When a child elects to share his or her writing, treat it with great care for the prize that it is. Never criticize a child's writing for misspellings or other errors. Find something about the child's writing to praise. "Pete, what a wonderful capital letter *O* you wrote to begin your sentence." When a child seeks help with his or her writing, frame the teach-

---

Classroom-Based Writing Topics

- A thank you note for a class visitor or field trip guide
- An invitation to come to the classroom
- A get-well card for a sick friend
- A list of things to do in dramatic play during center time
- A set of classroom rules or expected positive behaviors
- A list of things connected to the classroom theme (Our Favorite Colors, Our Names, The People in Our Neighborhood, Tools You Find in a Garage, Things You Find in a Diner)
- A recount of what happened during an experience (Our Field Trip to the Zoo, How We Made Pizza, What We Found Outside Today)

Storybook-Based Writing Topics

- Predictions about what the story will be about
- A letter to the author asking him or her a question about the story
- A letter to a character in the story
- A new story using the same structure of the story read with children creating new characters or new experiences
- A retelling of what the story was about
- Children's connections to the story (Things I Have in My Backyard, Things I Like to Collect, Things I Like to Eat)

FIGURE 6.8. Ideas for writing with young children.

able moment in a positive light. For example, "Sure, Pete, I can help you write the word *bear*. We can do it together. *Bear*. /b/ *ear*. /b/ *ear*. What sound do we hear at the beginning of the word *bear*?" And when a child is not in the mood to write, do not force him or her to write. Make a suggestion that he or she draw instead. Especially for young children, drawing still feels much more comfortable and safe than writing. Encourage the reluctant child to draw first and then ask if he or she would be interested in writing about his or her drawing. Respect the developmental step that each child can manage as a writer. As discussed above, teacher dictation is a good way to begin with new writers who may feel more comfortable drawing and talking about their artwork. A child can draw a picture and ask you as the teacher to record what he or she says about the picture below the drawing (see Figure 6.9 for an example). Then, as the child becomes more comfortable with writing he or she can begin to write about the drawing.

With these ground rules in mind, you need a context for small-group writing. Artwork is a great way to get children into writing (Love et al., 2007). Asking children to draw a picture and then to write about their picture is a natural activity that children enjoy. Whenever possible, you can ask children to draw something that is connected with your classroom theme or a classroom event, such as a field trip or class visitor. As children become more interested in writing, you can expand their repertoire by asking them to write letters to parents or friends. Letter writing becomes especially meaningful when children receive a reply to their letter. Setting up individual child mailboxes in

FIGURE 6.9. Sample student drawing with teacher dictation.

the classroom is a way to facilitate children sending mail to other children or to adults in the room. Finally, children also enjoy writing books. You can write books together as a class over several small-group settings, or individual children can write small books. Purchasing or making spiral-bound scrapbooks is a good format for a class book. Adapt ideas from a storybook you are reading in class as a focus for your class book. We have seen wonderful class renditions of *Brown Bear, Brown Bear, What Do You See?* (Martin & Carle, 2007b), *In the Tall, Tall Grass* (Fleming, 1991), and *My many Colored Days* (Seuss, 1996). Small books are perfect for individual children's writing. Creating books of two to three pages of half-size or small sheets of paper is easy, and children flock to the small size. With only a few pages to fill, little books give children a sense of accomplishment and confidence as writers when completed. Connect the activity to children's developing understanding of concepts of print by asking them to give their book a title and sign their name as author and illustrator. With large or small books, ask children to draw and write, provide the amount of help with writing requested by the child, return to read the books aloud in class to celebrate the writing, and place the completed books in the classroom library for children to read on their own.

We would also like to describe a specific method for helping young children write that can easily be used in small group settings. Kid Writing, also known as invented spelling, is an approach that asks children to focus on the sounds in the words they are writing (Feldgus & Cardonick, 1999). The process typically begins with having a child draw a picture. The teacher will then ask the child to explain what is happening in the picture and encourages the child to write a word, phrase, or sentence about the picture. In invented spelling, teachers tell children to write what they hear (See Figure 6.10 for an example.) As with introducing any new approach, it is a good idea for an adult to model several examples of writing using this approach for children to see. A teacher can stretch out the individual sounds in a word she is writing and represent each sound by a

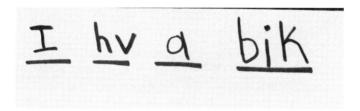

FIGURE 6.10. Example of child's inverted spelling.

letter or combination of letters as she models writing. As children write independently using invented spelling, conventional spelling becomes less important than writing what sounds the children hear in individual words. The teacher celebrates the fact that children are writing. The next step involves the teacher or teacher's aide. Once the child has written his sentence, an adult asks the child what he or she has written and asks if the child would like to see what the writing would look like in "adult writing." The teacher's dictation under the child's writing helps the teacher and child complete the last step, which is to reread the child's writing together.

Center Time

The writing that children can do independently or with teacher support during center time is play based. Children attribute meaning to their writing when it is genuinely important to the play situation (Burns, Griffin, & Snow, 1999). For example, children learn that when they go to a restaurant the waiter or waitress writes down their order. Using this information, children pretend to write down orders when they are playing waiter or waitress in a restaurant. Similarly, children learn that when you go to the doctor's office you fill out forms; children may have seen their parents do this when they have had a checkup. As a result, when children play doctor's office, they give their "patient" a clipboard with a piece of paper on it and ask him or her to sign his or her name. Therefore, the props and environmental print included in centers are extremely important. In order for literacy-rich play to develop, the centers need to be well stocked with writing utensils and supplies but also with theme-related props and signs that will motivate children to read and write (Vukelich & Christie, 2004). Figure 6.11 provides a list of writing props organized by common preschool themes. We have provided this list as an example; it is by no means exhaustive. Use your imagination and what you know about the real place you are trying to replicate when you are planning props for a new center. One suggestion we have is to go to the real place and act as a detective—observe, listen, take photographs, and write down everything you see that is literacy related. Talk to people who work in the setting. Many times if you tell people what you are trying to do

Common Preschool Theme	Writing Props
Outdoors/Nature/ Insects	Binoculars, magnifying glasses, butterfly nets, specimen jars, creature cages, field guides, camping and hiking environmental print signs, science journals
Transportation	Maps, written directions, taxi, bus, and rail fares, destination boards, arrival and departure signs, travel brochures, postcards, tickets, bus or rail schedules, travel journals
Food/Dining	Menus, restaurant signs, open/closed signs, today's specials signs, order pads, bills, receipts, play money, nutrition labels, recipes, cookbooks, hours of operation signs, food diaries
Doctor/Dentist/ Health	Magazines and books for waiting room, prescription pads, telephone and message pads, appointment book, clipboard for patient check-in, X-rays, scale, doctor's kit with tools, check-up forms, patient forms and files, eye charts, dental charts, height and weight charts
Neighborhood/Post Office	Post office costumes, envelopes, letters, mailing labels, postcards, packages, mail-sorter trays, stamps, hours of operation, cash register, play money, large mailbox, individual child mailboxes, scale, stamp prices and shipping costs, pick-up times for mail, address book, junk mail
Building/ Construction	Blueprints, appointment books, telephone, do-it-yourself books, tools, hard hats, safety signs, construction vehicles, contracts, caution tape, blocks, clipboard, chalk, rulers
Flowers/Planting	Seed catalogs, bulb catalogs, gardening books, aprons, gardening tools, soil, pots, watering cans, artificial flowers, plant markers, rulers, seeds, planting diaries
House/Home	Empty food containers, cookbooks, recipe cards, dishes, play food, play appliances, utensils, empty cleaner bottles, broom, mop, dustpan, telephone, notepad, phone books, books, magazines, newspaper, junk mail, coupons, clock, calendar, baby dolls, baby bottles, baby food jars, diapers, play stroller, play lawnmower, notes for the refrigerator, notes for the babysitter, phone list, magnets

FIGURE 6.11.   List of writing props by theme.

in the classroom they will have helpful insights into behind-the-scenes literacy activities or may even offer to provide you with a sample form. You can then use the notes you take to help you set up a center in the classroom. Figure 6.12 also lists a few books we have been able to find with creative suggestions for creating literacy-rich centers.

As an example, let's look at one dramatic play center that has been converted into a classroom post office. Prior to setting up the dramatic play area in her classroom, the teacher visited her local post office and created a list of all the literacy-related activities she saw going on in the post office and all of the props she could include in her dramatic play center. As part of her research, she visited the post office webpage to download sample forms to photocopy and include in her center. The teacher had funds available to purchase several things, including a mailbox; however, many of the props could just as easily have been made out of cardboard boxes. In fact, one clever thing the teacher did

Hereford, N. J., & Schall, J. (1998). *Dramatic play: A practical guide for teaching young children.* New York: Scholastic.
West, S., & Cox, A. (2004). *Literacy play: Over 300 dramatic play activities that teach pre-reading skills.* Beltsville, MD: Gryphon House.
Wiggins, A. K. (2006). *Preschoolers at play: Building language and literacy through dramatic play.* Greenville, SC: Super Duper.

FIGURE 6.12. Resources for creating literacy-rich dramatic play centers.

was to include a box with different slots for her children to sort mail (see Figure 6.13). In addition, the teacher pulled items from her regular classroom supply of toys that fit into the post office: a cash register, play money, customer costumes, and cloth bags for the mail carrier. The teacher also included a variety of writing utensils—pencils, crayons, markers, alphabet letter stamps, ink pads, colored pencils, and pens; and different types of paper—plain white paper, lined paper, construction paper, photocopied forms, envelopes, postcards, greeting cards, stationary, calendars, and appointment books (see Figure 6.14). Next, the teacher added word cards that included post office-related vocabulary words written with pictures next to each word. These served a dual purpose of reminding children of vocabulary words useful in the center and supporting their efforts to write. Last, the teacher worked with children to create environmental print likely to be found in a post office, such as a sign with hours of operation that the children chose. The end result of the teacher's efforts was a well-stocked, literacy-rich post office (see Figure 6.15 for an example of a class post office).

FIGURE 6.13. Box for sorting mail.

FIGURE 6.14. Writing utensils in the classroom post office.

FIGURE 6.15. Dramatic play center: Post office.

So, you have set up literacy-rich centers for children to play in; now, how do you get children writing? Unfortunately, it is not enough to set up a well-stocked dramatic play area and leave children to play and write, especially if children are unfamiliar with what goes on in the setting. The key to having successful writing experiences in the dramatic play center is for the teacher or teacher's aide to enter into play with the children. The teacher serves as a model for what kinds of activities, writing included, occur in the setting. We have seen teachers and teacher's aides effectively engage children in writing activities when they have taken on roles to play in the center. As you take on a role while playing with children, think of scenarios and authentic purposes for writing. For example, a teacher who entered dramatic play area with an ice cream shop theme enjoyed the dessert the cook prepared so much that she requested the recipe. The child promptly retrieved a piece of paper and a marker and wrote down his recipe (see Figure 6.16 for the child's recipe). Similarly, in the post office above, the teacher's aide entered the post office one day as a customer trying to mail a heavy package. Let's listen to her conversation with the children playing in the post office to see how she engaged the children in writing.

TEACHER AIDE: Hello, I am so glad it is my turn. This is such a heavy package. It was hard for me to bring it into the post office from my car.

CHILD: What can I help you with today?

TEACHER AIDE: I need to mail this package. My boss asked me to bring this package over here today from my office. She said it needed to be mailed right away. Do you need to know where it is going?

CHILD: Yes, where are you mailing it to?

FIGURE 6.16. Child's written recipe.

TEACHER AIDE: I need to mail it to China. I wonder how expensive it is going to be because it is so heavy and it is going very far away.

CHILD: Let's see. (*Takes the package onto his scale.*) That is going to be $50.

TEACHER AIDE: Oh, that is quite a lot of money. Would you write down the price on a receipt for me so that I can take it back to my boss? I want to show her how much it cost to mail this package.

CHILD: Sure. I can write it for you. (*Takes a small pad of paper and a marker to pretend to write the price.*)

Adult role play is critical for engaging children in writing activities during center time. In addition, there are several quick things you can do as a teacher to help facilitate children's writing. As a management tool for which children get to play in centers at what time, one teacher we know asks children to sign up for the center in which they would like to play. This serves as a waiting list of sorts. One of the adults in the room keeps an eye on time and helps facilitate movement down the list so that all children who have signed up for a time slot have an opportunity to play. Writing is involved because children must write as much of their name as they know how to: a first letter, a whole first name, or a first and last name. See Figure 6.17 for an example of a center sign-in sheet. As discussed in the post office example above, involving children in the task of creating environmental print is also an easy task in which the adult can support children's writing. Figure 6.18 provides an example of an hours of operation sign created for their zoo in a dramatic play. Also, creating forms that children can incorporate into their center play are constant reminders for children to write. You can create at least one, if not more, forms for any play theme. For example, in a restaurant theme, you can create menus, order forms, bill forms, and receipt forms. Keep in mind that the form should be short, one page at the most, and whenever possible include pictures for young children to associate with the words. Be sure to make enough copies for multiple children to use across multiple days. Figure 6.19 shows an example of a form a teacher made for children to use in a restaurant-themed center. The form includes pictures and written words of pretend foods in the center that the customers may want to order for their meal. The child is using a marker to check off what her customers are ordering.

Last, writing can be incorporated in multiple centers across the room by posting charts with questions for children to respond to while in the center playing independently or with adults. For example, at a block center, a large chart can ask children to create a blueprint prior to building, to draw what they built and label the parts, or to graph how tall their structure is. At a sensory table filled with water and plastic animals, a large chart can ask children to record what they caught with their nets while playing in the water or to graph how many of each type of fish they caught. At an art center, children

FIGURE 6.17. Center sign-in sheet.

FIGURE 6.18. Environmental print written by children.

FIGURE 6.19. Child completing a premade form.

can sign their name to their art, like a great artist does, and display their artwork and signed name on a large piece of chart paper for others to see. At a science center, a large chart can pose a question about a science experience that is occurring at the center. For example, Figure 6.20 shows a chart that asked children to make predictions about what they thought would happen to the ice left in the cup in the classroom. Children playing at the science center could observe the ice and then make a prediction by writing their name under one of three choices the teacher offered. When using large charts around the room during center time to encourage writing, be sure to introduce the chart to children prior to their playtime. Point out the new question posted and read aloud to children what the question asks them to think about, respond to, or write down. It may help to provide an example by writing down your own response or name for children to see. Make sure to provide a writing utensil close to the posted chart for easy access and throughout the center time to encourage children to write on the chart. Also, it is a good idea to come back to the chart after center time as a whole group to read what children have written or responded to as a whole group to celebrate the writing that has occurred.

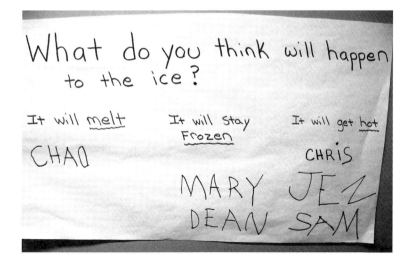

FIGURE 6.20. Science center prediction chart.

Additional Opportunities

Meaningful opportunities for children to write need not be limited to whole group, small group, or center time. One of the best ways to get children writing is to incorporate writing into the morning routine. Preschool children love to write their name. Teachers need to know who is present and who is absent each morning. Why not combine the two needs into a meaningful morning sign-in routine? We observed one preschool teacher who asked her children to go to the writing table after they had unpacked each morning upon arrival. At the beginning of the year, the teacher provided children with a name card with their first name printed in large black letters and a photograph of themselves (see Figure 6.21). The photograph helped children who could not yet recognize their name in print find their name card. The children sat down at the table and used their name card to either trace at first or later in the year write their name on a new slip of paper. Once students had signed their name, they returned their name card to a basket that permanently stayed at the writing table and placed their signed slip in a pocket chart on the rug. The teacher was then able to read the names aloud during morning group time to see who was present and who was absent. By reading the children's names aloud the teacher's actions indicated to the children that there was an important purpose for them to sign in each morning.

The teacher also changed the name cards periodically throughout the year on the basis of individual children's progress with writing. For example, the teacher noticed that one child could identify and write her first name easily. For this child, the teacher first removed the picture, challenging the child to locate her name by reading and identifying letters in her name rather than relying on the picture. Once the child could do this task comfortably,

FIGURE 6.21. Child's name card.

the teacher added the child's last name to her card in order to extend the writing task. The teacher changed children's name cards based on how each child was progressing individually, so at any given time of the year she had some name cards with pictures, some without photographs, and some with both first and last names written on them.

Writing can also occur outside. Just as children love to spread blankets under a tree and read books outside, they also love to take notebooks and pencils outside to write. One nice activity is to ask children to sit, close their eyes, and listen to the sounds of the world around them. Prompt children by periodically asking them to think about what they hear, what they smell, and what they feel. Once children have had a few minutes to experience the moment, ask them to open their eyes and write in their journals. They can draw pictures and write about something that they experienced in the location. This activity can then be repeated in different locations and then compared to see what children noticed differently depending on the location. Did they hear a bird next to the tree? Did a fish jump when they were next to the pond? How did the location change what they drew or wrote about? Participating in a sensory experience like this one helps children develop observational skills and also allows for a meaningful writing opportunity.

A favorite pastime of young explorers is keeping track of creatures and plant life found outside. Equipping children with magnifying glasses, binoculars, butterfly nets, bug jars, specimen containers, insect or bird field guides, and journals with pencils encourages children to explore the natural world around them. You never know what creature a child may find in the grass or mulch on the playground. You never know what creature may fly through the air. A perfect way to capture these incredible finds is through drawing and writing in weekend journals. Children also like to write about their own lives and experiences. Connecting home experiences with writing teaches children

FIGURE 6.22. Child's journal entry.

that writing can bring each child's home experiences to the classroom. See Figure 6.22 for an example of one child's journal writing about his family.

IMPLEMENTATION IN THREE CLASSROOMS

A Public School-Based Preschool: Pam

Given that Pam works with a population that might struggle with the academic demands of kindergarten instruction, Pam and her assistant Cheryl make it a priority to weave writing into their instruction. They know that children need to develop the insight that writing is a way to communicate thoughts and feelings and have the opportunities to represent these ideas with their own writing attempts. Together, Pam and Cheryl work to ensure that children have lots of opportunities to see them write and to engage in the "writing process" themselves. From the very beginning of the school year, children begin to see the connection between oral language and written language and that writing is a powerful form of expression.

First, Pam uses whole group and circle time to draw children's attention to the forms and functions of print. She labeled the entire classroom and takes time to introduce children to these labels during the first few weeks of school. She points out the word *door*, *window*, *trash can*, and *rocking chair*. Later, children will be encouraged to write their own labels for classroom items during center time. Cheryl takes the children on a walk around the building the first week of school and points out print in the building. Children then come back and talk about the print that they observed. Children also consistently interact with print around her whole-group carpet area. They "read" the days of the week, the months of the year, the weather, classmates names on the attendance chart, the thematic poem, and the Question of the Day.

Pam and Cheryl also take turns engaging children in a language experience approach (LEA) every week centered on a different topic. For example, the children go on a fall walk during the fall exploration unit to collect and observe various signs of fall. Back in the room after the walk, Pam models the oral language to print connection by thinking aloud a sign of fall that she observed on the walk. She might say, "I saw two leaves falling from the tree." Then she will say, "Now, I'm going to write that thought on our chart." Pam says each word aloud as she writes it on the chart. Then everyone reads it together as she tracks the print. Each child is then encouraged to provide his or her own observation and Pam (or Cheryl) records it word for word on the chart. Children are very proud of seeing their own words translated to print. They read the sentence together and ask the children to write their name next to his or her own sentence. Pam will continue to revisit the LEA over the next few days to have children read the sentences again and to draw attention to components of print and alphabet awareness.

Pam also views center time as an essential time to encourage children's very own writing attempts. One center in particular, the writing center, is a place where children's writing really blossoms. In the first few weeks of school, children are encouraged to write their name. Most children are writing the first letter of their name when they begin but after a few weeks of practice they are writing all of the letters in their name and spelling it aloud. Pam loves this transformation. Her children will use the Kid Writing program when they enter kindergarten so she uses this same idea but in a scaled-down format for prekindergarten. Each child has his or her own writing journal in a container in that center. Much like Kid Writing, she and Cheryl encourage the children to draw a picture and then talk about what is happening in the picture. Pam and Cheryl rotate working with children in the writing center every other day. They first label each part of the picture with the child and then ask the child to dictate a story based on his or her picture. Pam and Cheryl write each word on the other side of the journal and then read it back to them. She finds that children create longer sentences and stories to accompany the drawings as the year progresses. They also see the direct connection between oral language and print. Children are also encouraged to write target letters, or the focus letters of the week, and to read and write print that they view in the room.

A Head Start Center: Elaina

Working with a large population of children from impoverished backgrounds, Elaina knows that her children especially need exposure to writing. They need to see writing everywhere. For this reason, Elaina labels almost everything that does not move in the classroom prior to the first day of school. She creates labels with both the English and Spanish written words and a picture to help children associate the words with the picture. She writes children's names on their cubbies at the beginning of the year so that they can begin to recognize their name, and in the middle of the year when they can begin to write their own name Elaina encourages them to replace her name card with one the children have written. She posts environmental print she has written and that children have written around the room (see Figure 6.23 for an example). She creates literacy-rich, well-equipped dramatic play centers in the classroom. She knows her children need time to explore and experiment with the purposes and functions of writing, so she places writing utensils and writing paper in every classroom center to encourage children's explorations. She displays her dictation of children's writing and children's own writing along every wall in her classroom. She places class-made books in the class library. Elaina has found that children especially flock to scrapbooks she makes with children during small group in which she places copies of photographs she has taken of the children and asks the children to help her write captions under the photographs. And she seizes any and every opportunity that presents itself to complete a shared or interactive writing experience with her children.

Especially at the beginning of the school year, Elaina has many children who struggle with what writing is and with the fine-motor skills necessary for writing. To teach children about the many functions and purposes of writing, Elaina exposes children to print in the classroom—object labels, environmental print, signs in the dramatic play center, classroom rules, large-group writing experiences, and so on. She also asks her

FIGURE 6.23. Classroom environmental print.

teacher's aide on the bus and parents in their cars to point out road, store, and restaurant signs to children. She models writing for different purposes in large group as well as times when she is role-playing with children in dramatic play and other centers. For example, she writes letters when she visits the classroom post office and writes in her own science journal when she is at the science center. When appropriate, Elaina asks her children to help her write messages home to the parents informing them of upcoming events. Instead of writing an invitation to an upcoming event herself, Elaina enlists the help of children either in large group or during small-group time to compose an invitation to send home. To help children who are still developing the fine-motor skills necessary to write, Elaina makes sure she stocks her classroom with writing utensils of all sizes—large and small for different-sized fingers and hands. She also incorporates activities, games, and manipulative toys that develop fine-motor skills such as coloring, paint brushing, using small tweezers to feed a toy dog a bone, moving magnetic objects with magnet wands, pushing pegs into holes, and even hammering golf tees into Styrofoam. For children who want to write and have not yet mastered holding a pencil, Elaina supplies magnetic letters and small magnetic boards for children to write messages.

Elaina also strives to incorporate writing within the home–school connection. To facilitate this, she sends parents reminders to write in front of their children. It does not matter whether parents write in English or in Spanish, just as long as children see adult role models writing for important purposes. Elaina suggests that parents ask children to help them write lists for the grocery store, to-do lists, or greeting cards to relatives. She also encourages parents to reply to letters children write to them while in school by writing, even if it is one or two lines, a letter back to their child. At the same time, Elaina is realistic about the home lives of her children and periodically sends paper, even if it is scrap paper, home with her children who may not have anything to write on. Whenever Elaina makes a new supply of small books for her classroom, she makes an extra set so that each child has one blank book to take home and write in at home. She has also been successful in getting a local business to donate small notebooks and packs of crayons for children to keep each year.

A Private Preschool: Sarah

Sarah wants to increase her focus on emergent writing this year, but she is worried that it could easily turn into handwriting. In fact, some of Sarah's parents equate a rigorous curriculum with worksheets, and they press her for handwriting worksheets. Sarah is determined to both increase her class's writing skills and maintain a developmentally sensitive approach. She wants them to go to the kindergarten comfortable with writing and ready to learn more conventional letter formations. She also wants to provide the parents with evidence that their children's skills are developing *without* worksheets.

Because Sarah has so few materials in the classroom, she has to use chart-paper poems and stories for some circle-time activities. She decides that she can use this time to model writing more often than she has in the past. Instead of preparing the charts in advance, she can write some of them during circle time, showing the children exactly how she does it and involving them over time in shared writing experiences.

Sarah decides to start the year with journals in the writing center. Each child has a journal, which is a bound book with blank pages. At the beginning of the year, these are labeled and decorated. At the writing center, Maria engages the children in journal writing connected to their morning experiences—they draw and write about the morning's circle time, big book, or an event from the previous day. Maria has a date stamp, and she stamps each page so that Sarah can use them as a chronicle of each child's movement toward conventional writing.

The journals are perfect vehicles for scaffolded writing, and Maria helps only a few children at a time. In the 20-minute period, she has enough time to first have the children draw, and then label. She finds that drawing the lines for the children focuses their attention on the few words they have chosen. Because the center is already stocked with letter strips, the children have ready models for the letters they are trying to write. Maria resists her temptation to teach them handwriting. Rather, she teaches them (through her prompting) that their writing efforts are worthwhile.

In the arts-and-crafts center, Sarah takes responsibility for ensuring that each child learns to write his or her first name. She does this in a natural way, treating the children as artists who sign their work with their names. In fact, she has art books in the center, and she can show the children that artists do sign their works. Because the children use a variety of supplies in the center (markers, paint brushes, crayons), Sarah observes and supports the fine-motor skills required for writing, and provides multiple chances, in different mediums, for children to learn to write their names.

WHERE CAN I FIND MORE INFORMATION?

There are many sources of ideas about integrating writing into your classroom. Here are some that we recommend.

Web-Based

- Kid Writing
  kidwriting.homestead.com/
- Read Write Think
  www.readwritethink.org/
- Time 4 Learning
  www.time4learning.com/teaching-writing.shtml
- Washington Learning Systems
  www.walearning.com/parent-tools/preschool/

Text-Based

- Behymer, A. (2003). Kindergarten writing workshop. *Reading Teacher, 57*(1), 85–88.
- Bissex, G. (1980). *GNYS at work: A child learns to write and read.* Cambridge, MA: Harvard University Press.
- Calkins, L. M. (1986). *The art of teaching writing.* Portsmouth, NH: Heinemann.
- Clay, M. M. (1975). *What did I write?: Beginning reading behavior.* Portsmouth, NH: Heinemann.
- Dyson, A. H. (1989). *Multiple worlds of child writers: Friends learning to write.* New York: Teachers College Press.
- Feldgus, E. G., & Cardonick, I. (1999). *Kid writing: A systematic approach to phonics, journals, and writing workshop* (2nd ed.). DeSoto, TX: Wright Group/ McGraw-Hill.
- Graves, D. H. (1983). *Writing: Teachers and children at work.* Portsmouth, NH: Heinemann.
- McCarrier, A., Pinnell, G. S., & Fountas, I. C. (2000). *Interactive writing: How language and literacy come together, K–2.* Portsmouth, NH: Heinemann.
- Ray, K. W., & Glover, M. (2008). *Already ready: Nurturing writers in preschool and kindergarten.* Portsmouth, NH: Heinemann.
- Schickedanz, J. A., & Casbergue, R. M. (2004). *Writing in preschool: Learning to orchestrate meaning and marks.* Newark, DE: International Reading Association.
- Teale, W. H., & Sulzby, E. (1986). *Emergent literacy: Writing and reading.* Norwood, NJ: Ablex.

CHAPTER 7

Tracking Children's Progress

The Role of Assessment in Preschool Classrooms

The preschool years are marked with growth of many kinds, and each of them could be tracked through formal assessment measures: physical development, social and emotional development, self-regulation, fine- and gross-motor skills, and ability to attend. The level of attention to these areas and the choice of tools to assess them is likely determined by center directors or administrative agencies. In this chapter, we focus on tracking growth only in language and literacy, and specifically on the age-old teaching question: Are they learning what I am teaching? You will see that the answer to that question has immediate implications on what to do next in the preschool classroom.

While there is a growing consensus on how to build and use assessment systems in primary-grades classrooms, we approach literacy assessment in the preschool classroom with caution. It is not easy to assess the skills of 3- and 4-year-old children with any degree of accuracy; they simply do not understand the abstract talk that can be used in formal assessments. For example, a young child might not understand what it means to tell an examiner whether words have the same or different beginning sounds. They might not understand beginning, middle, or end. It might not make sense to them to point to a picture that shows excitement. Preschoolers live in the here and now, and formal assessment tasks are not always crafted well for them. To justify any classroom assessment in preschool it must be simple, it must be natural and game-like, and it must be useful. You will see that we argue that there is a fine line between assessment and instruction in preschool. Most of our assessment tasks will look exactly like the instructional ones. The difference is in the thinking and planning that happen afterward.

WHAT IS ASSESSMENT?

It may be tempting to say that assessment is testing. Assessment is actually more than testing. Assessment is the collection of information for reflection and decision making. Assessment can be formal or informal. A formal assessment has a set of administration directions and interpretation guidelines. An informal assessment is designed by and interpreted by the teacher. A formal assessment can answer normative questions (How is this child performing compared to other children of the same age?), criterion-referenced questions (How is this child understanding and internalizing the concepts I have taught?), or predictive questions (How likely is this child to be successful when formal literacy instruction begins in kindergarten?). The trick is to design an assessment system with the fewest possible tasks to answer the questions that are important in a particular preschool classroom, and to use tasks that are developmentally valid. In preschool, that means that the questions or items must make sense to the children, the environment must be comfortable, and the testers must be familiar with both the measures being used and the children being assessed (Epstein, Schweinhart, DeBruin-Parecki, & Robin, 2004).

Assessments are expensive in preschool. They must be given individually, so they take precious time away from the rest of the complicated work of the preschool day. They also take time to understand, so they take precious teacher planning time. Finally, they take time to interpret with stakeholders, especially caregivers who are keenly interested in their child's progress but may not understand the nuts and bolts of assessments. Our goal here is to link assessment so intimately to the instructional tasks in the preschool day that they are integrated into daily life, easy to interpret, and easy to communicate to others. In order to do that, we recommend that not all children need the same assessments, and not all children need to be assessed at the same time.

The primary grades have adopted a metric for assessment that includes four types: screenings, diagnostic assessments, progress monitoring assessments, and outcome assessments (Kame'enui et al., 2006). That metric can also be useful in preschool. Figure 7.1 shows the assessment types and previews the questions that each type of assessment can answer. Remember, though, that we have defined literacy development in preschool to include oral language and vocabulary, comprehension, print and alphabet awareness, phonological awareness, and writing. A more comprehensive listing of the assessment possibilities, then, is provided in Figure 7.2. You will note that we have already highlighted the assessments that we think are most useful and important.

We have chosen not to focus on screenings, although there are formal screening assessments available for preschool. Screenings should not be used unless their reliability and validity has been established formally; they are designed to be specific (they actually assess only the target area) and sensitive (they reliably sort children into categories) (Schatschneider, Petscher, & Williams, 2008). These requirements imply that screenings

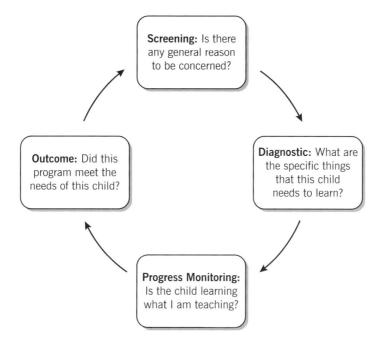

FIGURE 7.1. Preschool assessments by type.

	Screening	Diagnostic	Progress Monitor	Outcome
Oral Language			X	
Vocabulary			X	
Comprehension			X	
Print Concepts		X	X	
Phonological Awareness		X	X	
Alphabet Knowledge		X	X	
Writing			X	

FIGURE 7.2. Potential assessment targets in preschool.

cannot be designed by teachers. An example includes the Phonological Awareness Literacy Screening Pre-K (PALS PreK) (Invernizzi, Sullivan, & Meier, 2001). This screening system contains subtests in name writing, alphabet knowledge, beginning sound awareness, print and word awareness, rhyme awareness, and nursery rhyme awareness. Each of the items on these subtests underwent rigorous trials. Scores are meant to be used to set child-level and classroom-level goals. For 3- and 4-year-olds, some of whom have had very limited access to language and literacy, initial performance on a screening assessment is not as useful as data collected after 3 or 4 months of rich preschool experience. However, if your preschool mandates a set of formal screening measures, be sure that you use those measures to identify particular children who need even more of your language and literacy attention.

We also have chosen not to focus on outcome measures. Conceptually, the outcome measure for a preschool classroom that makes the most sense is an assessment of readiness for kindergarten in the schools that the children will attend. That means these measures will be associated very specifically with your neighborhood schools, and they may be better conducted at the beginning of the kindergarten year. However, knowing what those kindergarten assessments actually are *and* how they will be administered and used is a worthwhile investigative task for a preschool teacher; in fact, that information can form the basis of meaningful discussions with caregivers beginning around the middle of the 4-year-old preschool year.

In some programs, external parties will mandate outcome measures. That will likely be true in federally funded programs. In most cases, those assessments will be formal and standardized in nature, yielding either growth scores (subtracting fall scores from spring scores) or normative scores (comparing performance of your children with performance of other children in other settings). In that case, we urge caution in the interpretation of these assessments for individual children; outcome assessments such as these should be used to reflect on the extent to which the program met the needs of the children and to direct program improvements over time. We are more interested in the types of assessments that are more intimately related to day-to-day decisions about instruction.

WHY IS ONGOING ASSESSMENT IMPORTANT?

There are three main reasons why assessments are important in preschool—to plan literacy experiences and instruction, to reflect on its effects, and to identify those few children whose language and literacy should be evaluated more formally in order to access additional specialized educational services as soon as possible. Even the best observer can fail to see whether an individual child has mastered an early skill during a whole-group session. That is why we will argue that brief individual assessment sessions must be part of the preschool program. These few assessment moments with each child individually, conducted deliberately but playfully, answer important questions about where to go next in instruction.

ASSESSMENTS FOR PLANNING

The easiest assessments to give and to use for planning are assessments of print concepts, phonological awareness, and alphabet knowledge. If you think of these areas logically, you can see why. Each of these assessments provides information about whether an individual child knows something or not. There is relatively little gray area. If the child does not know it, the teaching implication is clear—teach it.

In Chapter 5 we described development and instruction of print concepts, those early prereading items that are so easily modeled during shared reading sessions with big books. Marie Clay (1993) pioneered assessment of these items, and her full assessment protocols are still available. We build on her work in our thinking about both instruction and assessment of these concepts. A slight modification of Figure 5.11 turns our description of how to teach book and print concepts into two useful assessment checklists, presented here in Figures 7.3 and 7.4. The book can be chosen by the child as a personal favorite to make the assessment more meaningful and contextualized. The teacher then sets the stage comfortably in a corner of the classroom or just outside, and simply engages in natural conversation, embedding the questions on the figure as they share the book. A simple yes or no decision can be recorded on the assessment sheet.

Results of these brief interactions will identify a group of children who need to learn both book and print concepts, a group who know book concepts but need print concepts, and a group who know both. Small-group work on these concepts, directly targeting these important items, can address this need. Then, after instruction, the teacher can readminister the assessment as a progress monitor, identifying the children who now know these concepts and those who still need more instruction. Once children have achieved book and print concepts, it is very unlikely that they will revert to not knowing them, so the cycle of screening, diagnosis, instruction, and progress monitoring is completed once children have demonstrated these concepts.

Remember from Chapter 4 that phonological awareness has a general developmental sequence. What that means is that these skills generally develop in the same order across individuals. In Figure 7.5 you will see a slight revision of Figure 4.1. We have simply replaced the instructional talk with items that allow you to answer the assessment question: Does this child know this or not? Because the items tend to be developmental, you can probably stop assessing once the answer is no. In other words, you need not waste time assessing phoneme-level skills for a child who does not have word awareness.

Child:		Date:
Book Conventions		
Show me the front of the book.	Yes	No
Show me the back of the book.	Yes	No
Show me the title.	Yes	No
Show me the title page.	Yes	No
The author of this book is _____. What does the author do?	Yes	No
The illustrator of this book is _____. What does the illustrator do?	Yes	No

FIGURE 7.3. Assessment checklist for book conventions.

Child:		Date:
Print Conventions		
Show me the top line of the print on a page.	Yes	No
Show me the bottom line of the print on a page.	Yes	No
If I am here at the beginning, which way will I read?	Yes	No
If I am at the end of this line, where will I read next?	Yes	No
This sentence says _____. Can you touch each word and read it back to me?	Yes	No
How many words are on this page?	Yes	No

FIGURE 7.4. Assessment checklist for print conventions.

Term	Definition	Sample Assessment Items
Syllable Awareness	Knowledge that words are made up of parts called syllables.	I am going to say a word and I want you to clap its parts. The word is *shoelace*. How many parts? How about *September*?
Rhyme Awareness	Ability to identify words with the same rime sound (vowel and following consonants).	I am going to show you three pictures [*frog, log, flag*]. Show me two that sound the same at the end.
Onset–Rime Awareness	Knowledge that one-syllable words can be divided into beginning sounds and then the vowel and what comes after.	What sound do you hear first in the word *foot*? What comes after the /f/?

What sound do you hear first in the word *bed*? What comes after the /b/? |
| Phoneme Awareness | Knowledge that words are composed of individual speech sounds that blend together. | I am going to say a word slowly and I want you to say it fast. My word is /d/ /o/ /g/. Can you say it fast? How about /p/ /i/ /g/?

I am going to say a word fast and I want you to say it slowly. *Moon*. Can you say it slowly? |

FIGURE 7.5. Assessment tasks for phonological awareness.

As in the case of book and print concepts, the results of these informal assessments can be used to group and teach. In addition to the whole-group tasks in which all children engage, small groups, focused on a specific skill, can address the specific area that children need to learn—the lowest-order area. For example, a child who has no word awareness likely also has no syllable or rhyme awareness. In order to build a strong foundation for these skills, moving back to word awareness is important for that child and likely some others in the class.

The final basic-skills assessment that creates a neat planning tool is assessments of alphabet knowledge. Developmentally, children will tend to first learn to sing the whole alphabet, then to say it, and then to say it while touching the letters. After that, they tend to learn to identify individual letter names (when the letters are presented in isolation) and then individual letter sounds. In the preschool classroom each of these attainments will only develop if it has been a target of instruction; you will have to choose the levels of alphabet assessment based on the alphabet-knowledge targets you have set in your instruction. As a general rule of thumb, though, it is helpful for beginning kindergarten children to be able to identify each letter of the alphabet and be ready to learn the letter sounds quickly.

The first level of assessment is, like our assessments of book and print conventions, a kind of all-or-nothing assessment. Like our earlier assessments, the task is informal and natural. Simply ask the child to sing the alphabet. If he or she can sing it, ask him or her to say it. If the child can say it, give him or her an alphabet strip and see whether he

Child:		Date:
Alphabet Knowledge		
Child can sing the alphabet song.	Yes	No
Child can say the alphabet.	Yes	No
Child can sing or say the alphabet while touching the letters.	Yes	No

FIGURE 7.6. Recording sheet for basic alphabet knowledge.

From *The Building Blocks of Preschool Success* by Katherine A. Beauchat, Katrin L. Blaney, and Sharon Walpole. Copyright 2010 by The Guilford Press. Permission to photocopy this figure is granted to purchasers of this book for personal use only (see copyright page for details). Purchasers may download a larger version of this figure from the book's page on The Guilford Press website.)

Child:		Date:		
Letter Names				
D	M	J	O	T
H	A	Q	X	F
L	V	K	P	N
S	B	G	R	U
I	W	C	Z	E
Y				

FIGURE 7.7. Recording sheet for letter names.

From *The Building Blocks of Preschool Success* by Katherine A. Beauchat, Katrin L. Blaney, and Sharon Walpole. Copyright 2010 by The Guilford Press. Permission to photocopy this figure is granted to purchasers of this book for personal use only (see copyright page for details). Purchasers may download a larger version of this figure from the book's page on The Guilford Press website.)

or she can say it and touch the individual letters. Figure 7.6 provides a simple recording sheet.

For preschoolers who can say the alphabet, it makes sense to figure out what letter names they know. Typically, capital letters are used in preschool assessments. It is important that they be presented in a random order so that you can be sure that you actually assess their letter-name knowledge rather than their knowledge of the alphabet as a whole. To focus the task, present the child with a copy of the letter sheet and say, "I have a page with letters on it. I want to see which ones you know. I am going to touch a letter, and if you know it, I want you tell me what letter it is." Figure 7.7 can be used in two copies. The teacher can hold one copy on a clipboard, circling the letters that the child does not know, while focusing the child's attention on the other copy.

Another way to use an alphabet knowledge assessment is to create an assessment that includes only the letters that you have taught. Whether children are remembering them or not provides insight into the success of your initial instruction and into your strategies for cumulative review. It is simple to build in 2 or 3 minutes of review of previously taught letters, either in circle time, during shared reading, or in a writing center. This form of curriculum-based assessment, if used for these kinds of simple adjustments to the curriculum, can increase the success of all children.

While the same template could also be used to identify letter sounds that a child knows, it will be rare that a preschool child progresses to this level. More importantly, it may be a poor decision to target letter sounds in preschool. A child with initial levels of phonological awareness and knowledge of most letter names will be poised for success in learning letter sounds quickly in kindergarten. Time in the preschool day would be better spent in language development activities.

To put these three simple assessments together, consider the classroom checklist presented in Figure 7.8. The checklist allows you to consider and summarize your individual assessments into a classroom one that can help you to form groups very quickly; we have prepared a blank document so that it can easily be copied and used. You can put a check for each area that a child still needs to work on. Then, if you look down a column, you have a group of children and a focus for instruction.

ASSESSMENTS TO REFLECT ON INSTRUCTION

Each of these simple assessments can be used to identify things that children need to learn. If you use those data to form small groups and then target your instruction, it makes sense to use assessments to evaluate the success of that instruction. In the preschool environment, teachers can use their aides and assistants to provide multiple targeted small-group sessions each day. Figure 7.9 shows the decision-making cycle that we use to guide our thinking.

Teacher: _____   Date: _____

Classroom Assessment Summary

Checks in the following cells indicate that children still need additional instruction and practice.

Children's Names	Book Concepts	Print Concepts	Sing the Alphabet	Say the Alphabet	Track the Alphabet

FIGURE 7.8. Assessment summary sheet.

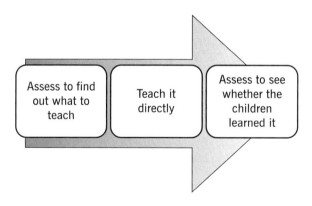

FIGURE 7.9. Decision making in preschool assessments.

For example, consider our assessment of print concepts. After giving the assessment to all children, perhaps five would have instructional needs in that area. Those five could be brought together for a brief shared storybook reading every day, with the teacher modeling and explaining the print concepts and providing opportunities for the children to explore and apply them. After 2 weeks, it would make sense to visit each of these five children in the book center and readminister the initial assessment. If any were still struggling, they could be given one-on-one sessions. All of the adults in the classroom could be tasked with providing brief and numerous opportunities for children to build the skills they lack. Then, after children have had time to benefit from these additional opportunities, they can be reassessed with the very same tools. That, conceptually, is progress monitoring at its best. It answers the question: Did they learn what I was teaching?

There are other ways to answer that question, some of which are more formal. Depending on the curriculum materials that are available in a given classroom, there may be progress monitoring assessments embedded. If there are, and they would be useful to guide instruction, use them. There are also assessments that you can download from the Internet (see, e.g., *www.igdi.ku.edu* and *www.cehd.umn.edu/ceed/projects/ggg/ default.html*. These assessments are called curriculum-based measurements (CBMs). Their strength, long argued as crucial, is that they test only what the teacher has been able to teach, and they test and retest it in exactly the same form as it has been taught (Bryan, Ergul, & Burstein, 2008). Often they represent individual progress over time on a simple graph such as the one represented in Figure 7.10. You will see in the figure that CBMs represented in this way show both achievement and general rate of improvement.

However, especially in preschool, it is important that teachers decide on how assessment data will be used to improve or target their instruction before they take the time to conduct the assessments.

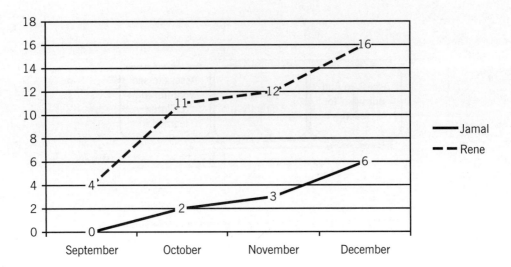

FIGURE 7.10. CBM representation for letter naming.

Less formal CBMs can also be constructed for higher-level skills. Consider the case of vocabulary knowledge. In Chapter 2 we discussed strategies for building knowledge of the meanings of specific words associated with a theme that would be interesting to young children. If the words themselves are important enough for teachers to teach individually, they are important enough for children to learn. If teachers choose the words themselves, it will be impossible to find a formal assessment of their meanings. If the words are chosen by the designers of a curriculum, a formal assessment may be available. Either way, assessment can help teachers know which words to reteach or revisit with which students. The challenge is that, as with print concepts or letter names, each individual word is its own assessment item. And word meanings are not a "yes or no" proposition; knowledge of a word's meaning grows over time with engaged opportunities. Figure 7.11 presents a continuum of word knowledge that is useful in designing vocabulary assessments for young children.

It may be that narrow knowledge in context will be the goal for many of the words teachers target; strong connected knowledge might be out of the reach of many preschoolers. However, given the resources gathered to teach interesting themes in preschool (storybooks, pictures, manipulatives, creative play centers) it makes sense to assess which words are known by which children while the resources for reteaching them are available.

A useful, reasonable way to monitor progress in learning specific word meanings is to use pictures to engage children in one-on-one discussions of word meanings. Figure 7.12 shows a record-keeping format. Children with narrow knowledge in context could demonstrate understanding in a brief discussion with a teacher using a storybook from

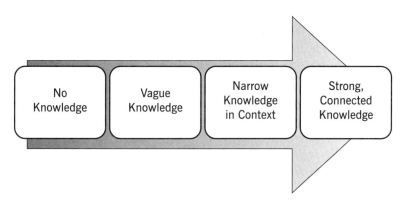

FIGURE 7.11. Continuum of word knowledge.

Child:			Date:	
Theme Vocabulary	Can Name It and Discuss It	Can Name It Independently	Can Identify It if the Teacher Names It	Does Not Know It

FIGURE 7.12. Record keeping for word meanings.

the theme, touching a particular picture, and asking the child to name it. A lower-order task would have the teacher naming the item and the child pointing to it. A stronger knowledge of the word's meaning would be demonstrated if the teacher simply asked the child what he or she knows about the word, with no pictures or props.

Another key area for tracking progress, oral language, may seem too daunting at first. You will recall in Chapter 2 that most of our suggestions for building oral language promoted you to invite talk and to extend it. We can use those same strategies for considering growth. Books provide a natural medium for what to talk about. A one-on-one conversation with a child, conducted naturally with a teacher who is familiar to and with the child, can provide evidence of language growth. Figure 7.13 provides a set of prompts that, when used with a familiar book, can elicit oral responses.

Once you have chosen a prompt and a time and space for eliciting oral language, you have a decision to make—will you transcribe the response (i.e., write it down verbatim) or record it? There are costs and benefits to each decision. Writing it down means that it is already done. You can reflect on it immediately. However, you may miss things if the child speaks quickly, and this will lead you to underestimate the response. Tape recording eliminates this problem, but then you have to make time to listen to the tape and write it down. Whatever decision you make, keeping a record of language over time will help you to identify children who are not making progress over time and plan to provide them additional language opportunities every day.

Progress in comprehension can be assessed in much the same way. Given a very familiar story (e.g., one that you have read and reread many times in shared storybook time) you can ask a child to pretend to be the teacher and read the story to you or to a stuffed animal. Such a session, while in itself a fantastic opportunity for a child to spend time producing language, provides you with a window into the extent to which the child is simply randomly associating words with the pictures or actually getting a sense of the story and of story language. Tape recordings, here, provide tangible evidence of development over time.

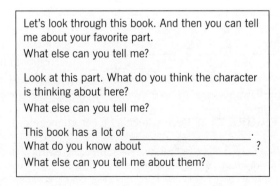

Let's look through this book. And then you can tell me about your favorite part.
What else can you tell me?

Look at this part. What do you think the character is thinking about here?
What else can you tell me?

This book has a lot of _____ .
What do you know about _____ ?
What else can you tell me about them?

FIGURE 7.13. Prompts for collecting oral language samples.

A final area in which it is important (and simple) to collect progress monitoring data is in the area of writing. Children's emergent writings, collected over time, can provide a compelling narrative of their language and literacy development. In Chapter 6, we have not advocated handwriting instruction, but we have advocated writing, both in shared writing formats and in authentic writing centers. Children will be able to draw and pretend to write; you can transcribe their pretend writing by asking them to read it to you. Dated and collected periodically, these writings provide a window into development that is concrete and rich with information about what children understand about the purposes and forms of language and literacy.

ASSESSMENTS TO IDENTIFY CHILDREN AT HIGH LEVELS OF RISK

One other role of classroom assessments in preschool is to use them to signal a need for additional assessments. A very small percentage of children have significant language disabilities and many of those will later have both language and literacy disabilities. The earlier these children are provided services by special educators and speech language pathologists, the better their long-term prognosis is. It is important to note that none of the simple assessments we have described above is sufficient for identifying a disability. That designation must come from longer, norm-referenced tests that cannot be given by preschool teachers. Educational psychologists and educational diagnosticians are trained to administer and interpret these assessments. Even for children attending private preschools, these services are available through the child's home public school district.

Although our informal screenings, diagnostic measures, and progress monitoring measures are not sufficient to identify children for special services, they can help decide who really needs to have additional assessment. That decision-making cycle is the heart of the new special education protocol called response to intervention (RTI). RTI initiatives are based on the notion that disabilities are identified only after appropriate instruction—not simply because children have low achievement. In preschool, that is abundantly clear. If you made referrals to special education based only on your children's September performance on literacy measures, you would identify children who have not had access to books at home or whose home language is not English as potentially disabled. Surely that is not true. Those children are poised to make especially rapid progress, given language and literacy-rich opportunities in your classroom.

That does not mean that your assessments are not important, especially if they are used to plan instruction. Given repeated small-group and individual attention, for a child who cannot learn any letter names or vocabulary words repeatedly taught and retaught, or who does not progress in language from one-word responses to questions, a preschool teacher may consider procedures for accessing additional testing. It is important, though, that the teacher is not confusing a lack of English skills with a lack of language skills. ELLs will be difficult to assess in the classroom until they mass enough English words. Luckily, in a language-rich preschool, that language development happens quickly.

HOW DO YOU ACTUALLY PLAN
AND IMPLEMENT AN ASSESSMENT SYSTEM?

At first blush, our suggestions for assessments might seem unreasonable. You have to decide what to choose among our suggestions. First, decide what data are important to collect in your classroom. Remember that just because data can be collected does not mean that they should. Consider your own capacity to work with your instructional team—your classroom assistants and aides—to use the data to group and to adjust instruction. If you cannot use the data, it does not make sense to collect it. Next, decide on how you will interact with parents and caregivers; collect only data that will be useful for you as you discuss each child's strengths over time.

Next, create an assessment portfolio for each child, with an assessment checklist on the front. A simple file folder for each child, stored in a file drawer or box, may be enough to start. Gather the materials that you will need, such as copies of the book and the print concept charts and the alphabet charts in this chapter, and place them in the folders. We know that your assessment minutes will be dear, and if you are not prepared to use them, they can easily be lost in the other demands of the day.

Next, make a reasonable schedule, one that builds in wiggle room, and use it to keep yourself on track with assessments. It does not make sense to assess preschoolers on the first days of school; you should plan to use that time to build community, classroom procedures, and to introduce shared reading to all of the children. Once children have acclimated to the setting and to the schedule, you can begin to collect information from them.

You cannot assess everything, or you will not have time to teach. Consider assessment cycles. Public schools tend to be organized into 36 instructional weeks, with either 6- or 9-week grading cycles; many preschools follow the same calendar. You can use that calendar to identify blocks of time, and then stagger your assessments within those blocks. We think that the best time for assessment is during center time. This will be a time that the teacher and the classroom aide can work as a team to ensure that all children's needs are being met. For example, the teacher might be conducting alphabet knowledge assessments in a quiet corner of the room while the classroom assistant is monitoring and interacting with the other children in the various centers. For the assessments that we have proposed in this chapter, 10 minutes is more than enough time to schedule.

Once a month, Pam and Cheryl use a CBM to assess children on the concepts directly taught during that month. These are administered during center time and take about 5–10 minutes per child. The CBM includes alphabetic recognition (cumulative review of letters introduced up to that time), letter sound awareness (cumulative review of letter-sounds introduced up to that time), and phonological awareness (rhyme and initial sound sorting). Based on these CBM results, she and Cheryl create new groupings and materials for small-group instruction. It also helps Cheryl to plan more targeted whole-group instruction and center-time activities. Cheryl and Pam also collect samples of student work during the week for each child's assessment portfolio as well as for the work sampling assessment system that her district has adopted.

Elaina collects two kinds of assessment information each month. On a weekly basis Elaina and her two classroom assistants collect informal observations on each child. The team records observations about each child's socioemotional, fine- and gross-motor, and cognitive development. At the end of each week, Elaina collects her team's observations and enters them into a computer database to keep track of each child's progress. The second type of assessment Elaina uses is a CBM designed with the help of the center director working with her. At the end of each month Elaina pulls each child over to work one on one with her for approximately 10 minutes during center time. Elaina administers the CBM right in the classroom. Elaina's CBM consists of two parts: alphabet knowledge and phonological awareness. This helps Elaina to plan subsequent instruction for whole-group and center-time play as well as for small-group instruction.

Sarah reserves 1 day each week for assessment during her center rotations. Because she has a partner during that time, each of them can collect information on different days. After 3 weeks, she and her partner and the children are comfortable with the center rotation, and they begin to collect information. They plan 3 weeks to assess all of the children on the book and print concepts and alphabet tasks summarized in Figure 7.8. For the next 3 weeks, the team will turn attention to oral language and comprehension. Sarah will use a vocabulary checklist during her rotation, and her partner will collect a first round of retellings of favorite storybooks in the library center.

HOW DO I SHARE ASSESSMENT INFORMATION?

When you share assessment information with the parents of preschoolers, it is important to highlight their child's growth over time rather than to compare their child to other children. The easiest way to do this is to use your assessment portfolio, where you have collected assessments over time. For example, if you decide to focus on a child's growth by using writing samples, line up the samples in your portfolio by date, and use them to guide a discussion of the things that the child is learning over time and to identify your own next targets. If you do that, some parents will be willing and able to assist you in accomplishing that next goal. For others, whose life situations make language and literacy work at home more difficult, you can simply ask for support in helping their child to be rested and ready for school each day so that his or her learning will be maximized.

WHERE CAN I FIND MORE INFORMATION?

Web-Based

- Center for RTI in Early Childhood
  www.crtiec.org
- Get it Got it Go
  www.crtiec.org
- PALS PreK
  pals.virginia.edu/tools-prek.html
- National Association for the Education of Young Children
  www.naeyc.org/positionstatements/cape

Text-Based (Real Cites)

- Clay, M. M. (1993). *An observation survey of early literacy achievement*. Portsmouth, NH: Heinemann.
- Enz, B. J., & Morrow, L. (2009). *Assessing preschool literacy development*. Newark, DE: International Reading Association.
- Pence, K. (Ed.). (2007). *Assessment in emergent and early literacy*. San Diego, CA: Plural Publishing.
- Schatschneider, C., Petscher, Y., & Williams, K. M. (2008). How to evaluate a screening process: The vocabulary of screening and what educators need to know. In L. M. Justice & C. Vukelich (Eds.), *Achieving excellence in preschool literacy instruction* (pp. 304–316). New York: Guilford Press.

CHAPTER 8

Making It Work for Adults and Children

It is one thing to think of the components of language development or literacy development separately, as we have done in the preceding chapters. It is another thing altogether to balance all of them every day among a group of active preschool children. And given the characteristics of the preschool workforce that we reviewed in Chapter 1, with typically high turnover and lack of formal opportunities for preservice and inservice training, it may seem overly optimistic to spend a chapter on planning. We recognize the very real challenges of the day-to-day demands of preschool teaching, but we think that starting with a big-picture plan, creating a workable schedule, reflecting on its successes and failures, collaborating with others to revise it, and engaging in continued professional learning will invigorate the preschool year—perhaps even keep some of you engaged enough to stay in preschool. Watching children make real progress in their language and literacy development is a reward with few rivals, especially because the children themselves greet their own accomplishments with such joy. As you have read in preceding chapters, this progress is also high stakes for children, particularly those at risk. Early success yields continued success, both in language and in literacy, and the preschool years are our first opportunity to make a difference.

GATHERING MATERIALS

As you have seen from our three model teachers, preschool classrooms can be very dissimilar. Some have core curriculum materials, and some don't. Some have extensive classroom libraries, and some don't. We think that many kinds of preschool classrooms can work for children, but that it is important to either organize or gather resources in advance so that the day's work can be child centered rather than curriculum centered.

The first task is identifying a series of themes or units that will unify language and literacy and play over time. If they are in the curriculum, it does not make sense to change them; if you have no curriculum, you have to choose them yourself. Either way, your choices are not necessarily high stakes. There are many topics that are interesting to young children, and you can choose those that maximize and integrate your existing resources.

Whether you have many materials or relatively few, they can likely be sorted into categories that serve different purposes. Having a big-picture plan will help you to cycle your materials, ensuring that new themes are greeted with new resources—keeping your classroom environment interesting. If you stick with preschool, your resources can be built over time. Figure 8.1 presents a template that you can use to organize your existing resources and to add to your collection if new monies become available to you. It may be useful to use one template to identify the items that you have, and another to identify the items that you wish you had.

You will see that you need books—big books, trade books, and little books—in order to make any language and literacy plan work. If you don't have them, get them at the local library. Once you have them, you have to decide how to use them. Since big books may be scarce, plan with them first. Sort your big books by theme because of their content. Within each theme, make sure that you have a sequence for using them. Then maximize the potential of each book. Which theme-based words can you teach? How

	Theme			
	Big Books	**Trade Books**	**Teaching Manipulatives**	**Creative Play**
Oral Language and Vocabulary	Target words	Target words	Picture cards to represent target words	Costumes, puppets, toys, magazines, art supplies, writing materials
Comprehension	Questions	Questions	Pictures for sequencing and sorting	
Phonological Awareness	Focus skill	Focus skill	Poems, picture cards, and objects to sort, markers for counting sounds, games, lists of words of different types	
Print Awareness	Pointer, Easel		Poems, little books, pointers	
Alphabet Awareness	Target letters	Target letters	Magnet letters, metal trays, alphabet strips, name puzzles	
Emergent Writing	Chart paper		Sentence frames, blank little books, plans for class books, writing utensils	

FIGURE 8.1. Resource planning template.

can you ask a variety of closed and open-ended questions? Which phonological tasks are best highlighted? Which words will allow you to build alphabet awareness? Keep track of your decisions both within the book (on sticky notes) and on a separate sheet of paper so that you can use the same plan next year. These same procedures will apply to your trade-book collection, and they will allow you to start every shared storybook reading and every read-aloud with a set of options for maximizing interactions.

If you are new to planning for phonological awareness and alphabet knowledge—the two key literacy skill sets for preschoolers—then remember to start with a plan. Alphabet awareness is about written letters. Preschoolers need to see, name, and explore letters. In order for them to engage in emergent writing, they have to begin to represent letter shapes on paper. While it is probably best to start with the letters in each child's name, you should also decide the order in which you will introduce the entire alphabet. That way, you can choose phonological awareness tasks that are matched to your target letters.

Phonological awareness is an oral proficiency. Children listen to and manipulate sounds in words. Early in the year, plan for the larger sound units: word, syllable, and rhyme awareness. The only materials you need are words and pictures, both from your read-alouds and in separate sets. Later in the year, you will need the same items (picture cards and word lists) but be sure to move to onsets and rimes, and maybe even to individual phonemes. A recipe box can be a great organizer for lists of words to use in oral word play, organized by theme. When it is possible, linking your phonological awareness lists to your target letters provides an added level of coherence to your children's first experiences with literacy.

SCHEDULING AND GROUPING

Preschool classrooms also differ in their schedules. Total time in school differs; requirements for meals, hygiene, and rest differs; access to outdoor play differs. Regardless of the constraints of the setting, though, preschoolers who are maximizing their language and literacy growth need time for shared storybook reading, for guided practice with language and literacy in one-on-one settings or in very small groups, and for consolidating and applying what they are learning in self-directed independent and peer play. Many preschool classrooms have more than one adult. If that is the case for you, we urge you to integrate your small-group and center schedules. Maximize the available adult–child interactions such that every adult in the room spends the most possible minutes each day engaged directly with children. Consider the two options in Figure 8.2. In the first plan, the teacher-centered plan, classroom assistants are used to help only with tasks and procedures. Their role during the small-group block is to keep children safe and engaged, following classroom rules as they move among centers. The teacher, then, works with a small group, uninterrupted, as the only person providing any structured language or

Teacher-Centered Plan	Collaborative Plan
Whole-group shared storybook reading and writing	Whole-group shared storybook reading and writing
Small-group teacher instruction, with classroom assistants monitoring center explorations for other children	Small-group adult interactions, with all adults working in a specific center directly with children

FIGURE 8.2. Two contrasting general schedules.

literacy instruction; on a given day, there is insufficient time for all children to have a turn in small-group instruction.

In the collaborative plan in Figure 8.2, all adults are centers. This type of collaboration allows for much more language in the classroom; all adults can listen to and speak to children *at the same time,* constantly providing them with additional language experiences and feedback. With two adults, it is possible to have two or three groups—two adult groups with half the class each or two adult groups and one independent group; with three adults, it is possible to have three or four groups with the same logic. Rather than having just one long group each day, children can rotate. Figure 8.3 charts this possibility.

The rotation below begs two very important questions: How should children be grouped? and How can the teacher provide differentiated instruction in all areas of the language and literacy plan? If the groups are to be stable, meaning that children move from one station to another as in Figure 8.3, they should probably be grouped heterogeneously; children with a range of language and literacy proficiencies should move together, with higher-achieving children providing strong peer models for children with more significant needs. In addition, the teacher should alternate his or her own role such that over the course of a week or 2 weeks the teacher works with each group in each area.

	Teacher: Phonological Awareness and Alphabet Knowledge	Assistant: Oral Language and Comprehension	Assistant: Writing	Centers: Creative Play
15 minutes	Group 1	Group 4	Group 3	Group 2
15 minutes	Group 2	Group 1	Group 4	Group 3
15 minutes	Group 3	Group 2	Group 1	Group 4
15 minutes	Group 4	Group 3	Group 2	Group 1

FIGURE 8.3. Possible small-group rotation for three adults.

	Teacher: Phonological Awareness and Alphabet Knowledge	Assistant: Oral Language and Comprehension	Assistant: Writing	Centers: Creative Play
15 minutes	Highest Achieving	Mixed Levels	Mixed Levels	Choice
15 minutes	Lowest Achieving	Mixed Levels	Mixed Levels	
15 minutes	Middle Achieving	Mixed Levels	Mixed Levels	
15 minutes	Middle Achieving	Mixed Levels	Mixed Levels	

FIGURE 8.4. Potential model for differentiation.

An alternative is to differentiate based more on skill needs. In a plan like that, all children would be playing in centers, and the teacher would call a group composed of children who need work in the same area while the classroom assistants call heterogeneous groups from the remaining children. Planning there is slightly more complicated, because each child can be in only one group at a time. Center rotation charts, clothespins, or pocket charts with children's names help in the planning. Figure 8.4 provides a potential model. In either case, children will need to learn how to work with one another and more independently, and teachers will need to be flexible about time and movement. In between or at the beginning of each instructional segment, children will benefit from some gross-motor movement; exercises, songs, and yoga stretches provide great transitions.

REFLECTING

The best-laid preschool plans have to be subject to change! There are two essential areas to consider: your own ability to enact your plan and the interaction of your plan with your children's skills. Either one could be cause for revisiting your overall plan; failure to get it right the first time is not a waste of time. Rather, failure to adjust when you know that your plan is not working is a waste of time—for you and for the children. Since neither you nor they have time to waste, reflecting on children's progress and expecting to make adjustments is an important disposition to foster within yourself and with your team.

Once you have made a plan and given it some time to work, there are two ways that you can reflect on whether it is reasonable. First, simply monitor the level of comfort that you and any adults working with you experience. After 2 or 3 weeks, the schedule should feel comfortable, with groups interacting productively and tasks accomplished at a reasonable pace. A feeling of community and competence is essential for both children and adults. Part of that comes from defining goals and responsibilities and then reaching them.

The second action you can take is a more conscious self-reflection. Tape record yourself and consider the extent to which your instructional talk is matching your instructional goals. It may be that too much time is spent on management and redirection and too little on language and literacy; that is a sure sign that children are not learning optimally. There are many possible reasons for that. One is that the activities are boring to the children, either because they are too easy or because they are too hard. Consider that possibility first. If the activities are too hard, try to step back developmentally and increase children's chances to participate actively. If they are too easy, increase the number of books you use, the amount of vocabulary you teach, or the level of phonological awareness you are targeting. Next consider whether there is too much or too little movement. The preschool classroom should never be a pressured academic learning environment. Young children who are alert and ready to learn can accomplish more in a few minutes of engaged time than they can in longer stretches of time when they are tired or distracted. Also consider that individual children (and adults!) can have bad days, where nothing seems to go exactly right. A good dose of empathy for that fact will go a long way toward a constructive, playful environment.

COLLABORATING

The richness of the preschool environment, with children and adults who are always moving (quite literally) can also be a source of stress. Some preschool teachers have the benefit of professional support systems through center directors, literacy coaches, or formal professional development plans. Others are more isolated, though. In few cases are the roles of the various adults in the preschool room clearly defined, and this fact can lead to confusion and lost opportunities. We have thought of the preschool day as a rich theater production, with changing props and evolving scripts. The actors have individual needs, and the schedules must be coordinated. There are multiple demands and multiple audiences. And like on Broadway, when the curtain rises, the show will begin—whether anyone is ready or not.

Conscious attention to collaboration will go a long way toward a successful day. Few teachers in any setting are actually trained to work with other adults, but preschool teachers have to jump right in. The schedules we presented in Chapter 1 detail the pressures on time in preschool, but finding consistent time to negotiate classroom roles and responsibilities each week, either before children arrive or after they leave, is essential. We suggest that teachers help their assistants to make and execute plans for work with children, that they ask for feedback and suggestions from their assistants, and that they involve assistants in as many instructional tasks as possible.

Collaboration with parents is also essential. Our model preschool teachers were careful to reach out to parents, to provide parents with materials to use at home, and to share information about children's progress with parents. In some cases, that means that preschool teachers have to overcome language and cultural barriers, and that will not be easy. However, experience tells us that respectful attempts to involve parents are repaid twofold; when you reach out to parents, including extra efforts to attend to their needs, you communicate your respect for them as their child's first teachers and also your care for their child's well-being. Interactions like these build strong home–school relations and help make children's transitions from home to preschool and from preschool to kindergarten much smoother.

LEARNING

Preschool classrooms are filled with opportunities for adults to learn about language and literacy development. One way to learn is by watching an individual child's development. Assessments of print and alphabet awareness will tell you how and how quickly children develop these skills; journals will show the development of emergent writing; retellings or transcribed language samples will show growth in oral language and comprehension. Eavesdropping during creative play will give you a window on a child's growing self-regulation and understanding of new concepts. Spying in the library corner will show you how a child comes to understand the purpose of print and identify his or her special interests.

Preschool curriculum materials provide a chance to learn. They target specific skills and concepts; they provide suggested classroom routines; they select texts for various purposes. Once you have experienced a full theme, and then several themes, you will be in a good position to understand the underlying logic that the instructional designers used. You will also be in a position to evaluate the match between that logic and the skills of your children. That type of thinking goes a long way toward maximizing the potential of preschool.

Preschool teachers can learn much about language and literacy from children's book authors. Taking the time to select beautifully written and beautifully illustrated books builds deep understanding of language. Using them in the classroom provides the rich vocabulary that is lacking in our oral language exchanges and that has the potential to change the rate at which preschoolers are acquiring word meanings. It also shows children the power of language and literacy such that they are more and more excited to participate in it.

We spend part of our days in direct classroom-based work and part in research. We hope that you will too. Preschool researchers are building the knowledge base for preschool teachers every day. In each of our chapters, we have identified print or web-based resources that you can consult to learn more. It is likely that you will be able to find something that really interests you and can explore it on your own or with colleagues. We urge you to consider your own learning and your own interests as essential to your preschool classroom; learning to teach is a task that is never completed.

Children's Literature

Aardema, V. (1975). *Why mosquitoes buzz in people's ears*. New York: Puffin.

Adams, P. (2007). *There was an old lady who swallowed a fly*. Whiltshire, UK: Child's Play International.

Andreae, G. (2001). *Giraffes can't dance*. New York: Orchard.

Asim, J. (2006). *Whose toes are those?* Boston: Little, Brown Young Readers.

Bang, M. (1999). *When Sophie gets angry—really, really angry*. New York: Scholastic.

Barner, B. (1999). *Bugs! Bugs! Bugs!* New York: Scholastic.

Barton, B. (1994). *Boats*. New York: HarperFestival.

Boekhoff, P. M. (2006). *What does a construction worker do?* Berkeley Heights, CA: Enslow Elementary.

Boyton, S. (1987). *A is for angry*. New York: Workman.

Brett, J. (1989). *The mitten*. New York: Putnam.

Brett, J. (2004). *The umbrella*. New York: Putnam.

Bridges, S. (2005). *I drive a bulldozer*. Mankato, MN: Picture Window Books.

Brown, M. (1991). *Big red barn*. New York: HarperFestival.

Brown, M. (1996). *Four fur feet*. New York: Hyperion.

Brown, M. W. (1977). *Goodnight moon*. New York: HarperCollins.

Brunelle, L. (1999). *The itsy-bitsy spider and a handful of finger rhymes*. San Francisco: Weldon Owen.

Carle, E. (1987). *The very hungry caterpillar*. New York: Penguin Group.

Carle, E. (1989). *The very busy spider*. New York: Philomel.

Carle, E. (1995). *The very lonely firefly*. New York: Philomel.

Carle, E. (1996). *The grouchy ladybug*. New York: Harper Collins.

Carle, E. (1997a). *From head to toe*. New York: HarperFestival.

Carle, E. (1997b). *Today is Monday*. New York: Putnam.

Carle, E. (1997). *Have you seen my cat?* New York: Aladdin.

Carle, E. (1998). *1, 2, 3 to the zoo*. New York: Penguin Group.

Carle, E. (1999). *Animals animals*. New York: Putnam Juvenile.

Christelow, E. (1989). *Five little monkeys jumping on the bed*. New York: Scholastic.

Collicutt, P. (2004). *This truck*. New York: Farrar, Straus & Giroux.

Crews, D. (1989). *Flying*. New York: Greenwillow Books.

Crews, D. (1991). *Truck*. New York: Greenwillow Books.

Crews, D. (1993). *School bus*. New York: Greenwillow Books.

Cronin, D. (2000). *Click, clack, moo: Cows that type*. New York: Scholastic.

Curtis, J. L. (1998). *Today I feel silly: And other moods that make my day*. New York: HarperCollins.

DePaola, T. (1975). *Strega Nona*. New York: Scholastic.

DePaola, T. (1978). *Pancakes for breakfast*. Boston: Houghton Mifflin Harcourt.

Dewdney, A. (2005). *Llama llama red pajama*. New York: Viking Juvenile.

Donaldson, J., & Scheffler, A. (1999). *The gruffalo*. London: Macmillan.

Dorros, A. (1997). *Abuela*. New York: Puffin.

Ehlert, L. (1988). *Planting a rainbow*. New York: Harcourt Children's Books.

Ehlert, L. (1996). *Eating the alphabet*. New York: Harcourt Brace.

Elting, M., & Folsom, M. (2005). *Q is for duck*. New York: Clarion Books.

Ernst, L. C. (1996). *The letters are lost*. New York: Viking Press.

Feelings, M., & Feelings, T. (1974). *Jambo means hello: Swahili alphabet book*. New York: Dial Press.

Fleming, D. (1991). *In the tall, tall grass*. New York: Henry Holt.

Fleming, D. (2006). *Alphabet under construction*. New York: Henry Holt.

Fredericks, A. (2001). *Under one rock, bugs, slugs, and other ughs*. Nevada City: Dawn Publications.

Freeman, D. (1978). *A rainbow of my own*. New York: Puffin.

Galdone. P. (2006). *The little red hen*. New York: Clarion.

Glaser, L. (1996). *Wonderful worms*. Boston: Houghton Miffin.

Gregor, A. (1959). *Animal babies*. New York: Scholastic.

Guarino, D. (2006). *Is your mama a llama?* New York: Scholastic.

Hague, K. (1984). *Alphabears*. New York: Henry Holt.

Hawkins, C. (2003). *Old MacDonald had a farm*. London: Egmont UK.

Henkes, K. (1991). *Chrysanthemum*. New York: Greenwillow Books.

Hoban, T. (1982). *A. b. see*. New York: Greenwillow Books.

Hoban, T. (1997). *Look book*. New York: Greenwillow Books.

Hoose, P., & Hoose, H. (1998). *Hey, little ant*. Berkeley, CA: Tricycle Press.

Howe, J. (1994). *I wish I were a butterfly*. San Diego, CA: Voyager Books.

Hutchins, P. (1971). *Rosie's walk*. New York: Simon & Schuster.

Johnson, S. T. (1995). *Alphabet city*. New York: Viking Press.

Juster, N. (2005). *The hello, goodbye window*. New York: Scholastic Trade.

Keats, E. (1998). *Peter's chair*. New York: Viking Juvenile.

Keats, E. (1999). *Over in the meadow*. New York: Puffin.

Kirk, D. (1998). *Miss Spider's abc*. New York: Scholastic Press.

Levenson, G. (2004). *Pumpkin circle*. Berkeley, CA: Tricycle Press.

Lichtenheld, T. (2007). *What are you so grumpy about?* Boston: Little, Brown Young Readers.

Lionni, L. (1963). *Swimmy*. New York: Scholastic.

Lionni, L. (1967). *Frederick*. New York: Random House.

Lionni, L. (1968). *The alphabet tree*. New York: Pantheon.

Lionni, L. (1969). *Alexander and the wind-up mouse*. New York: Scholastic.

Liu, J. S. (2002). *Yellow umbrella*. Brooklyn, NY: Kane/Miller.

Martin, B. (1989). *Chicka chicka boom boom*. New York: Simon & Schuster.

Martin, B., & Archambault, J. (1989). *Chicka chicka abc*. New York: Little Simon.

Martin, B., & Carle, E. (2006). *Panda bear, panda bear, what do you see?* New York: Henry Holt.

Martin, B., & Carle, E. (2007a). *Baby bear, baby bear, what do you see?* New York: Henry Holt.

Martin, B., & Carle, E. (2007b). *Brown bear, brown bear, what do you see?* New York: Holt, Rinehart & Winston.

Mayo, M. (2006). *Dig dig digging*. New York: Henry Holt.

McCloskey, R. (1976). *Blueberries for Sal*. New York: Scholastic.

McPhail, D. (1992). *The train*. Boston: Little, Brown.

Mitton, T., & Parker, A. (2003). *Tough trucks*. New York: Kingfisher.

Nayer, J. (1994). *A tree can be …* New York: Scholastic.

Neumeier, M., & Glaser, B. (1985). *Action alphabet*. New York: Greenwillow Books.

Numeroff, L. J. (1985). *If you give a mouse a cookie*. New York: Scholastic.

Numeroff, L. J. (1991). *If you give a moose a muffin*. New York: Scholastic.

Numeroff, L. J. (2000). *If you take a mouse to the movies*. New York: Scholastic.

Numeroff, L. J. (2002). *If you take a mouse to school*. New York: Scholastic.

Numeroff, L. J. (2008). *If you give a cat a cupcake*. New York: Laura Geringer Books.

Olson, K. C. (2004). *Construction countdown*. New York: Henry Holt.

Oxenbury, H. (1994). *The car trip*. New York: Puffin.

Pallotta, J. (1986). *The icky bug alphabet book*. Boston: Quinlan Press.

Patience, J. (1993). *An amazing alphabet*. Hills, MN: Crescent.

Pfister, M. (1992). *Rainbow fish*. New York: North-South Books, Inc.

Posada, M. (2000). *Dandelions, stars in the grass*. Minneapolis, MN: Carolrhoda Books.

Raffi. (1988). *Down by the bay*. New York: Crown Books for Young Readers.

Raffi. (2005). *If you're happy and you know it*. New York: Knopf Books for Young Readers.

Rankin, L. (1991). *The handmade alphabet*. New York: Dial Books.

Rathmann, P. (1995). *Officer buckle and Gloria*. New York: Scholastic.

Rathmann, P. (2000). *Good night, gorilla*. New York: Putnam Juvenile.

Ringgold, F. (1991). *Tar beach*. New York: Scholastic.

Rosen, M., & Oxenbury, H. (2003). *We're going on a bear hunt*. New York: Aladdin Paperbacks.

Roth, S. L. (2004). *Hard hat area*. London: Bloomsbury Children's Books.

Rylant, C. (1985). *The relatives came*. New York: Scholastic.

Scieszka, J. (1989). *The true story of the 3 little pigs*. New York: Puffin.

Sendak, M. (1963). *Where the wild things are*. New York: Harper Collins.

Sendak, M. (1992). *Alligators all around: An alphabet*. New York: Scholastic.

Seuss, Dr. (1963). *Hop on pop*. New York: Random House.

Seuss, Dr. (1996a). *Dr. Seuss's abc*. New York: Random House.

Seuss, Dr. (1996b). *My many colored days*. New York: Knopf.

Shannon, D. (1998). *No, David!* New York: Scholastic.

Shaw, N. (1986). *Sheep in a jeep*. Boston: Houghton Mifflin.

Slepian, J., & Seidler, A. (2001). *The hungry thing*. New York: Scholastic.

Sobel, J. (2006). *B is for bulldozer: A construction abc.* San Diego, CA: Voyager.

Spier, P. (2000). *Rain.* New York: Doubleday.

Steig, W. (1990). *Dr. De Soto.* New York: Farrar, Straus & Giroux.

Steig, W. (2005). *Sylvester and the magic pebble.* New York: Simon & Schuster.

Taback, S. (1999). *There was an old lady who swallowed a fly.* New York: Scholastic.

Taback, S. (2004). *This is the house that Jack built.* New York: Puffin.

Teague, M. (2002). *Dear Mrs. LaRue: Letters from obedience school.* New York: Scholastic.

Thomson, R. (1987). *All about abc.* Milwaukee, WI: G. Stevens.

Thompson, L. (2005). *Little Quack's bedtime.* New York: Simon & Schuster.

Van Allsburg, C. (1987). *The z was zapped.* Boston: Houghton Mifflin.

Viorst, J. (2009). *Alexander and the horrible, no good, very bad day.* New York: Simon & Schuster.

Westcott, N. B. (1992). *Peanut butter and jelly: A play rhyme.* London: Puffin.

Wiesner, D. (1997). *Tuesday.* New York: Clarion.

Wiesner, D. (2006) *Flotsam.* New York: Clarion Books.

Wood, A. (1999). *Silly Sally.* Boston: Red Wagon Books.

Wood, A. (2000). *The napping house.* New York: Harcourt Children's Books.

Wood, A. (2005). *The deep blue sea: A book of colors.* New York: Blue Sky Press.

Yolen, J. (1987). *Owl moon.* New York: Scholastic.

Yolen, J., & Teague, M. (2004). *How do dinosaurs count to ten?* New York: Scholastic.

Yoshi, (1998). *Who's hiding here?* New York: Simon & Schuster.

References

Adams, M. J. (1990). *Beginning to read: Thinking and learning about print*. Cambridge, MA: MIT Press.

American Library Association. *Children and young adult awards*. Retrieved September 3, 2009, from *www.ala.org/ala/awardsgrants/booksprintmedia/childrenyngadults/index.cfm*.

Arnold, J. M., Lonigan, C. J., Whitehurst, G. J., & Epstein, J. N. (1994). Accelerating language development through picture-book reading: Replication and extension to a videotape training format. *Journal of Educational Psychology, 86,* 235–243.

Ball, E. W., & Blachman, B. A. (1988). Phoneme segmentation training: Effect on reading readiness. *Annals of Dyslexia, 38,* 208–225.

Beauchat, K. A., Blamey, K. L., & Walpole, S. (2009, September). Building preschool children's language and literacy one storybook at a time. *The Reading Teacher, 63*(1), 26–39.

Beck, I. L., & McKeown, M. G. (2001). Text talk: Capturing the benefits of read-aloud experiences for young children. *The Reading Teacher, 55,* 10–20.

Beck, I. J., & McKeown, M. G. (2007). Increasing young low-income children's oral vocabulary repertoires through rich and focused instruction. *The Elementary School Journal, 107*(3), 251–271.

Beck, I.L., McKeown, M. G., & Kucan, L. (2002). *Bringing words to life: Robust vocabulary instruction*. New York: Guilford.

Block, C. C., Canizares, S., Church, E. B., & Lobo, B. (1981). *Scholastic Early Childhood Program*. New York: Scholastic.

Bodrova, E., & Leong, D. J. (2001). *Tools of the mind: A case study of implementing the Vygotskian approach in American early childhood and primary classrooms*. Geneva, Switzerland: UNESCO.

Bryan, T., Ergul, C., & Burstein, K. (2008). *Curriculum-based measurement of preschoolers' early literacy skills*. In L. M. Justice & C. Vukelich (Eds.), *Achieving excellence in preschool literacy instruction* (pp. 317–338). New York: Guilford Press.

Bureau of Labor Statistics. (2008). *Occupational Outlook Handbook 2008–09 Edition*. Retrieved May 26, 2009, from *www.bls.gov/oco/ocos069.htm*.

Burns, M. S., Griffin, P., & Snow, C. E. (Eds.). (1999). *Starting out right: A guide to promoting children's reading success*. Washington, DC: National Academy Press.

Bus, A. G. (2001). Joint caregiver–child storybook reading: A route to literacy development. In S. B. Neuman & D. K. Dickinson (Eds.), *Handbook of early literacy research* (pp. 179–191). New York: Guilford Press.

Clay, M. M. (1975). *What did I write?: Beginning reading behavior*. Portsmouth, NH: Heinemann.

Clay, M. M. (1993). *An observation survey of early literacy achievement*. Portsmouth, NH: Heinemann.

Dickinson, D., & Smith, M. (1994). Long-term effects of preschool teachers' book readings on low-income children's vocabulary and story comprehension. *Reading Research Quarterly, 29*, 104–122.

Dickinson, D. K., McCabe, A., Clark-Chiarelli, N., & Wolf, A. (2004). Cross-language transfer of phonological awareness in low-income Spanish and English bilingual preschool children. *Applied Psycholinguistics, 25*, 323–347.

Dodge, D. T., & Colker, L. J. (2000). *The creative curriculum for early childhood* (3rd ed.). Washington, DC: Teaching Strategies.

Elley, W. B. (1989). Vocabulary acquisition from listening to stories. *Reading Research Quarterly, 24*, 174–187.

Epstein, A. S., Schweinhart, L. J., DeBruin-Parecki, A., & Robin, K. B. (2004, July). *Preschool assessment: A guide to developing a balanced approach*. New Brunswick, NJ: National Institute for Early Education Research and High Scope Educational Foundation.

Ezell, H. K., & Justice, L. M. (1998). A pilot investigation of parents' questions about print and pictures to preschoolers with language delay. *Child Language Teaching and Therapy, 14*, 273–278.

Ezell, H. K., & Justice, L. M. (2000). Increasing the print focus of adult–child shared book reading through observational learning. *American Journal of Speech–Language Pathology, 9*, 36–47.

Feldgus, E.G., & Cardonick, I. (1999). *Kid writing: A systematic approach to phonics, journals, and writing workshop*. Bothell, WA: Wright Group.

Hansen, J. (2004). *"Tell me a story": Developmentally appropriate retelling strategies*. Newark, DE: International Reading Association.

Hargrave, A. C., & Senechal, M. (2000). A book reading intervention with preschool children who have limited vocabularies: The benefits of regular reading and dialogic reading. *Early Childhood Research Quarterly, 15*(1), 75–90.

Hart, B., & Risley, R. T. (1995). *Meaningful differences in the everyday experience of young American children*. Baltimore: Brookes.

Hereford, N. J., & Schall, J. (1998). *Dramatic play: A practical guide for teaching young children*. New York: Scholastic.

Holdaway, D. (1979). *The foundations of literacy*. Sydney, Australia: Ashton Scholastic.

International Reading Association and National Association for the Education of Young Children. (1998). Learning to read and write: Developmentally appropriate practices for young children. *The Reading Teacher, 52*, 193–216. (Also available in *Young Children, 53*(4), 75–88)

Invernizzi, M., Sullivan, A., & Meier, J. D. (2001). *Phonological awareness literary screening: Pre-kindergarten*. Charlottesville: University of Virginia.

Ivey, G. (2002). Building comprehension when they're still learning to read the words. In C. C.

Block & M. Pressley (Eds.), *Comprehension instruction: Research-based practices* (pp. 234–247). New York: Guilford Press.

Justice, L. M., Bowles, R. P., & Skibbe, L. E. (2006). Measuring preschool attainment of print-concept knowledge: A study of typical and at-risk 3- to 5-year-old children using item response theory. *Language, Speech and Hearing Services in Schools, 37,* 224–235.

Justice, L. M., & Kaderavek, J. N. (2004). Embedded–explicit emergent literacy intervention. *Language, Speech, and Hearing Services in Schools, 35,* 211–301.

Justice, L. M., Meier, J., & Walpole, S. (2005). Learning new words from storybooks: An efficacy study with at-risk kindergarteners. *Language, Speech, and Hearing Services in Schools, 36,* 17–32.

Justice, L. M., & Pullen, P. (2003). Promising interventions for promoting emergent literacy skills: Three evidence-based approaches. *Topics in Early Childhood Special Education, 23*(3), 99–113.

Kame'enui, E. J., Francis, D. J., Fuchs, L., Good, R. H., O'Connor, R. E., Simmons, D. C., et al. (2006). The adequacy of tools for assessing reading competence: A framework and review. *Educational Researcher, 35,* 3–11.

Karweit, N., & Wasik, B. (1996). The effects of story reading programs on literacy and language development of disadvantaged pre-schoolers. *Journal of Education for Students Placed At-Risk, 4,* 319–348.

Lonigan, C. J. (2008). *(Almost) everything you wanted to know about phonological awareness and were afraid to ask.* Paper presented at the Early Reading First Grantee Meeting, New Orleans, LA.

Lopez, L. M., & Greenfield, D. B. (2004). The cross-language transfer of phonological awareness skills of Hispanic Head Start children. *Bilingual Research Journal, 28,* 1–18.

Love, A., Burns, M. S., & Buell, M. J. (2007). Writing: Empowering literacy. *Young Children, 62*(1), 12–20.

Manis, F. R., Lindsey, K. A., & Bailey, C. E. (2004). Development of reading in grades K–2 in Spanish-speaking English-language learners. *Learning Disabilities Research and Practice, 19,* 214–224.

McCarrier, A., Pinnell, G. S., & Fountas, I. C. (2000). *Interactive writing: How language and literacy come together, K–2.* Portsmouth, NH: Heinemann.

McGee, L. M., & Schickedanz, J. A. (2007). Repeated interactive read-alouds in preschool and kindergarten. *The Reading Teacher, 60*(8), 742–751.

McKenna, M. C., Walpole, S., & Conradi, K. (Eds.). (2010). *Promoting early reading: Research, resources, and best practices.* New York: Guilford Press.

Morris, D., Bloodgood, J., & Perney, J. (2003). Kindergarten predictors of first- and second-grade reading achievement. *The Elementary School Journal, 104*(2), 93–109.

Morrow, L. M. (2009). *Literacy development in the early years: Helping children read and write* (6th ed.). Needham Heights, MA: Allyn & Bacon.

Morrow, L. M., Freitag, E., & Gambrell, L. (2009). *Using children's literature in preschool to develop comprehension: Understanding and enjoying books* (2nd ed.). Newark, DE: International Reading Association.

National Early Literacy Panel. (2007). *Developing early literacy: Report of the National Early Literacy Panel.* Washington, DC: National Institute for Literacy.

National Institute of Child Health and Human Development. (2000). *Teaching children to read: An evidence-based assessment of the scientific research literature on reading and its implications for reading instruction: Reports of the subgroups* (NIH Publication No. 00-4754). Washington, DC: U.S. Government Printing Office.

National Institute on Deafness and Other Communication Disorders. (2000). *Speech and language developmental milestones* (NIH Publication No. 00-4781). Retrieved May, 2009, from *www. nidcd.nih.gov/health/voice/speechandlanguage.asp*.

National Reading Panel. (2000). *Teaching children to read: An evidence-based assessment of the scientific research literature on reading and its implications for reading instruction: Reports of the subgroups*. Washington, DC: U.S. Government Printing Office.

Neuman, S. B. (1996). Children engaging in storybook reading: The influence of access to print resources, opportunity, and parental interaction. *Early Childhood Research Quarterly, 11,* 495–513.

Neuman, S. B. (1999). Books make a difference: A study of access to literacy. *Reading Research Quarterly, 34*(3), 286–311.

Newborg, J. (2006). *Battelle Developmental Inventory (BDI)*. Rolling Meadows, IL: Riverside.

Paris, A. H., & Paris, S. G. (2003). Assessing narrative comprehension in young children. *Reading Research Quarterly, 38*(1), 36–76.

Pressley, M. (2006). *Reading instruction that works: The case for balanced teaching!* (3rd ed.). New York: Guilford Press.

Pressley, M., & Hilden, K. (2002). How can children be taught to comprehend text better? In M. L. Kamil, J. B. Manning, & H. J. Walberg (Eds.), *Successful reading instruction* (pp. 33–53). Greenwich, CT: Information Age.

Read, C. (1971). Pre-school children's knowledge of English phonology. *Harvard Educational Review, 41,* 1–34.

Robbins, C., & Ehri, L. C. (xxxx). Reading storybooks to kindergarteners helps them learn new vocabulary words. *Journal of Educational Psychology, 86,* 54–64.

Rossetti, C. G. (1988). The caterpillar. In B. Schenk de Regniers, E. Moore, M. M. White, & J. Carr (Eds.), *Sing a song of popcorn: Every child's book of poems*. New York: Scholastic.

Russell J., McCoy, A., Pistorino, C., Wilkinson, A., Burghardt, J., Clark, M., et al. (2007). *National Evaluation of Early Reading First: Final Report, U. S. Department of Education, Institute of Education Sciences*. Washington, DC: U.S. Government Printing Office.

Schatschneider, C., Petscher, Y., & Williams, K. M. (2008). How to evaluate a screening process: The vocabulary of screening and what educators need to know. In L. M. Justice & C. Vukelich (Eds.), *Achieving excellence in preschool literacy instruction* (pp. 304–316). New York: Guilford Press.

Schumm, J. (Ed.). (2006). *Reading assessment and instruction for all learners*. New York: Guilford Press.

Snow, C. (1991). The theoretical basis for relationships between language and literacy in development. *Journal of Research in Childhood Education, 6,* 5–10.

Snow, C. (2002). *Reading for understanding: Toward a research and development program in reading comprehension*. Pittsburgh: RAND Corp.

Snow, C., Tabors, P., Nicholson, P., & Kurland, B. (1995). SHELL: Oral language and early literacy skills in kindergarten and first-grade children. *Journal of Research in Childhood Education, 10,* 37–48.

Sulzby, E. (1985). Children's emergent reading of favorite storybooks: A developmental study. *Reading Research Quarterly, 20,* 458–481.

Sulzby, E. (1990). Assessment of emergent writing and children's language while writing. In L. M. Morrow & J. Smith (Eds.), *Assessment for instruction in early literacy* (pp. 83–108). Englewood, NJ: Prentice-Hall.

University of Virginia. (2004). *Phonological Awareness Literacy Screening (PALS).* Charlottesville, VA: Author.

Vukelich, C., & Christie, J. (2004). *Building a foundation for preschool literacy: Effective instruction for children's reading and writing development.* Newark, DE: International Reading Association.

Vukelich, C., Han, M., Buell, M. J., & Moore, N. S. (2009). Tutoring: A value-added way to support Head Start preschoolers' language and early reading development. *NHSA Dialog, 12,* 192–209.

West, S., & Cox, A. (2004). *Literacy play: Over 300 dramatic play activities that teach pre-reading skills.* Beltsville, MD: Gryphon House.

Whitehurst, G. (1992). Dialogic reading: An effective way to read to preschoolers. Article retrieved February 26, 2010 from *http://www.readingrockets.org/article/400.*

Whitehurst, G. J., Arnold, D. S., Epstein, J. N., Angell, A. L., Smith, M., & Fischel, J. (1994a). A picture book reading intervention in day care and home for children from low-income families. *Developmental Psychology, 30,* 679–689.

Whitehurst, G. J., Epstein, J. N., Angell, A. L., Payne, A. C., Crone, D. A., & Fischel, J. E. (1994b). Outcomes of an emergent literacy intervention in Head Start. *Journal of Educational Psychology, 86,* 542–555.

Whitehurst, G. J., Falco, F. L., Lonigan, C., Fischel, J. E., DeBaryshe, B. D., Valdez-Menchaca, M. C., & Caulfield, M. B. (1988). Accelerating language development through picture-book reading. *Developmental Psychology, 24,* 552–559.

Whitehurst, G. J., & Lonigan, C. J. (2001). Emergent literacy: Development from prereaders to readers. In S. B. Neuman & D. K. Dickinson (Eds.), *Handbook of early literacy research* (pp. 11–29). New York: Guilford Press.

Wiggins, A. K. (2006). *Preschoolers at play: Building language and literacy through dramatic play.* Greenville, SC: Super Duper Publications.

Yopp, H. K., & Stapleton, L. (2008). Conciéncia fonémica en español [Phonemic awareness in Spanish]. *The Reading Teacher, 61*(5), 374–382.

Yopp, H. K., & Yopp, R. H. (2000). Supporting phonemic awareness development in the classroom. *The Reading Teacher, 54*(2), 130–143.

Index

Page numbers in *italic* refer to illustrations.